Praise for *The Global Nomad's G*

"Tina Quick's initiative and book is a brilliant revelation of the phenomena of Third Culture Kids and their many challenges to re-discover their roots and identity with surprising results. Any parent who has lived abroad and wants to repatriate their children for university should read this book. Moreover any young student aspiring to 'return' to their country of 'origin' would benefit from the very practical advice and guidance on how to cope with the myriad of emotions and how to reintegrate, something easily said but so difficult to actually do."

-Robyn Tyner, Director of IB Studies,
International School of Geneva

"This wonderful book appears six months too late, as my TCK son has recently gone to university and he and I both wish he could have been better prepared. The wisdom in these pages comes from the finest resources. I shall be recommending it to every parent and school leaver who crosses my path, believe me."

-Jo Parfitt, author of *A Career in Your Suitcase*

"One of the greatest needs of an adolescent is to belong. Place on top of that 'coming home' where you think you belong, only to quickly realize you are not sure where you belong. This book will be like your GPS system to finding that you truly do belong."

-Sandy Thomas, Director USA Girl Scouts Overseas,
President of Families in Global Transition

"This book is filled with superb materials to help global nomads stay the course during their transition to university. Tina Quick skilfully blends core concepts and research from the transition field together with her own experiences and insights. Readers will be encouraged by the many stories, practical examples, and wise suggestions. Use this book as a 'transition companion' to accompany you into the exciting and challenging adventure into university life as a global nomad. Don't leave home, wherever and whatever that is, without it!"

-Dr. Kelly O'Donnell, CEO/Consulting Psychologist,
Member Care Associates, Inc.

"It's about time this book was written. It is a long-overdue guide for university students facing re-entry."

-Brice Royer, founder of TCKID featured on the BBC, ABC,
The Telegraph and the U.S Department of Defense

"This book is a must-read for any TCK who is either on their way to college, or already there! Tina Quick covers all the important topics that a TCK will encounter in their adjustment to university life. I plan to be sure that every TCK student I work with on the college counseling side of my practice gets a copy of this book. I am sure they will find the advice within invaluable and, as a result, will have smoother transitions."
-Rebecca Grappo, M.Ed,
Founder – RNG International Educational Consultants

"This book is uniquely and sensitively tailored to the needs of students who are either 'returning' to their home countries or 'transitioning' to another host country. The sensitive observation shines through, and will resonate with the experience of the folk who are going through it today. There is also a wealth of wise and balanced qualifications, leaving room for the great variety of individual experience. It is realistic without being fatalistic; it should help a generation of students to make the very best of their college careers."
-Dr. Richard Pearce, International School of London,
Consultant on National and International Education,
co-author of "The Essential Guide for Teachers in International Schools"

"I wish we had this book when my kids were trying to figure out which country to go to for university! Anyone who is intending to head 'home' to one of their passport countries needs to read *The Global Nomad's Guide to University Transition*. Parents, you need to buy this book for your children's school. This guidebook to university transition teaches what it means to be resilient and globally normal in this next exciting stage of life."
-Kathleen McAnear Smith, author of *Parents on the Move!*

"Tina Quick's writing style is sincere and her seasoned expertise is evident. The stories and vignettes in her book show her well-honed knowledge of the transition process. Any TCK would benefit from this book."
-Beverly D. Roman, Consultant/Special Projects
BR Anchor Publishing

The

Global Nomad's Guide

to

UNIVERSITY

TRANSITION

Tina L. Quick

SUMMERTIME PUBLISHING
Great Britain

First edition May 2010

First Published Great Britain 2010
by Summertime Publishing

ISBN   978-1-904881-21-6

Printed by Lightning Source

Cover Designed by Creationbooth

Edited by Sally Rushmore

I dedicate this book to my family,

the loving constant throughout all our transitions.

Table of Contents

Foreword

In the more than twenty-five years I have worked with Third Culture Kids (TCKs) – children who grow up in cultures outside their parents "home" or passport culture(s) – and the adult TCKs (ATCKs) they become, I have heard one major recurrent theme: among the many transitions and relocations of their lives, the most difficult one for most is when they repatriate long term to the country which their passport declares as home but in which they may not have lived for much or all of their childhood. While expecting to go "home," they soon find that living a global lifestyle has shaped their thinking and outlook in ways that are different from their peers or educators who have lived in more traditional upbringings. The common greeting – "So where are you from?" – seems almost impossible to answer succinctly. Often TCKs soon realize there are cultural cues others assume "everyone knows" but they have no idea what they are.

Frequently, this repatriation, or re-entry time, is coupled with another major life transition experience – leaving home to begin university. While this time of being launched into early adulthood is an exciting period because of the promise of all that is ahead, combining these two major life events can also add unexpected stress as well. The unwritten rules and cultural expectations of this new environment are hard to operate by when you don't know what they are. Parents who grew up in this land may assume you already know these things because they do and forget to spell them out clearly.

And so, whether you are a TCK returning to your passport culture, a TCK facing the added stress of entering one more cultural world because you have chosen a university outside your passport culture, or even an international student who is also making a cross-cultural move while beginning university, this book is written for you, not about you. Tina has faced this situation in her own TCK experience and as she has raised her children in a global lifestyle. She knows the simple, practical steps needed by all who are changing cultural worlds and beginning university as they navigate these sometimes wavy waters with clarity and strength. I invite you to read this book knowing that it is written because she believes in the countless gifts a cross-cultural experience offers and wants to see you use those gifts well, and grow from the challenges in the process.

As one who also grew up as a TCK, I, wish you all the best as you begin this wonderful journey into your university experience. Like most of you, I would not trade my experience for anything and I look forward to seeing you not only survive but thrive and this is one tool that can help you do that.

Ruth E. Van Reken, Adult TCK
Co-author *Third Culture Kids: Growing Up Among Worlds* (rev.)
Co-founder Families in Global Transition

Acknowledgments

This book could not have been written without the innumerable third culture kids who felt safe enough to share their most personal and intimate stories with me. They selflessly put themselves in uncomfortable and vulnerable positions with the whole-hearted belief that their stories would help other students avoid what they suffered. My heartfelt thanks go out to each and every one of them. In order to respect and protect their privacy the names of those whose stories appear throughout these pages have been changed with the exception of my daughters and Brice Royer of TCKid.com whose mission it is to help TCKs like himself. You can read his personal story in Chapter 3. A special thanks to each of my daughters for allowing me to publicize some of their worst transition moments.

I also want to thank those TCKs who went through my "Transitioning Successfully for University" seminars and put the proof in the pudding. Their successful transitions were the impetus for writing this book in an effort to get these messages out to as many transitioning TCKs as possible.

Love and appreciation beyond words go to my loving and supportive husband who has believed in the value this project has for global nomads, their parents, educators, and counselors, as well as college and university staff on the receiving end since its first inception. I am so thankful for the time he has taken from his busy work life to brainstorm, review chapters, find resources, offer advice, and just listen to me.

I cannot begin to say how much I have appreciated the mentoring, encouraging and cheerleading Ruth Van Reken has done in support of me and this project. Her belief in the value of the book has truly carried me through. Her willingness to share the wisdom, insight and lessons learned over the years has helped make the information presented here as useful, practical and genuine as possible.

I also want to thank Barbara Schaetti for taking the time to read over the chapters and give her "Final Reflections." Barbara's TCK background, her work in the field of transitions and her groundbreaking work on TCK identity development (Chapter 7) puts her at the forefront of understanding the issues TCKs face upon repatriation. I am truly grateful for her support.

A huge thanks goes to contributing guest author, Sylvia Vriesendorp, for her chapter on personality differences (Chapter 10). Ever since Sylvia first administered and briefed my husband and me on the Myers Briggs, I personally felt everyone should undergo some such personality type indicator at some point in their lives. It would certainly be helpful to couples contemplating marriage, working teams of corporations, and anyone else sharing time and space together such as university roommates.

Thanks and appreciation go to Maureen Tillman of "College with Confidence" for her contributions on depression in Chapter 4 and to Dr. Rachel Timmons for her input and permission to use portions of her Reacculturation Rubric in Chapter 7.

My sincere thanks goes to David Hudson for allowing me to put into print his profound and touching poem on what "The Great American Teen Novel" would look like (Chapter 4). His insightful words reach far beyond his tender young age to unambiguously demonstrate what emotional turmoil one can experience upon re-entry.

I am indebted to Libby Stephens and Janet Blomberg for allowing me to take part in Interaction International's Transition/Re-entry Seminar. It was there that my passion was ignited for this work.

I would like to thank others who have spent time with me on the phone, over Skype, on email, and in restaurants and cafés to share their experiences, survey results, research, theses and theories on this topic. This would include Laura Saylor who put Boston College's first TCK orientation together, Catherine Epstein, Laila Plamondon, David Wickstrom, Esther Schubert, Ann Baker Cottrell, Lois Bushong, and Anne Copeland.

I truly appreciate all those who have reviewed my work, sent in their comments and shared with me their enthusiasm, thoughts and experiences. Thanks go to Chelsea Co, Timothy Fuderich, Becky Grappo, Mary Langford, Kelly O' Donnell, Doug Ota, Robin Pascoe, Richard Pearce, Beverly Roman, Brice Royer, Sandy Thomas, and Robyn Tyner.

I am grateful to my colleague and friend, Dr. Michèle O'Donnell, for introducing me to the world of intercultural readiness by helping me prepare my own family for re-entry. Her knowledge, enthusiasm, and passion for helping others in transition have inspired me to take a leap of faith in choosing to pursue this new career path.

I would like to thank Annie Chamberlain from Bank of America for spending time explaining the in's and out's of banking intricacies and how to address students' needs for the information presented in Chapter 9.

A big thank you goes to Sally Rushmore for her professional expertise, insight, and advice in editing this text, to Graham Booth for this beautiful book cover, and to my publishing coach, Jo Parfitt, for guiding me all along the journey with her experience, expertise, and encouragement. Without all of you, this project would not have come to fruition.

Preface

This book is written specifically *to* TCKs and their parents. It has been written with third culture kids/global nomads repatriating to their home country for college/university as the primary audience, but TCKs transitioning to another host country as a "foreign student" or "international student" will find it just as useful. Many of the same issues surface because both categories of students are making a double transition: (1) a life stage change as well as (2) a cultural change. Both the repatriating TCK and the foreign student face culture shock, or transition shock, as I like to call it, but the foreign student expects it whereas the TCK typically does not. All TCKs will appreciate reading about the challenges they may face while finding friends and building relationships, learning how they relate differently from students who have never left their home culture, and discovering the best ways to deal with the question, "Where are you from?"

If the college/university-bound student's family happens to repatriate at the same time, younger secondary school-aged siblings will also benefit from the pages of this book. Many of the same psychosocial issues will apply to them as well.

My hope is that institutions of higher education will also understand the value of learning about the journey home for these global nomads in order to better support them. Since they are neither truly from their home country nor from their host country, it is too easy for them to fall through the cracks.

International students in the traditional sense – coming from their home country to a host country for higher education – will also benefit from understanding what happens during the five stages of transition. There are many books for foreign students studying abroad; however, none of them evaluates closely the psychosocial and emotional issues of being away from home in the way this one does when delving into the details of the transition cycle. When I have put on international orientations for colleges receiving foreign nationals, the session on the five stages of transition seems to be the one students most appreciate.

The other major audience for this book is parents. I highly encourage parents to read the entire book to know exactly what they can expect their student to be dealing with as an independent, young adult far away from home, perhaps for the first time. Chapter 11 addresses specific parental issues and concerns relevant to preparing and supporting your university-bound student.

Much of the phenomena I speak of in these pages will happen in whichever country you are repatriating to. As I am more familiar with life in North America, I present the information from that point of reference and add in, where I am able, information from other countries. I also invite students to transfer this information to reflect their particular experiences.

How to Use This Book

As with any book, the most logical manner to read this one is from the front cover to the back cover and that is my suggestion as the chapters follow a progression of thoughts. I would be daft to think the majority of you will follow my advice, so I have attempted to write this book for the cover-to-cover reader as well as the student who will pick it up only to find a quick answer to a problem or issue. If you sense some repetition between the chapters, be assured it was intentional.

As Chapter 11 is directed toward parents, students may opt out of reading it, but there is always something to be learned by understanding both perspectives. As I mentioned earlier, I also suggest parents read through the entire book so they can understand the issues specific to the TCK student.

Chapter 1 is a TCK fundamentals session for those who may just now be learning that there is a term for people who have lived the lifestyle they have lived. Even those well-versed in the TCK profile would benefit from the short review as it is fundamental for understanding what issues exist and why.

I truly believe that if every TCK understood four simple truths, they would have a much smoother transition. The first of these four 'pearls,' as I like to call them, is the transition cycle. Chapters 2 through 5 explain the transition experience as depicted by the five very predictable stages of Dave Pollock's (co-author, *Third Culture Kids: The Experience of Growing Up Among Worlds*) transition cycle. These chapters are relevant to *anyone* making a cross-cultural adjustment and would pertain to all families and students, TCKs or not. Each chapter includes what the international sojourner can expect to experience in that particular stage as well as practical advice for managing it.

The second 'pearl' worth understanding is unresolved grief. Grief that comes from living the international lifestyle of a TCK is described in Chapter 3. Students will gain an understanding of what happens when grief is not dealt with properly and what can be done to confront it and move through it.

Chapter 6 addresses the most popular topic of all international students – relationships. The chapter is filled with lots of 'a-ha' moments and advice, mostly contributions from other TCKs who have gone before. The third 'pearl' of wisdom – how global nomads relate differently from their home-country peers is fully explored in two arenas:

– why TCKs sometimes find disconnects with peers while trying to build relationships and

– a myth-buster of the supposed 'superficiality' of home-country peers TCKs so often complain about.

Chapter 7 introduces the latest tools and strategies available to international sojourners. The first is Dr. Barbara Schaetti's TCK Identity Development model, the fourth 'pearl' global nomads need to comprehend to better understand themselves and their reactions as they reacculturate. This model explains "encounter" – when TCKs realize they are different from others which commonly occurs upon repatriation for university. Dr. Rachel Timmons' Reacculturation rubric is introduced as a hands-on tool that will help you assess and chart your progress in repatriation adjustment.

Chapters 8 and 9 delve into practical issues of college/university life. Ignorance is not bliss. Students need to take charge of preparing for the shift in lifestyle. Parents need to plan how they will help their student deal with those changes. These chapters are not intended to give definitive advice on the issues presented, but are instead meant to guide students and parents to know which questions they should be asking and to give some ideas as to where they can look for answers and obtain the most current information.

In Chapter 10, guest author Sylvia Vreisendorp explains personality differences and how they play out on the university campus. Everyone needs to understand himself or herself before he or she can expect to get along with and appreciate others and their differences. This chapter gives you a head start.

As was mentioned earlier, Chapter 11 is specific to parental issues and concerns. The university transition can be just as difficult, if not more so, for parents. Useful advice and food for thought will help you plan out how to prepare and support your student from afar.

It is nearly impossible to cover every issue that will come up over the course of university study, but the purpose of this book is to get students and their parents underway and to help them navigate the transition with a steady rudder. I encourage students to take the book along with them to college/university and for parents to keep a copy on hand for quick reference and reassurance that all is normal – and, indeed, even expected – and will pass in time.

With this book in hand, stories of hopelessness and suicidal thinking like the one you will read in the introduction need not be repeated. This book empowers the student to be proactive in his or her adjustment process and paves the way for parents to appropriately support their offspring along their journey.

Introduction

"I had a really difficult time at college," Tammy said as she stared down into her cup of coffee. "I didn't really enjoy it at all. Everyone told me it would be the best years of my life, but I couldn't wait for it to be over." Tammy was referring to the transition from having spent eight years in Africa where she attended an international school to re-entering her home country for college.

I asked her what she found to be so difficult about her re-entry. She recalled that she immediately sensed a "disconnect" between herself and her home-country peers. "It became more and more uncomfortable to try to relate to them. I finally decided there was something wrong with me that I couldn't connect with anyone," she recalled.

Tammy ended up spending most of her time alone. The isolation eventually spiraled into a deep depression. In the hope of finding help she reached out to her parents, who were an ocean away, and tried to explain to them what she was going through.

"I'm really depressed. I don't feel like I can get my course work finished. I feel like I can't even get out of bed," were the words she used when she eventually plucked up the courage to call. Her parents tried to encourage her but didn't recognize the fact that she needed professional help. Tammy explained that she eventually became so depressed that she formulated a plan to kill herself. One evening she was ready to go through with it. She had started running the water in the bath tub and got the razor out she would use to slit her wrists. She had even researched how to cut herself to make sure she would hit the arteries and not just the tendons and superficial veins.

I was choked with emotion as I contemplated how this beautiful, gifted, young woman could possibly fathom taking her own life. With tears in my eyes, I reached across the table, placed my hand on hers and asked, "What stopped you from going through with it?"

She sat there staring blankly out the window before finally answering, "Frankly, I was afraid I wouldn't be successful and, if that happened, then people would think I was crazy. Then I would have been considered weird *and* crazy."

Tammy eventually found a good mental health counselor who was able to help her. She continued to have many ups and downs after graduation, but today she is stable and recently married. She offered to share her story with the hope that it would help others avoid what she suffered.

"I wish there had been a book like this when I left for college," she says. "They told me at my school that it was going to be difficult, but I didn't believe it. After all, I was in an international school where we all spoke English. I didn't expect there to be such a big difference back home. I wished I had paid more attention and taken it seriously."

In the five years following my family's re-entry to the U.S. and, as a result of living in Boston which has over 200 colleges and universities, I found I was coming into contact with more and more college students who had lived the expatriate life. I kept hearing familiar patterns to their stories, some far worse than others, but too many were stories of silent suffering, sadness, loneliness or, in extreme cases such as Tammy's, severe depression. These were young adults who had spent incredibly rich childhoods in other countries and cultures. They spoke a variety of languages, understood that there are many ways of doing, living and believing that are not necessarily wrong but just different from their home-country norms. They sported hidden diversity that made them good bridge builders, ambassadors and communicators. But somehow upon returning to their "home" culture, they found themselves misunderstood, weird, strange, standing out as being different, misfits in the very place where they had always imagined they belonged. Their stories and experiences, together with my own family's experiences, convinced me that this population of repatriates needed to benefit from what those who had gone before them had learned along their journey.

We first left the U.S. for Peshawar, Pakistan when my oldest daughter was three years old, my middle child 15 months old and the youngest was not yet conceived. We were prematurely forced out of Pakistan when President George Bush declared war in the Persian Gulf. All American families were evacuated back to the U.S. We then had the opportunity to go to Nairobi, Kenya, where we enjoyed four incredible years. But the place my daughters really call home is Geneva, Switzerland. Actually it was a combination of two countries because we lived in neighboring France. Our house was literally a stone's throw from the border crossing.

After spending nearly ten years there, the opportunity presented itself for us to move back to the U.S. The timing was perfect in the sense that our oldest daughter, Janneke, was preparing to go off to college in the U.S. and it would be wonderful to be on the same side of the big pond together. Also my husband's and my parents were beginning to need more care and attention and we were feeling the need to be closer to them. However, my middle daughter, Katrina, had two years left of high school and my youngest daughter, Kacie, would be re-entering in the last year of middle school. Yikes!

Upon hearing the news that my family was repatriating after having lived abroad for 15 years my psychologist friend, Michèle O'Donnell, offered to give me a re-entry tutorial. Michèle, a counselor to missionary families and hugely familiar with the issues associated with re-entry, took me through the work of Dave Pollock (Interaction International). She explained in detail the five stages of transition and how to "leave well in order to enter well." I soaked up every word Michèle uttered, studied every diagram and chart she presented and started researching to find out more about what expatriates face when they return "home." I put quotes around the word *home* because, although it was the country of the passport we carried, it did not feel like home to us because we had been away from it for so long. It certainly was not home to any of our girls at that point in their lives because none of the three had lived there since they were old enough to remember.

I was particularly interested in the effects the move would have on my children, global citizens who had never really lived in or gone to school in their passport country. During our time in Geneva, when my three daughters were still in primary school, I heard someone speak about "Third Culture Kids" (TCKs), but I never read or heard anything more about them after that and I forgot about the term. But during Michèle's tutorial she kept bringing up the terms TCKs and global nomads (GNs) and I realized that this was a subject I was going to have to investigate. Living overseas for all or most of their lives had impacted my children in ways I needed to understand and, as it turns out, they needed to understand as well in order to be able to relate to their home-country peers without feeling like complete aliens.

Living abroad had given my children a wealth of languages, peoples, customs, traditions and places (exotic and not so exotic), but no sense of who they really were as Americans. They had become global citizens, internationals who crossed borders and cultures with as much comfort and ease as their home-country peers crossed town lines. Returning to live in a country they only knew from home leave visits every one to two years meant having to learn a whole new culture even though it was somewhat familiar to them. That turned out to be the tricky part. Because they were familiar with our home-country culture they were tricked into believing they would be able to settle right in and even relished the thought of living the American life. It didn't take long, however, before reality set in. They were no longer Americans. They were international nomads, "belonging everywhere and nowhere at the same time."

I knew the adjustment to our home country was going to be tough, but through Michèle's tutelage and the subsequent research I had done, I acquired the necessary insight to help them through it. The result was that the road, although not completely smooth, contained fewer bumps and surprises, and we had the tools we needed for navigating the potholes.

The purpose in writing this book goes back to what Tammy and many other repatriating TCKs have said, "I wish someone had told me what I could expect...I wish there had been a book I could have taken to university with me...I wish someone had come to my classroom and told us about re-entry..." The bottom line is that students really do not think they need to be told how to re-enter or move on to another country they think they know. Experiences tell us otherwise. As the Billy Wilder quote goes, "Hindsight is always twenty-twenty."

Institutions on the receiving end also need to take the global nomad's transition into consideration. The terms 'third culture kid' and 'global nomad' are still relatively unknown on campuses around the world. University mental health counselors need to understand the TCK experience in order to understand the special issues of TCKs/GNs and the reasons for those issues. Global nomads don't fit the typical labels and boxes many domestic student issues fall into.

Ideally students and parents will read this book well before departure, as it is full of information on how to leave well, but if denial wins out, the book can still go with the student to university and be there as a resource when the going gets tough. Some students will do all they can to prepare for leaving and others will have a wait-and-see attitude about it all. "I'll read it if I need it," they will say and that's absolutely fine. Whichever the case may be, reading this book can mean all the difference between just surviving and actually thriving in the university transition.

It is important to note that everyone is different. Not everyone has the same experience, but those who do run into problems are frequently very surprised by it. Some global nomads will actually fare better in their adjustment than their home-country peers because their international background has helped them be resilient. They have come to expect change throughout their lives and have learned to deal with relocations and all the change that surrounds a move. The things I talk about in this book may or may not happen to you, but it is good to know what other TCKs have gone through to avoid unwanted surprises and to learn from their experiences.

While experts say the repatriation experience is just as, if not more, difficult than going abroad, armed with the knowledge of what happens during transition, knowing what to expect, and understanding that it is completely normal can prevent, or at the very least, mitigate the challenges students will face. Some students will seemingly breeze through the five stages of transition. Others will spend months or even years getting through them. This book is filled with the experiences of others who have taken the journey before you. Hopefully, their journeys will have helped pave the road of transition to be straighter and smoother for you.

Tina Quick
Founder, International Family Transitions
www.internationalfamilytransitions.com

Chapter 1

The World of the Global Nomad

"A transition can be said to occur if an event or non-event results in a change in assumptions about oneself and the world and thus requires a corresponding change in one's behaviors and relationships."
Nancy Schlossberg, Counseling Psychologist

My first adult overseas posting could have ended in disaster if someone had not forewarned me what I could expect to experience. My husband and I were preparing to move our very young family to Peshawar, Pakistan, widely acknowledged as being quite a difficult place to live, especially for women. I did a reconnaissance trip beforehand and was *not* looking forward to going. Somehow in all the preparations for leaving I became excited to go and was actually looking forward to the adventure. Just before our departure, a colleague of my husband turned to me at our farewell party and said, "At just about three months, you're going to hate it there, will get depressed, and want to come home." I was quite taken aback and wasn't quite sure how to respond. To tell you the truth, I was a bit ticked off. How could he possibly predict how I or any other person for that matter would feel? He had just burst my bubble of enthusiasm. Before I could think of anything to say, he took another breath and said, "But don't worry about it. It will pass and you'll get through it."

Thank goodness this gentleman had the foresight to let me know I could expect this to happen because when we arrived in Pakistan, it really took some getting used to. Nothing was the same. It was an entirely different way of life for us. Everything changed from the way we had to brush our teeth, to the shopping and preparing of food, to how we were expected to dress and act in public. I could go on and on, but you get the picture.

At first, everything was so quaint and different. I enjoyed hearing the sound of horses' hooves coming down the street pulling carriages of passengers or carts of food. I loved watching the donkey carts and rickshaws, the graceful flow of women's burkas (an enveloping outer garment Muslim women wear to remain totally covered when going out in public) and best of all, having house help. But then after some time, I felt myself getting a little blue for no obvious reason whatsoever. I tried to pull myself out of it, but I only became even sadder. Then I remembered what the gentleman had said to me. I started counting. He was right. I had been in Peshawar for just about three months. He said this was going to happen. Of course, I didn't believe him at the time, but here it was three months and I was experiencing exactly what he had predicted. What made it all manageable was that I also remembered that he had told me it would pass. I honestly think if I had not known that, I would have packed up my children and gone home, leaving my husband there alone.

You are most likely reading this book because you are an internationally mobile young person who is about to undergo a major life transition that involves not only a lifestyle change, but a cultural change as well. How wonderful to be your age and in your position of finishing secondary school and preparing for your launch into independent adulthood. Most adults I know would love to once more be where you are right now. You have undoubtedly had one adult or another wistfully say to you, "These will be the best four years of your life." And they have every potential to be if you are properly prepared. You are taking the necessary steps that can lead you where you want to go and these pages will help you get there.

 Dig Deeper: Preparing ahead of time helps reduce the number of unwanted surprises and roadblocks you may otherwise run into. Knowing what to expect, helps you to appreciate that various events and feelings are completely normal.

What is a Global Nomad/Third Culture Kid?

Some of you may have heard these interchangeable terms before and know a little or a lot about their profile. Others of you may be hearing for the first time that you have a name. Sociologists call people who grow up outside their parents' home culture or cultures *global nomads* (GNs) or *third culture kids* (TCKs). Whatever your case may be, this book is designed for you and for this particular stage in your life because your global experiences have created benefits and challenges you can build on and grow from as you transition from life abroad back to your home country or on to another host country.

International Mobility Experiences

There are three different types of experiences relating to international mobility for attending university:

(1) Repatriating TCKs,

(2) Transitioning TCKs,

(3) International or foreign students (FS).

(1) Repatriating TCKs – If you have been living in a country other than that which is stamped on the cover of your passport and are returning to that country for college or university, you are a repatriating TCK. An American TCK by the name of Rita is such an example. Her family moved to France when she was nine years old and then to India when she was 14. Rita decided to repatriate to the U.S. to attend university after graduation from her international secondary school in India. The repatriating TCK may be returning to their passport country with or without his/her parents.

(2) Transitioning TCKs – If you have been living outside your passport country but, instead of returning to your home country, have decided to attend university in another host country, you will be a transitioning TCK. You, like Theo, the Kenyan teenager I met who had grown up in Germany and was planning to attend university in the U.K., are transitioning. Your university will most likely consider you to be an international or "foreign student" (FS) because you hold a passport from another country. This might be technically accurate but at the core you are really a "transitioning TCK."

(3) International or foreign students – If you are a student who has grown up in your passport country and are choosing to make an international move (expatriating) for the first time as you enroll in university, you will be known as an international student. Because your passport is not from the country where you have chosen to attend university, you clearly fall into the FS category. For instance, someone who has spent their entire life in China and expatriates to study abroad is referred to as an international or foreign student. In some ways, your transition is more straight forward and clearly delineated. People in your new host country will expect you to have some adjustment issues, whereas TCKs returning "home" will have very similar issues to yours but most people will not understand. TCKs sometimes fall between the cracks because universities and TCKs themselves do not recognize that they don't know the culture of their passport country as well those around them assume they do.

Commonality in the Experiences

While you may have different backgrounds and experiences, what you all have in common is each of you is making a cross-cultural transition for university. While most of what is discussed throughout these pages is particularly focused on GNs/TCKs who are going back to attend university in their passport culture, I invite those of you with slightly different experiences to apply the principles of each story to your own life as well. While the majority of my examples are taken from TCKs who have repatriated to the U.S, the scenarios are applicable to most any TCK returning to his or her home country.

 Try This: Whatever your particular international experience is, try applying the principles discussed throughout this book to fit your situation.

Not Fitting In

"I had something of a difficult transition into college. I didn't really feel comfortable [at university] until sometime into the fall semester of my second year, but perhaps that is normal? I had difficulty figuring out where I best fit in. I didn't feel understood by most of my peers, and I didn't understand how to relate to people who grew up in this more or less single culture country. I felt like an anomaly. I didn't expect to have such challenges so that probably made it more difficult."

Rita, American TCK who lived in France and India
and repatriated for university.

Internationally mobile young people often grapple with certain issues that those who have been born and bred in one country may not experience, such as, "Where on earth do I belong?" This can be an especially tough question when you are supposedly returning "home." After years of answering the question, "Where are you from?" by stating the country written on your passport, you may feel like anything but that nationality when you return. You may feel more like an "international student." Even though she was fluent in French, Rita said she didn't feel very French, and she certainly wasn't very Indian, but once back in America, she didn't feel at all American either.

The Good News

Rita's experience is not unusual. After having lived a most interesting and rich life outside their passport culture(s), when TCKs repatriate, it takes a while to feel as if they fit into what is supposed to be their own culture. The good news is that research has shown that people who receive cross-cultural training and preparation shortly before or after their international relocation have a smoother transition (more on this in Chapter 2). This holds true for you when you repatriate, transition or expatriate for university. Knowing what to expect, appreciating that your responses are normal, and having tools and strategies for dealing with the change will keep the roadblocks and unwanted surprises to a minimum. Let's look at such an example:

5

Leslie is an American TCK who grew up in England and France but decided to return to the United States for college. Leslie's parents knew that there were some normal challenges that TCKs often face when combining repatriation with starting university. They encouraged her to attend a program designed especially for students who had been living outside of their passport country but were repatriating for higher education. They chose a week-long Transition / Re-entry seminar, where TCKs from around the globe came together to learn about some of the useful gifts their international experience has added to their lives as well as how to deal well with the particular challenges that are also a normal part of this lifestyle. It was here that Leslie learned what to expect in the cycle of adjustment that comes with a relocation that is doubly impacted by a change of cultures.

As a result of attending the Transition/Re-entry Seminar Leslie settled into her new surroundings extremely well. She says,

"I had no problems settling in. I love my university. After the first long break when I went home I wasn't sure which room felt more like home – my bedroom at my house in France or my dorm room here on campus. I learned a lot about relationships and was even able to offer some answers and give advice to some of my new international friends who found themselves overwhelmed and perplexed at some of the ways American students interacted."

Leslie is now in her third year at college. She has become a counselor at her university's International Orientation program, and is highly involved in the International Club on campus.

A Double Adjustment

Regardless of which internationally mobile student category you fit in, you not only have the upcoming adjustment to university life to deal with but an added adjustment to a foreign culture. Even if you are a GN/TCK returning to your home country it may be foreign to you in many respects. Through no fault of their own, global nomads often know more about other places, peoples, cultures and languages than they do their own passport country. This can lead to cultural imbalance, identity issues, and being misunderstood by home-country peers which can then lead to the feeling of not fitting in or not belonging which I talk about in detail in Chapter 5.

Brent has an American father and a Thai mother and lived in Pakistan, the U.S., and Switzerland during his childhood. Brent is currently in his fourth year of college in the U.S. and tells us some of his story.

"My Thai mother and American father each provided me with a very balanced upbringing insofar that I experienced aspects of both their cultures. I lived in the U.S. for a short period of time when I was elementary age and I came back to the U.S. every other year for home leave. I was deemed American by my international school friends because that's what was written on my passport and I had an American accent which stood out in a school where there weren't many.

Coming into a small college, it was quickly apparent how different I was from my fellow classmates. People would point out my differences, whether it was my speech, dress, mannerisms, or opinion, by coining the phrase, "You're so Euro." It was just a way for them to justify my differences, which took me aback since in my Swiss international school such labeling didn't exist because everyone was different. There was a pressure (which admittedly, was mostly self-imposed) to conform. But I think that is the case with everyone who finds themselves in an environment that is shockingly different from the one they are accustomed to."

I think of Brent as my "poster child" because he is the quintessential third culture kid returning to his passport country for college. I knew him in his Swiss international high school as a dynamic, intelligent, talented, and gifted student who was a bit of a "class clown," pulling stunts that would have even his teachers laughing with him rather than becoming angry at him. Brent did not receive any type of re-entry training before the start of college and as is many times the case, he had a difficult time with his transition and was eventually treated for depression. You will hear more about his journey and his advice to you throughout these pages.

This phenomenon is not unique to students who return to the United States or Canada. TCK Jennifer, whose mother is English and father is Zimbabwean, was also raised in Europe but attended a university in the United Kingdom. Jennifer had

> *"I was so frustrated. They would invite me to tea and not talk about anything substantial. It was a waste of my time."*
> Jennifer, bi-cultural TCK

difficulty relating to her U.K. peers because she saw them as shallow, boring and immature. No one showed any interest in getting to know her on a deeper level. She found herself impatient with their insular way of thinking. They did not seem to know what was going on in the world and didn't have any goals for their lives other than finishing "uni" with a degree. Unfortunately Jennifer wrote off her home-country peers and spent her university years only with other internationals. I say 'unfortunately' because, as you will later learn, it may take longer to get to know your home-country-peers, but it is worth the time and effort because everyone has something to offer and to teach you.

Why a Cross-Cultural Childhood Matters

Some of you may be thinking about adults who move to a new culture for the first time and how difficult that is. So why don't we make a big fuss over that? The answer is, we do. Adults go through major culture shock and they must go through a period of adjustment which is not always easy. The difference is that adults have already established their value system, sense of cultural identity and core relationships with family and friends in the home culture. An adult understands that he or she is an English person who happens to be living in Japan or a Kenyan living in Germany and so on. Third culture kids live in a world that changes culturally and physically during their ever-important formative years. The book, *Third Culture Kids: Growing Up Among Worlds* by David Pollock and Ruth Van Reken is filled with many 'a-ha' moments for me. This is the first:

> For TCKs, the moving back and forth from one culture to another happens before they have completed the critical developmental task of forming a sense of their own personal or cultural identity.

In other words, they are not sure of who they are and exactly where they belong – a quandary that does not usually crop up until they repatriate, oftentimes for higher education. Until this time they haven't had to examine the issue of belonging. Many TCKs feel they are more a part of the host culture in which they have been immersed than the culture or cultures their parents hail from.

> While living in Japan one African/American little girl used to tell her mother that she was Japanese. As much as her mother tried to explain that that was not the case, the girl insisted. It wasn't until her mother heard about the TCK experience that she finally understood what her daughter meant and felt.

Belonging to the Third Culture Tribe

What is the Third Culture?

People ask all the time, "What exactly is the 'third culture'?" Social scientist Ruth Hill-Useem coined the term "third culture" in the 1950's when she went to India for a year to study expatriates. She discovered that expatriates (people living outside their own country) preferred to hang out with, or spend time with, other expatriates even though they were from different cultures and countries. The expats had formed an interstitial lifestyle that was different from either their home or host cultures, but it was one that they shared together in that particular setting.

Dr. Useem continued to study expatriates when she returned to North America and found that while the repatriated parents were eventually able to slip back into their home culture, the children had a much more difficult time adjusting to that culture. The children were actually more comfortable being with others who had been in a similar situation.

Dr. Useem came to identity three distinctly separate cultures these children had been exposed to:

- The "first culture" refers to the home or passport culture.

- The "second culture" is all of the places a child has ever lived.

- The "third culture" is the *community* of people who have done the same thing.

What she discovered is that the *sense of belonging* is found neither in the home culture nor in the host culture, but *with others who share the experience of living outside their passport cultures.*

The Expanded Definition

Dave Pollock, interculturalist and founder of Interaction International (*an organization dedicated to being a catalyst to help all organizations who send families with children overseas know how to do it better*), spent a lot of time in Nairobi, Kenya, in the 1970's working with expatriate students. He began to notice issues and attitudes with which these students and others like them in other parts of the world struggled. Upon returning to the U.S. he started Interaction International to help these kids even as they grew into adults and still struggled with issues from their childhoods.

Together with Ruth Van Reken, who grew up in Nigeria and struggled with the same issues from her childhood, Dave wrote *Third Culture Kids: Growing Up Among Worlds* and gave us this expanded definition of a Third Culture Kid:

> A Third Culture Kid (TCK) is a person who has spent a significant part of his or her developmental years outside the parents' passport culture. The TCK builds relationships to all of the cultures, while not having full ownership in any. Although elements from each culture are assimilated into the TCK's life experience, the sense of belonging is in relationship to others of similar background.

Basically what Useem, Pollock and Van Reken are all saying is a child is taken from the country of his or her parents or parent (the first culture) and raised in a host or multiple host countries (the second culture), but belonging is in that community of people who have shared a similar way of living. Finding commonality with others is what gives the sense of belonging regardless of their national, ethnic or cultural heritage. Together these students form a common, shared set of experiences.

What Does it Mean to be a Third Culture Kid?

Whether you are a student, a parent, an educator or a counselor, if you have not already done so, I would highly recommend that you read Pollock and Van Reken's *Third Culture Kids: Growing Up Among Worlds.* In fact, if it has been awhile since you first read it, I would encourage you to read it again. The first time I read the "purple book," as it is affectionately referred to by many, I read it through the lens of a mother's perspective. I am the mother of three TCKs and we were in the process of repatriating. The second time I read it, I did so to be prepared for a workshop I was attending. The third time I read through it, I did so for enjoyment.

It was only upon the third reading that it struck me that my name was written all over those pages. I too, am a TCK and I had not fully appreciated how that had impacted my life. I finally understood so many things about myself that I didn't even have words for before. Known by many as the definitive resource on third culture kids, their book answers the many "how's" and "why's" about children in their developmental years who are affected by a cross-cultural, highly mobile lifestyle. Since understanding the TCK profile is imperative to understanding so much of what happens during the transition to higher education, it is worth briefly summarizing Pollock and Van Reken's TCK profile before going any further.

The Basics

If you have only now discovered that there is a vocabulary, a language, and in fact, a culture for the lifestyle you've been living, then what follows is, for you, a much abbreviated foundational session. It is important to remember that when we generalize about a group of people, we cannot speak for the individuals themselves. Everyone is different and may not demonstrate the same traits or tendencies as the majority of the group. The TCK experience can be incredibly enriching for some, a real struggle for others and somewhere in between for still others.

Let's start by going back to Pollock's expanded TCK definition and look closely at the last phrase: "*...the sense of belonging is in relationship to others of similar background.*" Remember what Dr. Useem found in her research – that third culture kids preferred to hang out with kids who had had a similar experience? Libby Stephens from Interaction International and a colleague of the late Dave Pollock says, "You can put two TCKs in a room with 200 other people and within minutes they will find each other."

TCKs have been around since the beginning of time. According to JustLanded.com, by the time this book is published more than 200 million people will be living abroad and the global relocation trend surveys indicate that those numbers continue to grow every year. Many famous people you know today have spent all or parts of their childhoods in a foreign country.

One of the best known TCKs is U.S. President Barack Obama who spent four of his pre-teen years growing up in Jakarta. Shortly after the 2008 presidential elections, a colleague who was following President Obama's cabinet and staff appointments pointed out that approximately half of his first fifteen appointments were adult TCKs (ATCKs). For those of us who work with TCKs it came as no surprise and was a real validation of Dr. Pollock's definition.

Cultural Confusion

Another '"a-ha" statement that strikes me from Pollock and Van Reken's "purple book" is this:

> One of the major developmental tasks that help us form our sense of identity and belonging is to successfully learn the basic cultural rules of our society while we are children, to internalize those principles and practices as we move through adolescence, and then use them as the basis for how we live and act as adults.

What happens if those rules keep changing because the TCK keeps moving from one culture into another, even if it is from host to home culture and back again? You get it – cultural confusion.

Two Realities of Being a TCK

Pollock and Van Reken definitively state that two basic realities shape the formation of a TCK's life:

1. *They live in a genuinely cross-cultural world.* The typical TCK has made many cross-cultural relocations. Right now you may be saying to yourself, "She's not talking about me. I was born and raised in my host country. It's the only place I consider home." But think about it for a minute. Do you not go back to your parents' passport country or countries to visit relatives every year or every other year? The typical TCK will come back "home" as their parents may call it, even though it may feel like anything but home to the TCK, regularly for an extended period of time, whether it is on furlough, home leave, Christmas vacation or family events. For instance my family would spend 6-8 weeks every other summer back "home" to catch up with extended family and friends. If you went to a boarding school, you were coming and going on holiday breaks between your school and where your parents were living or from school to your passport country. Wherever you came and went to and from, you most likely encountered crossing one or more cultures.

2. *They live in a highly mobile world.* When TCKs move back and forth between host and home countries they must say good-bye to their friends in the host country and hello to grandparents, aunts, uncles, cousins and maybe old friends in the "home" country. Then, when the time comes to return to their host country, it means another round of good-byes to family and hellos to the friends they left behind. Even if this particular type of mobility does not apply to the TCK, they still undoubtedly have experiences with people whom they care about moving in and out of their lives with a certain amount of frequency. Teachers, mentors, best friends, coaches, pastors, beloved neighbors are seemingly constantly coming and going in that very transient third culture. This is one of the reasons international schools can be so

13

welcoming for new students. Everyone there has been new at one point in time and understands how it feels.

Share It: In the back of their minds is a constant awareness that their best friend may have to pack up and leave any day. So the circle of friends is ever changing and enlarging to take in newcomers.

Internationally Mobile Childhood: The Plus Side

I often like to ask TCKs I am working with to brainstorm about the gifts, opportunities or benefits they have gained from their international lifestyles. The obvious ones come up first:

> *"Third culture kids will always be third culture kids. When they grow up they become adult third culture kids (ATCKs)."*
> Dave Pollock

- Learning new languages

- Meeting new people

- Learning first-hand how other cultures operate

- Seeing and experiencing many "exotic" places

- Having confidence in travel and starting anew

- Having friends all over the world

- Learning to bc creative

- Understanding that there can be more than one way to look at the same thing

- Being good storytellers

The highly mobile, international lifestyle of the TCK has other, hidden benefits which serve them well in life such as:

Cross-Cultural Skills

Because many TCKs have been educated alongside children of other nationalities and races, they understand that friendship extends past all traditional racial and cultural boundaries. They come to appreciate diversity and understand that if someone believes or acts differently from

14

them, there is a reason for it. This is why they make natural bridge builders – because they are comfortable with diversity they are able to bridge the gap between cultures.

Barely a newscast goes by that we don't witness President Obama doing this. In his acceptance speech at the Democratic National Convention he said, "There will no longer be red states (Republican) and blue states (Democratic), but the United States." Shortly after taking office he gave his first TV interview to an Arab satellite channel and relayed the message that his approach would be to listen to other countries and not force U.S. policy. He made it clear that the U.S. was not an enemy of Islam. He drew ties to his familiarity with Islam (he has family members who are Muslims) and his knowledge of the Muslim world (lived in Indonesia for four years). This bridge building ability influenced his consideration for the Nobel Peace Prize he was awarded less than a year after taking office.

Observational Skills

TCKs are like cultural chameleons – they wait and watch to determine which cultural color they must turn into in order to fit in. The power of observation is a skill that serves third culture kids well throughout life, whether it is when attending a new school (e.g. college/university), a social gathering with an unfamiliar group of people, or a new job. Rather than barging in on the scene and boldly making their presence known, they instead learn to wait and see how things work in this new place.

And then sometimes, such as was the case with my oldest daughter's friend from Cameroon who grew up in Europe, this desire to fit in is sometimes so acute that TCKs forfeit their ability to remain true to themselves. In Cameroon there are two working languages – English and French – and 230 other languages. This young lady had a thick African accent even though she spoke beautiful French and English. She went off to university in England after graduation from secondary school. When we saw her two years later she had the thickest, most proper English accent one could ever want. When my daughter pointed it out to her, she didn't even realize it, nor could she change it. In her desire to fit in, she subconsciously adopted the ways of her new host country to the point of taking on an accent she did not own.

Adaptability

Surviving chronic change can bring resilience. The typical TCK experience means repeatedly having to cope with new situations. This is one reason many TCKs actually manage the university transition better than their home-country peers.

 Share it: TCKs sometimes fare better than their domestic peers in managing the university transition because they are used to coping with change.

Social Skills

On the one hand, TCKs can appear to be socially slow during their chameleon stage. On the other hand they can be very socially competent and confident, particularly in comparison to their home-country peers. TCKs are often mistaken for being older, which translates to more mature, than they are because they are comfortable with looking an adult in the eye and holding an intelligent conversation with them, something domestic peers often struggle with.

The Flip Side

At this point you may be thinking, "She's way off target. She's not talking about me." Just like anyone else TCKs respond to a given situation in a variety of ways. While some will grow from their multiple moves and constantly changing cultures, others will be practically paralyzed by them. Some will be outgoing and adventurous, others will withdraw and become incredibly shy and still others will experience everything in between.

The Emotional Toll

What follows are some of the responses TCKs have brainstormed to the question, "What are some of the down sides of a being a TCK?"

- Having to say frequent good-byes

- Having to find new friends

- Leaving pets and people behind

- Having to wear masks

- Being abnormally normal

- Being culturally imbalanced

- Being all too familiar with pain

- Not knowing my own country as well as other places lived in

- Being critical of many things but especially of home-country peers

Arrogance – Real or Perceived

Sometimes a TCK will admit to and throw the word 'arrogance' into the mix. This can be real or perceived. *Real* arrogance is when they forget that their cross-cultural lifestyle has given them a broader view of the world and they become impatient and even judgmental of others when they can only see things from a narrow or one-sided perspective. A condescending attitude rapidly develops due to their impatience with what they equate as ignorance, particularly on the part of home-country peers.

On the other hand, TCKs are often *perceived* as being arrogant – boastful, haughty and just plain showing off – when they are only trying to share their life experiences with others not familiar with the international lifestyle. These are the only stories they have to tell and they don't think of them as being so unusual. It is not surprising that TCKs feel more comfortable being with other internationally oriented people who can relate to the places a TCK has been, the food he or she has eaten, or even the airplane and bathroom stories they so enjoy sharing. They too, are "abnormally normal."

Experience versus Identity

You are a global citizen, global nomad, third culture kid who has adopted languages, customs, and belief systems of other cultures in addition to those of your home culture. They have shaped you, just as everyone's experiences have shaped them, to be the individual human being that you are. These experiences and influences have helped you develop your unique gifts, talents and interests that could have been very different if you had never gone abroad.

While your world view and conceptual thinking may not be like those of your peers back home and you may not share popular culture or common experiences with them, what you do share is humanity. Each of you is, first and foremost, a person. You all have the same relational, emotional, spiritual, creative, intellectual, physical, and other basic needs. TCKs fundamentally then are not different as people but their experiences have been different.

Being a TCK is not to be equated with an identity. It does not define who you are. And you are not a victim because you are a TCK. Having led a TCK lifestyle is a beautiful gift as long as you have the knowledge and self-awareness to work positively with it. There can be a tendency for people to blame their problems on life experiences they could not control and use them as an excuse to explain away their issues. Minorities, immigrants or refugees could look at themselves the same way and say they have issues because of their circumstances. Everyone has issues regardless of their experiences. Being a TCK is only *one* part of you.

 Beware: While it is important to understand the language of TCKs, try not to translate your TCK experience into your identity.

TCKs are not alone in their search for identity which often accompanies the college years. Brent, the quintessential TCK at the beginning of the chapter says this of the identity search and the college experience:

"College is different for everyone as it has a culture of its own. There are kids who live forty minutes from my campus who are depressed and hate college. Everyone has their own reasons, but this just goes to show that TCKs are not unique in this light. Everyone is struggling to define themselves as they try to find who they are or want to be. Some are quicker to find it, but ultimately everyone will."

TCKs as a Sub-Group

In her circuit of domestic and international speaking engagements, Ruth Van Reken was consistently having people come up to her after her talk and saying things like, "I have never left my home country and yet, I have experienced the exact same things you are talking about with TCKs. Why is that?"

Ruth began examining the question and currently lectures on the outcomes of her research on kids who cross cultures regularly without ever leaving their home countries. She explains that before the onset of World War II most people were born and raised in stable communities, often living with or near many family members. Due to the fact that very little mobility took place, these communities were highly mono-cultural. Because of that, people had a strong sense of who they were, how they related to those around them, how they differed from people in other communities, and what the social rules, values, and traditions were. They enjoyed a sense of belonging and a definite sense of who they were.

Changing Cultural Boundaries

Prior to World War II:

- Travel was limited mainly to business reasons.

- Children grew up in very stable, monocultural communities.

- There was not a lot of cultural mixing.

- There were clear delineations between "us" and "them."

- There was a strong sense of cultural and personal identity.

After World War II:

- Modes and routes of transportation – airplanes, railways, highways and engine powered ships – had dramatically increased.

- Travel for work, holidays, and other occasions proportionately increased.

- Immigration, which had all but ended before the start of the war, began to climb steadily.

As a result:

- Cultural boundaries began changing and were no longer clear.

- Cultural mixing was causing the "us/them" delineations to break down.

- Diversity became more widespread.

- Sense of personal identity became a challenge.

An airplane or bus ride from one part of the country to another became equivalent to foreign travel because the cultural rules were different in this new place.

This was the case when my husband took a job with the U.S. Government's Indian Health Services in the little, sleepy town of Talihina, Oklahoma. We had stepped out of the culture of the Deep South where he had been doing his Family Practice residency and into the land of cowboys and Native American Indians. When we weren't in hospital garb we learned how to dress in jeans, cowboy boots and hats. We learned to compete in rodeo games, do the two-step at the local honky-tonk café and eat fried dough. Along with adapting to the visible layers of that culture we also had to learn what was considered taboo in order to get along in the community and make friends. This culture was so foreign to us that I often refer to it as my first expatriate posting.

Others face huge cultural differences by relocating from one end of their town to the other. And in some towns the diversity has increased to the point that people make a cultural shift the moment they walk out their doors in the morning and return to their own culture in the evening. My youngest daughter has a Vietnamese friend, Lisa, who walks out into middle class, mostly white suburbia in the morning to go to school and returns to "little Vietnam" each evening. Despite having lived here for years, her parents still speak little or no English and keep the culture of their homeland within the walls of their home. This girl is crossing cultures every day. As a result, her personal identity is challenged. Because she has no one at home to help with scholastic challenges, Lisa asked me to look over her college admission essays. I was startled to realize that for all intents and purposes, I was reading about the life of a Caucasian American girl. Nowhere did she make reference to her cultural diversity, something colleges are specifically interested in these days.

Cross-Cultural Kids

Lisa and others like her are what Van Reken has defined in the 2009 revised edition of *Third Culture Kids* as "Cross-Cultural Kids" (CCKs): "A person who has lived in or meaningfully interacted with two or more cultural environments for a significant period of time during their first 18 years." Among others, these could be:

- Traditional TCKs

- Domestic TCKs (like Lisa)

- Children of immigrants

- Children of refugee

- Children of minorities

- Children of bi-cultural parents

The interesting thing is that children may have a foot in several of these categories. Look again at U.S. President Obama. He is the child of bi-cultural parents, lived as a TCK in Indonesia, and had a parent of a racial minority. It is no surprise that, regardless of the sub-group, CCKs struggle with issues of identity and belonging.

Peter is a young man from the Philippines who had lived a TCK lifestyle but spent his secondary school years back in his home country. After attending a private international school offering the International Baccalaureate (IB) program rather than attending a local secondary school (he is what Ruth terms an "Educational CCK") he decided to stay in his passport country for university. He related how strange it felt to him to hear his native language, something he only spoke at home, being spoken in his classes and around campus. He was embarrassed to speak it because he wasn't familiar with the slang and, according to his extended family members, sounded like an old man. Peter also tells of difficulties fitting in until he found an internationally-oriented group of students to hang out with. He says now that he is glad he stayed in his home country because he has learned more about it and appreciates it more.

21

You are a human being who has the need for relationships and a sense of belonging like everyone else has. If you move, you lose those relationships or they change and you don't know where you fit anymore. Your lifestyle has had a lot of that and if you learn to navigate it well, you can help others who are going through it too, albeit perhaps in different ways. It may be reassuring to know that you will meet others on your college or university campuses who may be experiencing the same things you are going through even if they do not share an international background. If you understand your own experiences, you might be able to give others an understanding of themselves as well.

What You Should Know:

- If you have not already done so, I highly recommend you read *Third Culture Kids: Growing Up Among Worlds.*

- Your international experiences have made you different from most of your peers at college/university. Learning to live out those differences positively will help you thrive in your new setting.

- Remember that it is not you but your experiences that make it difficult for others to relate to you and you to others.

- There are others with cross-cultural experiences who may be facing the same issues you are. You can put your knowledge to use to help other cross-cultural kids and international students.

Resources:

Books

- *Third Culture Kids: Growing Up Among Worlds*, revised, by David C. Pollock and Ruth E. Van Reken, Nicholas Brealey, 2009.

Magazines

- *Among Worlds Magazine* by Interaction International – addresses ATCK issues.

- *Interact Magazine* by Interaction International – magazine for TCKs, their parents, caregivers and educators who deal with the challenges TCKs face. To order either of these magazines go to www.interactionintl.org.

Websites

- www.TCKid.com

- www.TCKacademy.com

- www.interactionintl.org

- www.TCKworld.com

- www.justlanded.com

Chapter 2

The Transition Experience

"Transitions can be keenly anticipated or feared. They can be stepping stones to maturity and new stages of life or they can be fraught with uncertainty and inconclusiveness and laced with pain."

William D. Taylor, *'A TCP String of Five Pearls'*,

Interact, Dec. 1994

Your upcoming transition from high school to college or university may seem like a journey into the deep unknown, but over the next few chapters you will come to know what you can expect to feel over the next year and beyond. As William D. Taylor's quote indicates, transitions can be keenly anticipated rather than feared. Our largest fears in life are based on the fact that we don't know what to expect – fear of the unknown. Knowing in advance what lies ahead prepares you for the challenges and allows for fewer unwanted surprises. Once you understand what takes place throughout transition you will know that your reactions are completely normal and that you will get through it.

The Cycle of Transition

Any transition is a cycle. The Encarta Dictionary describes a transition as "a process or period in which something undergoes a change and passes from one state, stage, form, or activity to another." Transitions take place when a family member is added or lost, a job is lost, a marriage or divorce takes place or a serious illness strikes. We witness transitions as "stepping stones to maturity" when children pass from infants to toddlers to adolescents to young adults. Transitions surround us without our even realizing it. They are a normal and expected part of life.

Ever since I was introduced to Dave Pollock's five stages of the transition cycle, I have seen it evidenced in so many aspects of life. I watched as my parents went through it from involvement to re-involvement when they moved out of their home and into an assisted living community. A good friend who survived breast cancer explained to me how she experienced the five stages as she withdrew from friends and responsibilities to undergo chemo and radiation therapy and then came back "to the land of the living" when she realized she had it beaten.

The five stages of transition as Dr. Pollock outlines them are:

1. Involvement Stage

2. Leaving Stage

3. Transition Stage

4. Entering Stage

5. Re-involvement Stage

If you were to attempt to draw a diagram of the transition cycle, it might look something like this:

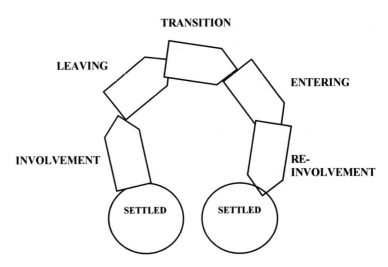

Fig. 2.1 Transition Cycle

While transitions are never easy, understanding that you can expect to pass through these five predictable stages is reassuring. Everyone is different and will pass through each stage in varying degrees. Some will breeze through them and others may get stuck in one particular stage or another. Some will even bounce around between the stages until they reach adjustment.

Figure 2.1 is fairly autocratic in that it implies you have moved from one place of belonging to another place of belonging or gone from one "home" to another "home." Any TCK can tell you that is not always necessarily the reality of relocations. Some would argue that TCKs are forever in transition, never truly able to commit to one particular place before they have to pack up again and move to yet another, even if it is just going from host country to passport country for the summer and back again. Which one truly is "home"? This is part of what leads to the rootlessness and restlessness TCKs often experience.

Everyone Goes Through It

Understanding the five stages of transition will help you to anticipate and manage the change that goes along with them. For the purposes of your upcoming career at college or university, we will use the word 'transition' to refer to the change you are about to undergo. Keep in mind that these stages are not unique to TCKs or international students. Every first-year college student is going through the same cycle. In fact, after giving a Transition/Re-entry Seminar at a Swiss international school, the coordinator who arranged for me to come and speak was approached by local Swiss students and asked if there could be a seminar to prepare them for attending university in their own country. Maureen Tillman, author of "College With Confidence," is a licensed clinical social worker who understands well what it takes even for domestic students to make successful university transitions. She has a comprehensive psychotherapy service that supports American students and parents through the college experience, and I can tell you that she stays very busy.

 Tip to Remember: Every first-year student on campus is making a transition and will also go through the five stages of the transition cycle.

On the other hand TCKs are always telling me about home-country peers at their universities who struggle with the cultural transition as well. When someone moves from one area to another of a sizeable country such as the U.S. or Canada, it can be equally disorienting because they have, for all intents and purposes, entered another culture. Some TCKs have been able to relate the experiences of their struggling peers to their own which resulted in helpful bonding.

 Tip to Remember: Even domestic students may struggle with the adjustment to university, particularly if they are coming from one culturally distinct part of the country to another. With your TCK background, you can help them make the cultural shift.

Schools also have their own cultures. I recently had a conversation with a father whose daughter had been born and raised in the U.S. and was struggling in her first year of university. Since she had spent her high school years away at a boarding school, he felt she would be better prepared for the transition than her hometown peers who attended all four years at the local high school. Her struggle was in leaving the very democratic and egalitarian culture of her boarding school for the highly competitive and elitist culture that pervaded her university. Culture is everywhere.

The Five Stages

Following are the five stages as adapted from Pollock and Van Reken's *Third Culture Kids* and Jean Larsen's *Transitions and TCKs:*

Stage 1 – Involvement

This is the state of normalcy as you know it. It may be where you are right now. You are settled, involved in your community, school, etc. This stage is characterized by a sense of belonging and participation. It's really the last place you can call "home."

Stage 2 – Leaving

Leaving begins the moment you are aware of an upcoming change. It can begin as early as 3-6 months before actually leaving. This is a time characterized by a loosening of emotional ties, distancing from others and relinquishing responsibilities.

Stage 3 – Transition

The transition stage begins the moment you leave one place and ends once you decide, consciously or unconsciously, to settle in and truly become a part of your new place. This stage is characterized by chaos and ambiguity.

Stage 4 – Entering

Things are no longer chaotic but you are still feeling marginal and uncertain during entering. You are looking for mentors and friends in this stage to help fulfill your desire to settle in and connect with others.

Stage 5 – Re-involvement

Re-involvement is a position of feeling settled again. You feel a sense of belonging and participation in your new surroundings. You can now call this new place "home."

If you were to draw out the emotional responses you can expect to go through in each of the five different stages, with the dark line indicating level of feeling, it would look something like the graph (Fig. 2.2) on the next page.

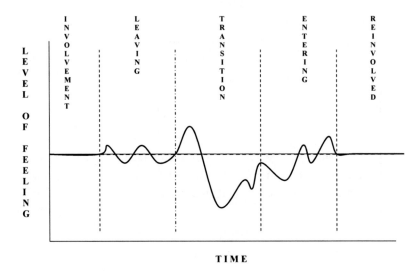

Fig. 2.2 Emotional Response to Stages of Transition

How to Have a Positive Experience

While transitions are never easy, and they can be quite uncomfortable as you can see from Figure 2.2 above, there is good news. Research has shown that people who receive cross-cultural training before making an international move have a much smoother adjustment. In fact, research from The Interchange Institute's 2004 Prudential Financial relocation study, *Many Expatriates Many Voices*, shows that expatriates who received cross-cultural training described themselves as having a more positive experience and better adjustment to their new surroundings than those who did not. Their Mental Health Inventory scores were higher and levels of depression lower. Eric Kruger, President of Compass Cross-Cultural Coaching, notes from his own experience in working with expatriate families that emotional responses to the transition cycle after receiving training could be charted out to look more like the curves of the dashed line in Figure 2.3.

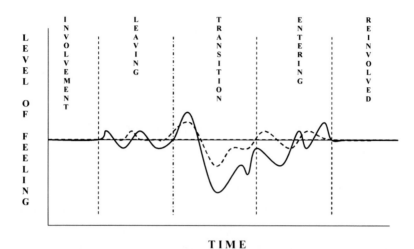

**Fig. 2.3 Comparison of
Emotional Responses to Stages of Transition
Before and After Cross-Cultural Training**

You can see that the training does not completely take away the vacillating emotional responses, but the ups are not nearly as high and the downs not nearly as low, and the responses are more rounded than they were without training. Knowing you can expect to experience ups and downs, highs and lows in the transition/adjustment cycle enables you to recognize when it is happening to you and assists you in normalizing your experiences.

Remember the opening story of the book? Thank goodness the gentleman at the party had the foresight to let me know some of the feelings I could expect when we arrived in Pakistan, and through the first few months. That was enough preparation to enable me to take a deep breath and survive until I lived through that part of that particular stage.

Leslie, the American TCK from Chapter 1 who went through a week-long Transition/Re-entry course tells other repatriating TCKs, "As a result of the training I received I knew what I could expect to feel. I had no problems settling and I love my new school."

> **Share it:** TCKs are often better equipped to handle transition because they have had to do it so often during their childhoods.

That is the intent of talking about each of the five stages of transition. If you know what to expect ahead of time, it reduces the number and intensity of surprises and road-blocks you may otherwise encounter. Knowing what to expect also helps you to appreciate that it is completely normal.

The Involvement Stage

Take a minute to think back on the last place you truly felt was home – a place that felt secure, intimate and where you were affirmed as a person. Others knew and appreciated what a special person you are. They were aware of your special characteristics, gifts and talents. You had relationships with others that attached you emotionally to that place. You had roles, responsibilities, and a reputation. You belonged. That place might very well be where you are right now or perhaps it was another time and place.

Really think about that place. What did it feel like? Was the climate hot and humid? Was it cold and breezy? What kinds of sounds did you hear? What were the smells? What kind of food did you eat? What kinds of animals were there? Who were the people? What were the stories you shared with these people? What did your house look like? What did you enjoy doing there?

Now come back to the present and ask yourself how it feels or felt in your safe place. You truly are or were (whatever your particularly situation is) involved in this place. People see you as being included. You have a reputation and a position in the school or other social community. You have/had good friends who listen/ed to your woes and who could confide in you. You feel committed to life in this place.

This is the first stage of the transition cycle – the stage of involvement. It may seem odd to give this experience (if you can call it that) a name depicting a stage because to you it is just going about living a normal kind of life. However, by recognizing this as a starting point, it sets the stage for what changes, how it changes and when it changes. Read on.

What You Should Know:

- Life is full of transitions.

- Every first-year student will experience a major lifestyle change and will go through the five stages of the transition cycle. You are not the only one.

- Understanding what happens in the stages of transition will help in your adjustment process.

Resources:

Book

- *Third Culture Kids: Growing Up Among Worlds*, by David C. Pollock and Ruth E. Van Reken, Nicholas Brealey, 2009.

Website

- www.interchangeinstitute.org – a not for profit research organization whose mission is to promote dialogue and facilitate understanding between people who move to a new country and their new communities.

Chapter 3

Itchy Feet to Dragging Feet

The Leaving Stage

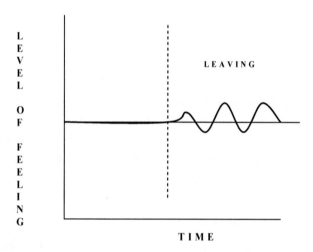

"I have only two days left in China. I don't exactly know how to verbalize my feelings but overall I am very sad. I also feel estranged to myself which has caused me to worry about how my family will view me when I get home. I am flying back home which is also a strange concept. I am excited yet nervous at going back to a place I so loved and then being away and then coming back.

I just cried hard for the past 45 minutes and I have no appetite. I don't quite understand why I am so sad. I should be happy. I have had the most incredible experience, one which has been life-changing, gratifying, enlightening and rewarding.

> Images and moments of my time in China keep coming to mind which triggers the tears and the pain in my chest. I run through many memories from beginning to end. I miss the group."
>
> *Marie, an American/British TCK,*
> *Semester abroad journal entry*

Marie, the daughter of an American mother and a British father who spent all of her childhood in Switzerland, is attending a small liberal arts college on the east coast of the U.S. She asked me to read journal entries she had written during her semester abroad to China. She needed to talk with someone who could help her make sense of the emotions she experienced during the different phases of her travels. Through the sensitive, insightful and descriptive entries in those crinkled and folded pages I was able to follow her journey through each of the three most difficult stages of transition – leaving, transition and entering. Whether you are leaving for a foreign culture or returning to a familiar one, you cannot avoid experiencing the transition cycle. She described her feelings so clearly, I requested her permission to reprint sections of her journals to help you, the reader, as you experience or anticipate your own transition.

Conflicted Emotions

Typically, the leaving stage of the transition cycle begins the moment you are aware of an upcoming change. Notice, Marie is profoundly sad two days before leaving her beloved China. For graduating high school students like you, the thought of leaving home for college or university has most likely been in the back of your minds ever since you started making those campus visits the summer before your last year of secondary school.

Denial

No doubt the sense of anticipation and excitement you experienced while doing all those college tours was infiltrated with a bit of denial. "No, this isn't really going to happen to me. Everybody else goes off to college, but I really don't need to think about it seriously yet." And yet you went through the motions of filling out those applications, writing essays and waiting anxiously for the daily mail to arrive to see if you had been accepted by the school of your choice.

Itchy Feet

Do you remember right about mid-year of your last year of secondary school when you were practically screaming, "I am so sick of school. I can't *wait* to get out of here!" But once those college/university acceptances started rolling in, a good dose of reality came with them. You practically did a 180 degree turnaround – "I really am going…but I'm not ready! I'm too young!"

Sound familiar? The academic lethargy and mini-rebellion that popped up from seemingly nowhere around the winter holidays is suddenly upstaged by the urge to act like a clingy two-year-old just about spring break time. Not only that but parents will attest to the emotional swings of the "I want out now" and the "I'm not ready to leave" extremes on a day-to-day, hour-to-hour, or even minute-to-minute basis.

Dragging Feet

There is no more denying it. You must select which college or university you would really prefer to attend for the next three to four years of your life. Once that commitment is made you are firmly planted in the leaving stage.

Separating and Distancing

The leaving stage is characterized by a loosening of emotional ties and distancing from family, friends and relationships. This behavior is quite unconscious and is a form of self-protection – from your own feelings. I watched as each of my three daughters went about this typical withdrawing in their own style. Janneke, my normally jovial, sweet, loving, eldest daughter became so irritable and downright annoying that I was convinced she was demon-possessed. She must have, somewhere back in the caverns of her mind, thought that by acting out, her family would be relieved to see her finally leave home to go off to college, thereby, making her departure easier on us.

My middle daughter, Katrina, handled it quite differently. She spent the entire summer before college hanging out incessantly with her friends. She didn't loosen any ties with them, only her family. In fact, if anything, she and her secondary school buddies became even tighter over the summer than they were in the two years they spent together before graduation. She was pleasant enough when she was around, but that wasn't very often. Any time we would ask her for a little family-together time, she would have to inform us that well-laid plans with friends could not be changed.

Kacie, my youngest daughter became a recluse at home. She came home from school or sports practice and went directly to her room to study. Her only appearance to spend time with family was mealtime.

Every time I slipped upstairs to check on her, I found her reading or doing homework. She had always been a good student, but she had also enjoyed sitting at the kitchen table to do homework so we could occasionally chat as I fixed dinner.

When I pointed out her long absences, she sighed and replied with a hint of sadness, "I'm sorry. I don't mean to be distant." Then I realized this was her way of disengaging and separating from us, her parents.

 Beware: Everyone goes through distancing and separating differently. It could be evidenced by withdrawal, frequent crying or sadness, becoming clingy with family or friends or even becoming angry and starting fights with those you love.

Surrendering Roles and Responsibilities

You may be experiencing a great deal of loss as your secondary school experience draws to a close. My daughter Kacie had a huge hole in her life when the basketball season ended. Basketball had been her major love for six years so when she relinquished her role and responsibilities as co-captain of the team, she felt lost. As a last-year student, she was not eligible for post-season play, so she struggled to find ways to fill the void in her life and to get into shape for college try-outs in the fall. Whatever roles and responsibilities you have had will end soon and you may wander the halls feeling like a "has-been."

Loss of Status and Identity

The inevitable transition can no longer be denied as you find yourself coming to the end of your student council position, drama production duties, or vocal or band responsibilities and making way for underclassmen to take over. You may feel some distancing or exclusion as others move into the roles you are vacating. You may realize you aren't needed anymore as younger students take over the responsibilities you used to have. You are, in effect, giving up your status, position, and even your identity. You were known in this place, valued for what you brought to the school community. Now you are heading off where no one knows anything about you.

 Beware: While handing over your roles and responsibilities might feel like a load off your shoulders at first, it may leave you feeling lost, unneeded, frustrated or even angry about the way the underclassman is handling the role.

This might be a good thing for some of you graduates. Perhaps you did not land so well in this place or never really gelled with the community like you did in your last host country. Maybe you were unfairly labeled or chose the wrong people to hang out with and acquired an undesirable reputation. This is a chance to start over with a clean slate. Since first-year college students don't know anything about each other, they are all on equal footing.

Conflicted Emotions

You might find that graduation is a very conflicted time for you. While ceremonies, celebrations, and festivities are taking place and everything is pointing to the promise of the future, you may be grieving the past and may try to hold onto it as long as possible. You may circulate yearbooks for signing, take tons of photographs for your albums and postpone your good-byes as long as possible. To parents, the summer after graduation may seem interminable. All your sons and daughters may want to do is hang out with their friends before they must, one by one, leave for university.

Beware: It is not uncommon for couples to start fighting as an unconscious effort to distance themselves from the inevitable pain of separation, so much so that those who had originally planned to stay together despite the distance actually end up apart. This brings more grieving and sadness.

This is also a particularly rocky time for romantic relationships. The decision must be made as to whether to try to manage a long-distance romance or break it up. If you and your significant other decide to break up, then you must decide when to do so and how to do it amicably. (More on romance in Chapter 6.)

Unresolved Grief – Leave and Grieve Well

If sorting out their personal identity is the greatest challenge TCKs face (see Chapter One), the second is unresolved grief, although most of the time, they may not even realize it. The high mobility lifestyle of a TCK brings with it a lot of loss. I give you a Dave Pollock quote from the TCK book which stuns me every time I read it:

> For most TCKs the collection of significant losses and separations before the end of adolescence is often more than most people experience in a lifetime.

Imagine that before reaching age 18, most of you will have experienced more loss than most people do in their entire lives. These losses are both tangible and intangible. The tangible losses are numerous and easily recognized – houses, pets, friends, possessions, places, foods, languages, and

> *"It was like I was walking around with this big ball of grief and I didn't know where to put it."*
> American ATCK who grew up in Africa, repatriated to the U.S. for college and struggled with depression and suicidal thoughts.

schools to name a few. The hidden losses are more obscure. Think about it, with one plane ride, everything is lost – an entire world, a lifestyle, having status and a reputation, sights, sounds and smells, events and celebrations, a history and so much more.

A mother tells the story of her daughter who kept a field hockey stick next to her bed as she anticipated the start of the season in the fall of the next school year. She was going to try out for the team. But her family was relocated over the summer to a country where field hockey wasn't offered at her school. That stick stayed next to her bed for many months in her new home as a memory of an intangible loss – the past that never was.

Grieve Well

We, as humans, need to grieve our losses. We can get stuck emotionally until we recognize our loss and grieve for it. Grief validates all the good in our lives. Grieving well means

- recognizing and naming the loss,

- mourning the loss,

- accepting the loss,

- coming to closure, and

- moving forward to the next developmental stage.

 Share It: Allowing yourself to go through the stages of grief validates the positive that you are leaving behind, allowing you to acknowledge the loss and move forward.

Lack of Time to Grieve

Unfortunately TCKs have little or no time to grieve. Today's travel is usually done by airplanes rather than boats as in days past. So, a few hours to a day at most is all the time they have to name their losses and deal with their grief before they land in their new host country and hit the ground running to learn the in's and out's of a new place and its culture.

 Dig Deeper: Due to the speed of travel today, we do not have the downtime to embrace our losses and grieve as we are already dealing with the adjustments of the new place.

Lack of Comfort

Without realizing it, parents often do not allow themselves or their children to grieve. They tend to focus on the cognitive reasons for the move, rather than on the emotions created by the move. They can be so anxious for their children to settle in that instead of comforting them and acknowledging their fears and sadness, they encourage them by saying things like, "Don't worry, you will make new friends soon." Or they may negate the grief by telling their children that the family is moving for a good reason, such as, "Daddy's work is going to help lots of poor and hungry people in this new place."

It could be that parents often focus almost exclusively on the cognitive because it is too painful for them to work through their own feelings of loss. If parents recognize loss in their own world, they acknowledge the associated grief. If they comfort their children they are saying that they accept and understand their grief. Since they don't want their children to be sad about leaving, they deny their own grief for the good of the whole family.

 Dig Deeper: At times parents will deny their own grief for the stability of the family. However, if a parent allows their grief to surface, it can start the process for the whole family to validate the positive in their experiences. Refer to the earlier section on how to grieve well.

Delayed Grief

Grieving openly is good grief, but when grief is pushed under the carpet or placed somewhere else in our minds to come back to later and coming back to it never happens, we have unresolved grief – grief that has not been dealt with. Unresolved grief can emerge later in life in destructive forms such as anger, rebellion, depression, isolation and even physical ailments. Such is the story of Brice, a typical TCK.

Brice's father is half French and half Vietnamese and his mother is Ethiopian. He moved seven times before his 18th birthday with his father's job as a United Nations peacekeeper. He remembers being plunked down at nine years of age in a Canadian school classroom speaking no English whatsoever. He moved around again after that.

Never really having a sense of where home was, at age 19 he decided to go to university in Canada, the country where his mother was living. Just before the start of university he was suddenly stricken with pain in his hands. The pain became so severe that it was completely incapacitating. The first doctor he went to thought it may be multiple sclerosis, a degenerative nerve disease that leads to physical and cognitive disability and has no known cure. After two agonizing weeks, all test results came back negative. For two years Brice consulted with a variety of physicians with no answers as to what was causing his debilitating pain. He had to wear braces on both hands and couldn't even lift a glass of water to his lips.

Then one day Brice's mother convinced him to accompany her to visit family in England. While there he realized that he didn't belong in England either. He didn't know where he belonged. So he started a search on the web for other people like himself. He discovered he was a third culture kid and he had been through a lot. He then proceeded to find a park next to an airport and spent the next two hours screaming at the top of his lungs and sobbing. He then came back to where he was staying and began journaling. The pain in his hands came but he pushed on. This kept up until there was no more pain.

What Brice discovered is that the pain in his hands was caused by unresolved grief. Today Brice manages TCKid.com, a website devoted to helping people like himself.

Marie, our TCK who spent a semester abroad sums up good grief in this journal entry:

> "I have come to realize the sadness and tears are, more than anything, another expression of my happiness/gratitude/dumb-struckness/amazement/overwhelming feeling of being blessed and watched over. It is such a strong combination of emotions that the only effective way of manifesting itself is through tears. Sadness appears when something great ends."

No Funerals

Life is filled with loss and resulting grief. It can be as serious as a loss of health, loss of a job, a death or a divorce. Or it could be disappointments like not getting the role you wanted in the school play or not getting accepted at the college of your choice. Making an international relocation is considered a major life event which triggers grief. It ranks right up there with death and divorce. You leave behind friends, routines, familiarity, favorite places, lifestyles, status, roles, responsibilities and so much more, but there are no rituals or ceremonies for grieving the loss. All the makings of a funeral are there, but there is no open expression of the grief that is felt.

 Try This: Force yourself to come face-to-face with your losses by putting a name on them. Embrace the sadness so you can validate the good and move ahead in your life.

To compound the grief even further, from the perspective of the non-international, there is seemingly no logical reason to grieve. To them you have been fortunate to have had this incredible opportunity. What do you have to be so negative about?

Confronting Grief

Give yourself permission to grieve. Spend some time with the losses and disappointments you are facing. Put a name on what they are, e.g. "I was known as the best female athlete in my school." "I don't know if I'll ever see my best friend again." "I'll miss my boyfriend…favorite teacher …or coach." "I always directed the annual fashion show." One by one, list the losses, cry, talk to someone who will listen and offer comfort, draw, journal, write poetry, compose music describing the losses, whatever helps you confront the loss and come to closure with it.

 Tip to Remember: Grieving is a process which takes time. Don't rush it.

If you feel you are stuck in your grief, seek professional help from a counselor who understands TCKs. There are those times when a TCK/ATCK cannot figure out exactly what their losses are because they have been repeatedly told they should not be so negative. The grief is then so suppressed that they have a difficult time going there on their own. This is when a professional therapist can come alongside them and walk with them on this journey of discovering those hidden losses.

As you can see in Marie's journal entry below that immediately followed the one at the beginning of this chapter, she, without even realizing it, was facing her fears and losses, while at the same validating her experiences and recognizing the value of having taken the journey.

"Why are you so sad?

- I am afraid that I will never see some people again.

- I know that my life will never be the same. I should be happy; that's a good thing.

→ But more than that I feel like I am going back to people (family and friends) that haven't changed. But I will be different and that makes me feel like there will be distance and a lack of understanding.

- I feel different in so many ways and as a result I feel disoriented, stuck between two worlds, not knowing what to think about either one.

How do you feel different?

- I feel more confident.

- More mature

- More adaptable to different people

- I don't look at my culture the same way; there are such different ways of living and seeing the world."

Build Your RAFT

Dave Pollock used to say that "you need to leave well in order to enter well." In other words, how you leave one place has a profound effect on how you enter the next. He developed a model anyone going through transition could

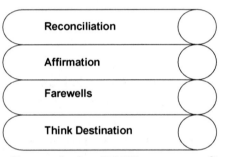

Reconciliation

Affirmation

Farewells

Think Destination

use to help them leave well. He used the **RAFT** acronym for **Reconciliation**, **Affirmation**, **Farewells**, and **Think Destination**. He discussed it in detail in the TCK book and I summarize briefly below.

Reconciliation

Do not leave a place with undone issues or unfinished business. There are many ways to resolve issues and resentments and reconcile your relationships. Whether it is the good, old-fashioned method of coming up to someone face-to-face and asking for or giving forgiveness or sending a note, it will free you to move forward. Sometimes friends and others hurt, embarrass, harass, bully or manipulate you and don't even realize what they have done. Or you have somehow caused a good relationship to go sour without understanding why. It could have been something said as a joke or even a cultural misunderstanding. You feel the coolness and the loss of closeness you once had with this person but don't understand what

46

happened. Perhaps it was too uncomfortable to say anything at the time and the crevasse in the friendship grew bigger and bigger over time.

Beware: Do not leave with unfinished business that can lead to relationship problems later in life.

Now is the time to approach that person and discuss it. It is never too late to restore relationships. Tell that person what you perceived they may have done, how it made you feel and tell him or her that you forgive him or her. On the other hand, if someone has pulled away from you, approach him and ask for forgiveness. This is all very difficult. It is not easy to humble yourself and open yourself up to be so vulnerable. But it really does free you when you forgive and grant forgiveness.

Try This: However uncomfortable it may be, you need to make relationships right with people in order to move forward in your life and enter well in your next environment.

Affirmation

Just as giving and receiving forgiveness liberates and heals you, so does affirming people that have been important to you. Telling friends, teachers, neighbors, pastors, coaches, mentors and others how much you appreciate and respect them makes you and them feel better about saying good-bye.

Try This: Be sure to tell others how much they have meant to you before you leave.

Just as there are many ways to ask for forgiveness, there are unlimited methods for affirming people. A small gift with a note or a hug will suffice as will flowers, baked goods or a personal memento of times spent together.

Tip to Remember: Teachers always get a big smile on their faces when they see notes from their departing students setting on their desks on the last day of school.

Farewells

Many cultures have wisely built traditions around saying proper farewells to help people move forward on their journeys. One of the most effective I have ever experienced incorporated reconciliation, affirmation and farewells into one gesture. When my family was leaving Switzerland a couple who had served as medical missionaries in Nepal for many years invited us over for a farewell dinner. As soon as we entered their home, the hostess came up to me and my daughters and laid scarves around our necks. She laid a necktie around my husband's neck and said, "In Nepal there is a tradition when people leave. If I had a lei of flowers, I would have put them around your necks, but I don't so please accept these." Then she bowed in front of us with her hands held, palms together, in front of her and said, "Please forgive me for any wrongs I have done you and I forgive you for any wrongs you have done me. I have truly appreciated and valued our friendship. Now go in peace." That certainly wrapped it all up for us! We were all very touched.

Farewells To People

High school friends will be scattering across the globe to start university. This is a particularly tearful time for TCKs.

Tip to Remember: Parties are also a great way to gather friends together in one place and say goodbye all at once. Be sure to spend a few minutes one-on-one with each person at the party doing appropriate farewells including giving and requesting forgiveness as well as giving and receiving affirmations. Having a party without speaking to all of your guests can do more harm than good.

Perhaps your family has decided this is a good time for another move and you may not see these friends again. You won't be coming back on holiday breaks and meeting up again. This is what happened to Brent whom you met at the beginning of the first chapter.

Brent was very bitter over not being able to return to this beloved country where he felt he belonged and being able to see all his friends again. He struggled with losing his past.

> "I was angry and bitter that my parents were moving. I knew all my friends would be together over the school breaks and I wouldn't be able to be with them. This was the only place I felt was home and my parents were taking that away from me."

Even if your family is staying in your host country, you may or may not get to hang out with your secondary school buddies during your university breaks. Schools in the United Kingdom and Europe are on different schedules than those in North America. American and Canadian schools do not have the same vacation schedules. Your friends may not be home when you are. There is also a tendency as the years go by for students to get involved in other pursuits at break times, especially over the summer. They do internships, have short study trips, get involved in volunteer work in other countries (something particularly pertinent to TCKs who have a keen sense of global responsibility) and don't spend much time back with their families. They are pursuing their areas of study and thinking about how they can build on their experiences for their futures. But you may be surprised at the ways and means by which you do run into your international friends throughout your college years. It is a small world, but you still need to say good-bye, so be sure to spend some time with your best buddies before you go your separate ways.

 Share It: It may be painful, but you need to say good-bye so you can come to closure, especially if your entire family is relocating and you will not be returning to this place.

Farewells To Places, Pets, and Possessions

It is important to have farewells with our pets, especially if they must remain behind and the family is moving on. Be sure to visit all your favorite haunts, particularly if you will not be returning. Do all your favorite activities in those places one last time.

You can't bring all of your favorite possessions to college or university with you. Think about the size of those dormitory rooms and apartments. But you do need to bring things with you that bring you comfort and tie you to your past. These are sacred objects that are going to come in handy when making the transition. These could be photos, trophies, scrapbooks, yearbooks, treasured childhood stuffed animals (I know one boy currently in his third year at college who sleeps with his favorite teddy and he's apparently not the only male student with a soft toy), anything you consider special and makes you feel good to have around. I know of one family who went around taking pictures of every room of the house just as it was when they lived there so the children would have that to look back on when they missed it, and they were only moving one street away!

 Tip to Remember: Plan to take favorite items with you that tie you to your past and bring you comfort.

Think Destination

The last log that forms your RAFT is to think about your destination.

Research Your New Environs

- Find out as much as you can about the college/university you will be attending, the town or city it is in, the state and even the country *before* you get there.

- Get a feel for the lay of the land so it will not be so

"Having gone through a bad repatriation, I suppose I could have a few recommendations based on my experience: Look forward. My mindset wasn't ready to leave and I avoided thinking about the inevitable future for which I was unprepared upon arrival and for the following months."
TCKid's Uncle Dan, Daniel Nguyen-Phuoc, TCK.

difficult to get your bearings when you first arrive. The internet and multimedia services are a good place to start.

- Buy a traveler's guide to your new country even if it is your home country because you don't know it as well as you think you do. You need to treat your home country the same as you would a foreign country because in many ways it will be foreign to you.

- Ask your school to send you the Handbook for International Students, even if you are repatriating.

- Use the information available on your college or university website, particularly the pages for international students. Read every page of the website, the booklets and handouts your school sends and whatever other information you can get your hands on.

- Even if you consider yourself to be 100% native in your passport country, think about approaching it as a foreign student. We will talk about this more when we discuss International Orientation in Chapter 6.

- Find someone you can actually talk to and ask questions before arriving. It is a great way to relieve anxieties about the unknown.

  - Most colleges and universities are very happy to help locate someone near you, whether it is an alumnus or a current student who can answer your questions.

  - With the ability to communicate via the internet using Skype, Skype out, VoIP, chatting or emailing, distance isn't usually a problem.

  - Don't hesitate to ask whatever is on your mind for fear of sounding stupid.

  - You could even contact someone from the International Students and Scholars Office. They are used to being asked all kinds of questions without making judgments.

What Will You Need?

- Start thinking about what you will need in your new surroundings. There will be many things you never had to consider when going back on home leave for summer or holiday times. You didn't have to. Your parents always handled those details. But now it is your turn, your responsibility to think about those particulars. What do you need to bring with you? What will you put into storage or leave at home? What will you take as opposed to buying once you've arrived? Following is a list of just some of the things you will want to think about:

    - Furniture items such as lamps, chairs, futons

    - Computer, printer, office supplies

    - Clothes for all seasons or just to get you to winter vacation?

    - Bedding

    - A mini-fridge and/or microwave

    - Storage containers for clothing, personal items, and even food

    - Bathroom supplies

    - Special objects from your past

- Will you need to replace all your electrical appliances to conform with a change in voltage?

Other Practicalities

- How will you be getting to your campus?

- What will you do in case of an emergency? Who will you use as an emergency contact?

- What will be your system for communicating back home?

- Banking needs – checking account, credit card, ATM debit card? Will your parents be putting money into an account? How will they do that? How will you receive money from other sources?

Going through and strapping each of the four logs together to form a RAFT (reconciliation, affirmation, farewells, and think destination) will ensure that you not only leave well, but that your transition journey will be a psychologically healthy one that will help you enter well on the other side. Allowing yourself to reconcile relationships, affirm those important to you, say farewell and process the grief that goes along with it will bring validation to your past, release you from it and let you move forward in healthy ways.

What You Should Know:

- The process of leaving needs to be taken seriously.

- Complete all four logs of the RAFT model – Reconciliation, Affirmation, Farewells, Think Destination – to help you leave well so you can enter well on the other side of the transition.

Resources:

Book

- *Third Culture Kids: Growing Up Among Worlds* (Rev.) by Dave C. Pollock and Ruth E. Van Reken, Nicholas Brealey, 2009.

Website

- www.TCKid.com – a non-profit community of over 21,000 members dedicated to help third culture kids connect and find a sense of belonging. It has been featured on the BBC, ABC News, *The Telegraph*, The U.S. Department of Defense and *Education Week*.

Chapter 4

Fish Out of Water

The Transition Stage

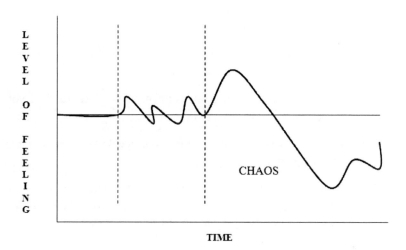

> "I am sitting on the plane flying from Hong Kong to Kunming. I had a good flight from San Francisco to China and had a fair amount of sleep. It is now 1:05 pm (4:00 am in SF) so I am very tired but the idea that I am in China is still overwhelming. I cannot believe that I have made this dream come true and that I am living it at this very moment. I feel so grateful for this opportunity and can't wait to see what the rest of the trip will hold..."
>
> *Marie, semester abroad journal entry*

It is clear to see from the journal entry above that this young woman is at the start of the transition stage, which begins the moment you leave a place. It ends once you have the desire, whether it is conscious or unconscious, to connect with, commit to and participate in the new place.

Chaos and Ambiguity

The most common characteristic of the transition stage is utter *chaos*. Think about some of the other times you have made an international relocation, even if it was just to go back to your passport country to visit family and friends. You land and everything you have been used to has completely changed. In one plane ride:

- You have lost your status, roles, and routines, and the comfort and self-confidence that go along with them.

- You don't know how to get from point A to point B. In fact, you may not even know what point B is.

- You may not feel completely comfortable speaking in your home country language.

- Chances are you need to familiarize yourself with the monetary system, public transportation procedures, phones, food, banking and postal procedures, social etiquette, customs, and more.

Unexpected Shock

While TCKs transitioning to another country and FSs expect everything to be new and different, all of this can be a real shock to the TCK who has come "home." You may have expected that you would know your passport country well, but are now finding (or may find) that you feel very much like a foreigner. TCKs are typically more observant than your domestic peers. It is a skill you own, a benefit of your cross-cultural and highly mobile childhood. You have had to be observant in order to see what was happening around you and to understand the reasons for what you saw. You have learned, sometimes the hard way, that you need to watch and wait in order to fit in and not break the social rules of your new culture.

Oddly enough, TCKs are slower to use this skill in their home country. You know a lot about other cultures, but don't realize that you don't know your "own" that well.

 Caution: TCKs must treat their passport culture the same way they would any other foreign culture. This is *big*.

Things Change

Things have changed while you've been away. You've changed while you've been away. Your international experience has given you different sets of rules, norms and customs. One very thoughtful person at my husband's office had the foresight to hand us a book when we returned in 2004 to the same city we had left 15 years before. It was the Interchange Institute's book by Dr. Anne Copeland and Helenann Wright: *Welcome to Boston: a Guide for International Newcomers*. I was grateful that this person considered me an international newcomer rather than just another American who would have no difficulties returning home. If I hadn't read the book, I would have made many more cultural *faux pas* than I actually did.

Things had changed so much in the years we had been away. As a small example, when my family left the U.S. the tipping rate was 10% or 15% if the service was particularly good. When we returned, the rate had gone up to 15-20%. If I had stayed with the old rates I could have left a long trail of angry wait staff, cab drivers and others!

 Tip to Remember: Buy a guidebook to the country where you will be attending university, even if it is your *home* country.

Transition Shock

The Transition stage is also where culture shock begins to take place. The Encarta Dictionary defines culture shock as

> *"Enter as a foreigner – not as a hidden immigrant."*
> Uncle Dan,
> TCKid.com

"the feelings of confusion and anxiety experienced by somebody suddenly encountering an unfamiliar cultural environment." You may remember going through culture shock when you first moved abroad. You may even have had some training before leaving so you came to expect the different stages of culture shock. You are not immune to experiencing this shock again upon repatriation, only now it is in reverse. Repatriation is widely viewed as being just as or more difficult than expatriation. It is the same experience, but this time it is happening in your own country where you supposedly know everything. This is why it is such a jolt and can go unrecognized for quite some time. You are not expecting it.

The diagram below, adapted from L. Robert Kohl's *Survival Kit for Overseas Living,* shows the stages of culture shock or country shock. When it is experienced upon repatriation it is often referred to as reverse culture shock or re-entry shock. Regardless of the name, the experience is the same whether you are a foreign student entering a first or second host country or a TCK repatriating to your home country. For this reason I prefer to refer to it as transition shock. The difference is that the foreign student expects he or she will have to deal with it while it often takes the repatriate by surprise.

Progression of time →

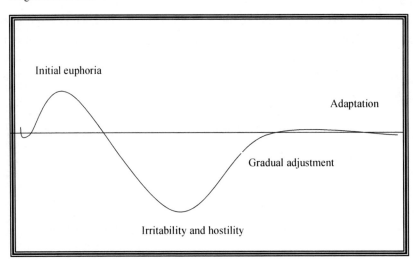

Initial euphoria

Adaptation

Gradual adjustment

Irritability and hostility

Fig. 4.1 Transition Shock

The horizontal axis is indicative of the progression of time. I prefer not to indicate weeks or months here because each person progresses to and through transition shock differently and in varying time spans. Some people will get through it in a few weeks or months and others will take up to as many as three years. It is also important to note that it is possible to go back and forth between the different phases. The mid-line represents normal level of feeling. Brent from Chapter 1 who is now in his fourth year of college says he is still in transition. Other TCKs I've interviewed were barely affected at all.

Try This: Remember the good news – now that you are becoming informed as to what happens in transitions, your reactions will most likely not be as marked as those in our case studies who had had no preparation.

The Honeymoon Stage

As you can see from the diagram, the initial rise of the curve at the beginning of the time interval indicates arrival in the home or host country when there is an initial euphoria. Some interculturalists refer to this as the "Fun" or "Honeymoon" stage where everything is exciting, new, and fun. You feel like a tourist. Over time this euphoria begins to give way to feelings of irritability and hostility. Things you once thought were quaint now begin to grate on your nerves.

Expatriates in France often say they initially admired the *joie de vivre* the French celebrated with the 35-hour work week and two-hour lunch breaks. They, too, partook in long, relaxing lunches in cafés and restaurants when they first arrived. Once they were settled with work and household responsibilities they found themselves irritated at the thought that everything shut down for two hours in the middle of the day. That was often the point in their day when they were ready to make business calls or run errands, but would be disappointed and aggravated to discover the business closed. Or worse yet, if the store, shop or business had been open on Saturday, they remained closed Sunday to Tuesday.

This happens when you return home as well. At first there is excitement over the food or shopping, television and other forms of entertainment that either was not available, lacked quality or was too expensive in your last host country. You enjoy being able to speak in your mother tongue again and be understood. You might eat out a lot at all your favorite restaurants. Then one day you wake up and feel yourself having a mind shift.

The Dip

Suddenly everything and everybody seems so materialistic, shallow, ethnocentric, and bigoted and the list goes on and on. You find yourself being extremely judgmental and critical of your homeland and the people around you. You may think your compatriots eat too much of all the wrong foods. You are disgusted by the TV commercials you once thought were funny and entertaining. You are repelled by the way your peers all wear the same shoes or jackets with the *right* designer logo. You swear you will never be a conformist and will maintain your own style at all costs. Craig Storti in *The Art of Coming Home,* says that being critical of home works well at keeping it at arm's length because you are still very much missing your host country. In fact for many, you might even consider it to be *your* country rather than just a host country.

> *"Until you are ready to embrace home, perhaps it is better that its charms elude you."*
> Craig Storti in *The Art of Coming Home*

This is the crisis stage of transition shock. It is indicated by the curve, mentioned earlier, a dip down from the normal level of feeling. You are still feeling overwhelmed with all the changes. You also feel marginalized, at the edges of society, like a minority. That's because you are. Your overseas life has changed you, and people don't understand what kind of influence an international upbringing has had on you, so you appear a little 'weird.' You are the "hidden immigrants" we will talk about in Chapter 5.

Fight or Flight

Not everyone has as deep a dip as shown in Fig. 4.1, especially after cross-cultural training, but common reactions to this crisis stage are what give it the nickname of the "Fight or Flight" stage. This is when you resist the adjustment and want to return to your host country and old friends. You may become angry and start mocking your home country culture, something which can be very dangerous. You may become terribly unhappy – even depressed, and as a result, you just want to escape and withdraw from it all. You may end up isolating yourself, avoiding others, or refusing invitations, all which lead to loneliness and despair. A very telling and powerful example of this is the following poem written by a 13 year-old American boy who had repatriated from the Middle East six months before. The homework assignment was to write about what "the Great American Teen Novel" would be about when it was written.

The Great American Teen Novel
By David Hudson

When they finally write the Great American Teen Novel
there will be boys and girls from remote countries

These boys and girls are stuck, sucked into America
Their prison
Their torture

They look around and see happy American teens
They look different
They feel different

They push away from American culture, the crowds, the groups
They start to suffocate, drown in the crowds
They feel hopeless, insignificant, tiny
They scream and pound against the walls of their prison
Their cell

Miserable, disheveled, upset, destroyed
Uprooted from their home
Depressed, shaking the bars of their prison, yelling, screaming
Wanting out

The groups of American teens walk past, happy chatting
Teens

The outsiders feel lonely, homesick
Slowly, slowly they give in, they stop pushing
They sink down
Down,
Into American teen culture

They give up
They think they want to die
But then they realize that life is OK
They come up,
Up
They adjust
They live

They even smile.

I love this insightful expression of what this child was experiencing throughout the shock of transition.

- He obviously went through the dip and wanted to flee – "yelling, screaming, wanting out."

- He expressed marginalization – "They look different...They feel different," "the outsiders feel lonely, homesick."

- He wrote about profound unhappiness, depression and isolation.

Freeze and Friends

Linda Maguire, one of my intercultural colleagues, often adds the term "Freeze and Friends" to depict this part of the curve. What helps when you are in the bottom of this curve is to be able to spend time with caring *friends* who will listen. This could be friends you have left behind in your host country, other classmates who are also off to university and perhaps experiencing similar reactions, relatives, student advisors on your college campus, or new friends you have made. There is a possibility that you could get stuck or *freeze* in this stage and not move forward.

I reiterate the story I tell in Chapter 1 about the man who warned me that I would experience culture shock when moving to Pakistan. What saved my marriage and family togetherness and kept us in-country was knowing (1) culture shock was going to happen and (2) I would get through it. Had he not informed me of both, I would not have realized that it was a normal and expected part of relocating and I might have become terribly depressed and decided to leave my husband there by himself. Since you are reading about it now and know that you might feel depressed, you too will know it will pass.

 Beware: When you first move to the new culture, you may find everything is new, fun, and exciting. Over time this euphoria gives way to feelings of irritability and hostility. You may even feel marginalized, like a minority. You may have an enormous urge to return to the culture from which you most recently came. Or, you may become depressed or angry. Knowing this will pass should encourage you to be patient and look for resources to help you get through it.

Knowledge empowers us to overcome adversity. Knowing it will pass encourages us to be patient and look for resources to help us get through it. Families who understand that their repatriated child may experience reverse culture shock or transition shock can be on the ready to lend an ear, be empathetic, and successfully encourage their students.

Gradual Adjustment

After taking a deep dip, the line in Fig. 4.1 indicating level of feeling is slowly scaling upward to feeling normal again. In reality what takes place is a series of further ups and downs as is indicated in the depiction of the transition stage at the very beginning of this chapter. The highs and lows will eventually become less and less frequent over time. *Emotional instability* is another trademark of the transition stage, but remember it is predictable and expected. The first few weeks and months are full of wildly fluctuating emotions. Students can be thrilled and excited about many aspects of their campus, love all their classes, be making new friends and joining new activities one day and be full of insecurity and sadness the next. Feelings of self-doubt begin to take over:

- Everyone here is so much smarter than me.

- I chose the wrong school.

- Everyone seems to be doing well but me.

- Everyone else has found friends. Why haven't I?

- I don't belong here. I want to transfer.

Typical Reactions

Students may feel:

- Fear – worry they will not succeed academically or socially in this place.

- Disappointment – perhaps the school, the people, the classes or the experiences have not met up to their expectations.

- Low self-esteem – arises from feeling marginalized.

Eventually, and this can be weeks or months depending on the individual student, negativities begin to melt away and you begin to see the value in both your new home and the place where you have come from. Just as the upswing in the curve in Fig. 4.1 reflects the gradual adaptation or adjustment of transition shock, so do the words of David's poem – "They come up, Up...They adjust...They live...They even smile."

There may still be much you don't care for in this new place, but you can now sort out things you were not so fond of overseas either. Your perspective is changing. You are balancing your experiences. You begin to relax and develop some routines which help bring structure and propel you forward.

 Tip to Remember: Give yourself some time. "This too shall pass." Your perspective will change as you process and balance present experiences with past experiences.

Cultural Incidents

On top of everything else you have to deal with when entering or re-entering a country, cultural misunderstandings or incidents, as Craig Storti describes in his book, *The Art of Crossing Cultures,* are taking place left and right. Again, because you *think* you know your passport culture well, or because you think you are competent enough or should be competent enough to handle any adjustment well, the result is shock and surprise when something catches you off guard. It can be something as simple as feeling so overwhelmed in the grocery or department store at the choice of products you came to purchase that you cannot possibly decide on the best product so you leave without buying anything. I have personally had the experience of hyperventilating in the feminine products aisle of Wal-Mart when back on home leave from Kenya where those choices had just not been available.

Type I Cultural Incidents

Storti explains that there are two types of cultural incidents: Type I and Type II. Type I cultural incidents occur when we react to the behavior of the people of the local culture. These types of incidents typically take place when we first move to a foreign country where we are not yet familiar with the cultural customs and traditions. An example of this comes to mind when my family moved to Pakistan. Housing was provided for us but we were responsible for furnishing it ourselves. As we mostly owned antiques that had been handed down through my husband's family, we chose to keep those in storage rather than take them to a hot, dry and dusty climate. I decided to go out furniture shopping on my own and was lucky enough to quickly find a lovely shop that had nearly everything I would need. The owner was very attentive and after some minutes of my browsing around was so kind as to offer me some hot chai. So, I sat and engaged in conversation with him until he reached over and began to rub my thigh. What do you do in a situation like this? As for me, I quickly hightailed it out of there without making any purchases and was very reluctant to ever go shopping again!

Type II Cultural Incidents

Type II cultural incidents occur when the local people react to *our* behavior. From all the stories I have heard from foreign students entering a new culture and TCKs who have repatriated for college and university, this type of cultural misunderstanding affects them the most frequently. It can be as simple as getting laughed at in the U.S. for asking a classmate for a "rubber" (which means "eraser" in the U.K. but means "condom" in the U.S.) or asking someone to "knock me up" at 7:00 a.m. (which means "wake me up" in the U.K., but means "get me pregnant" in the U.S.). Both these U.K. English words have completely different connotations in the U.S.

Language is commonly at the root of cultural misunderstandings but so are customary ways of greeting people or saying good-bye. There are misunderstandings when someone you've just met for the first time comes at you to kiss you farewell on each cheek or when someone who has been used to bowing receives a big hug.

I love to share the water fountain story Libby Stephens tells at the Interaction International Transition /Re-entry Seminars as a good example of a Type II incident.

> Libby had been living in Europe for a couple of years when she returned to the U.S. for home leave one summer. She had decided to visit a museum one very hot and dry day. She had been touring the museum for some time when she spotted a much needed water fountain. She, for some reason, approached the water fountain by clasping her hands behind her back and bending ever so slowly at the waist as she waited for the water to spring out. She had just witnessed all the automatic changes in the airport restrooms and her jet lagged mind must have somehow thought everything in the U.S. was now automated as well.
>
> When nothing happened, she backed up and looked for a button or handle to push to start the water flowing. By this time a line of hot and thirty museum goers was beginning to form behind her. Seeing nothing, she again approached the fountain but this time started waving her hands all around where she thought there may be infrared detection lights set up. Still nothing happened.

> Libby backed up a second time to try to understand how to make the fountain work. Finally the gentleman in the now very long line behind her said, "It's the bar on the front!" Libby took a few quick gulps (certainly not the amount of water she really needed to quench her thirst) and walked away completely mortified.

Examples

Following are some examples of cultural incidents that have either happened to me or to others I know and how I would classify them according to Storti's categories of Type I or Type II incidents:

TYPE I INCIDENTS	TYPE II INCIDENTS
• Being greeted with a hug when you are used to a handshake. • Feeling offended because someone eats in front of you without offering you any. • Having to jockey for position while waiting your turn to be served instead of standing in a queue (a line).	• Wrongly assuming the gratuity has been included in the restaurant bill so you leave only the small change. • Showing up 20 minutes late for a meeting where it is considered unprofessional to be late. • Using a common word or phrase that, in that culture, translates to something rude or vulgar.

Expecting Cultural Sameness

Storti explains that cultural incidents occur because either we expect other people to behave like we do (Type I) or other people expect us to behave as they do (Type II). In either case the reaction is anger, frustration, worry, fear, concern, horror, shame, or laughter. Whether we are the perpetrators of the reaction (Type II) or the person having the reaction (Type I), we are the focus. It is not unusual to have feelings of self-doubt and lose your self-confidence when these things are routinely taking place. As a result, there may be a tendency to isolate yourself in the hope of avoiding them.

Cultural Effectiveness

Cultural effectiveness is attained by becoming aware of these reactions and realizing that cultural incidents occur because we are expecting cultural sameness. Once we understand that, we are motivated to learn about the culture, or in the case of the repatriated person, re-learn one's own culture.

Tip to Remember: Don't be afraid to ask questions in order to better understand the culture.

After my disastrous Pakistani shopping trip I began recounting the tale to other expatriates who explained, much to my dismay, what *I* had done wrong. If I had been more aware of the Muslim culture, I would have known that it is considered improper for a woman to be out on her own, much less be friendly and chatty with a man alone in his shop. Only women of ill repute are expected to be that irreverent!

As time progresses, we eventually come to expect the local people to behave as themselves and fewer Type I cultural incidents occur. For repatriates, Type II incidents slowly dissipate as we re-learn the cultural norms of our society and behave accordingly. Let me remind you again, it is necessary to treat your home country the way you would any other foreign country because it is foreign to you in many ways.

Hitting the Dip

Once the honeymoon period is over reality begins to set in and feelings of fun and excitement give way to a whole spectrum of emotions. Let's have a look at the types of emotional reactions you may encounter once the newness has worn off.

Flip Flopping Emotions

Human beings bring order into their lives by creating routines. These routines become so well-rehearsed that you get to the point where you no longer need to keep them on a conscious level in order to repeat them. There are likely to be times you will find yourself inadvertently slipping back into a routine that worked well in your last place of belonging but is totally out of context in this new place. You may sometimes even find yourself speaking in the language (or accent) of your last host country. Perhaps you just cannot remember the word you are searching for in your home language and another language pops out instead. Confusion and embarrassment may be the standard as you flail around trying to figure out the proper way to greet or thank someone because what was once routine for you and took no conscious effort is now a deliberate thought process.

A particular but unexpected smell may set off your olfactory nerve or a familiar sound will momentarily transport you back to your host country and have your emotions flip flopping back and forth. You may even have recurring dreams of the country you have left and those dreams may be in the other language you spoke as we can see from Marie, our semester abroad student. She flip flops between cultures in this dream which, despite studying in English for the past three years, was all in French.

"This morning I had a wonderful, yet terribly upsetting dream. It was divided into three parts. The first was of me and [name of friend] walking very happily, arm in arm [in China]. Once that moment and the security of knowing [our relationship was good] were finally engrained into my heart, I began to run. I ran all the way to Switzerland, across mountains and snow, passing people along the way encouraging and cheering me on. Once I arrived in Switzerland, I stopped to say hello to some family friends and their daughter who happened to be very sick. By using my new knowledge of Chinese medicine I analyzed all her symptoms and asked her to stick her tongue out only to find it was white. I gave the prescribed medicine and blessed her and she was cured!!"

Exaggerated Responses

There are so many things coming at you at once in this new place that it feels quite overwhelming and even the slightest mishap or obstacle can suddenly become an enormous problem. The student's response to this can be just as exaggerated as the problem. It may appear that the situation is completely unsolvable and is just the worst thing that could possibly happen right now.

Let me illustrate with an example of my then-16-year-old daughter, Katrina, who was starting her next-to-last year of high school when we repatriated to the U.S. – her first time in an American public school.

> Every day during the first week of school she came home in tears, but this particular day was different. She burst through the front door and ran upstairs to her bedroom, slamming the door behind her. I could hear her sobbing two floors down. I slowly made my way up the staircase to inquire what was so terrible.
>
> "It's my locker!" she screamed.
>
> "Okay," I said, "what's wrong with your locker?" I was imagining all kinds of horrific things such as the inside being filled with disgusting graffiti or rotting cafeteria leftovers.
>
> Finally she blurted out between sobs, "It's on the first floor!"
>
> I thought that was a fairly reasonable place to have a locker since everyone entered and exited via the first floor. But as it turned out, all of her classes were on the second and third floors and the school was so large that she couldn't possibly have time to get to her locker between classes. This meant lugging all her books around all day long. As far as she was concerned, this was the end of the world! She just couldn't cope anymore.

The truth was that she was dealing with so much all at once that this was the "straw that broke the camel's back" – a little thing that became more than she could bear – and she had no reserves left to deal with it. All it took was a quick visit to the guidance counselor to sort out some other concerns such as appropriate level of classes (fallout of being in an English curriculum international school and returning to the American curriculum) and getting a new locker on the second floor.

It may be the most diminutive detail that throws you off balance, but it personifies all you have had to deal with up to that point and you feel you just cannot take anymore.

Caution: The learning curve is steep when internationals first enter or global nomads re-enter. There are so many things coming at you at once that it feels quite overwhelming and even the slightest mishap or obstacle suddenly becomes an enormous problem. It is normal to feel this way. It will eventually settle down and you will be able to laugh at your experiences.

Homesickness and How to Beat It

What do you do when homesickness hits? Homesickness is tough to avoid – not just for international students but all students. Many domestic students are also far away from home, maybe for the first time. Homesickness is an expression of grief. You are grieving over your losses. Domestic students share many of the same losses that you do – home, family, friends, routines, and way of life. Not everyone will necessarily experience homesickness, but for those who do, it will manifest itself in different ways for

> *"There are times when you can decide to be homesick. Choose to be homesick – don't let it choose you!"*
> Libby Stephens,
> Interaction Intl.

different people. For some it will be preoccupying thoughts of home. For others it may be frequent phone calls home and a feeling of uneasiness or discomfort. For most of us, especially women, it is manifested in a good cry and generally feeling blue.

How to beat homesickness:

- Plan a time when you don't have to be anywhere for a while

- Put your favorite music on

- Look at your photo albums and school yearbooks

- Have a good cry

 Try This: Instead of trying to fight off home-sickness, pick a good time and just give in to it.

Once you've done that, perhaps get on the internet and chat with your old friends and see what they are up to or call home and have a nice, long talk with your family…then go cry again. It's okay to give in to it and do it right rather than trying to beat it back and be on the losing end of things. By allowing yourself to openly grieve you are validating all the joy and good things from home. They are worth being sad over. Then take a deep breath and move on. Overwhelming homesickness may come back a few more times and you can give in to it again, but if it hangs around without letting go despite your efforts to deal with it, then think about talking with someone who can help, whether it is an upper-class student, an advisor, a friend, a coach, a professor or a counselor. You are not alone and people are happy to be helpful to students at this difficult stage.

The Blues and How to Shake Them

Blue days, crying spells and mood swings are normal in the transition stage. Nothing-is-right-in-the-world days are normal, but they are usually interspersed with good or just-okay days. Remember that the big time blues may show up at 6-12 weeks or more due to the downward dip in the curve of transition shock. A second dip sometimes recurs at around six months. This is normal. I like to tell students who cannot go home for that first vacation when the campus clears out that they need to make other arrangements to get away. This may happen in the fall when a short, four-day weekend is given as a reprieve just before or after fall weekend when parents and alumni visit. North American college campuses also tend to clear out at Thanksgiving and four days is just too short a break for an international student to make a visit home.

 Try This: If you cannot go home for short breaks try to make plans to visit friends or relatives who live in the country rather than stay on a deserted campus or in a lonely apartment. It may be a good time to visit a former classmate who is also attending college in the same country. Perhaps you could visit a nearby city you have always wanted to spend time in. Some proactive colleges arrange such excursions for students rather than leave it up to them to figure out for themselves.

Many professors and other university staff recognize how difficult it is for students who have nowhere to go at Thanksgiving and invite them to their homes for the day. Another time they are likely to offer their home is at Parents' Weekend when everyone else is walking around campus with their parents and siblings but not the international student whose parents couldn't just hop a flight across the ocean for the weekend. Many colleges and universities have churches in the area that organize families who will look out for students at these times and also offer a get-away and a home-cooked meal.

How to shake the blues:

- Engage in activities that bring you joy.

- Look for volunteer opportunities such as community service projects – colleges are full of them.

- Get your mind off things by going to a comedy film or out with new friends.

- Push yourself to go out and socialize even if you don't feel like it. It usually turns out to be a better time than you thought.

- Try identifying all the good that has come from this change in your life.

Along with the losses of what you have left behind is a realm of gains. What are some of the positive things that have come out of this experience? You may be missing your old friends, but you are making new ones, seeing new places and having some exciting new experiences. Don't give up. You will get through it. As Scarlet O'Hara says in one of her worst moments in the movie, *Gone with the Wind*, "Tomorrow is always another day!"

Thoughts of Transferring

Many students begin entertaining thoughts about transferring out to another school during this time. The majority of them don't actually follow through because things start to get better. Panic phone calls home to sympathetic parents are not uncommon. They just need someone to talk to. Our semester abroad student's journal entry at this time eloquently sums up the typical feelings in the transition stage:

> "Maybe it's because I haven't really found a group of people I can really stick with but I really do feel like a fish out of water. I want to see and learn and there is excitement and enthusiasm with that but still there is this feeling of discomfort, being so insecure, not knowing how to behave, how to act, how to hold myself. This is probably why it has made interacting with a group of people so difficult. I am often lost for words and do not know what to say to most of them. I am very self-conscious and often find myself alone. Making new friends has never been difficult but here I am encountering quite a bit of difficulty getting to know people and asking the right questions. Everything is so new and different that I somehow feel different and I have a hard time knowing what to do. I guess I must just wait and be patient and try to relax a bit…"
>
> *Marie, semester abroad journal entry*

Marie was incredibly insightful. She was feeling the chaos and not understanding why everything was so much more difficult for her in this new place, but she figured out she just needed to "wait and be patient." She recognized that her feelings would pass and that things would get easier.

Everyone Goes Through It

This is such a difficult time for students because they are desperately missing their best friends and want someone to talk to. They haven't yet made a good friend with whom they feel they can share their feelings. No one wants

> *"Everybody tells you college will be the best years of your life, but no one talks about how hard it is at first. I remember the first time someone had the nerve to speak up about it. We were all sitting around in the library talking about how great our first year of college had been and one girl actually came out and said it, "Yeah, but those first three months were awful."* Catherine Epstein, domestic student, Vassar College, 2007

to be with a 'downer dude' so everyone keeps their best face on 100% of the time, which gives the false impression that everyone is doing just fine. Caving in to peer pressure and bowing to experimentation with drugs or alcohol are common reactions to feelings of loneliness and wanting to fit in. Out of control parties are prime examples of outlets for students trying to escape reality or hide their insecurities. See Chapter 9 for more on "drugs, sex, rock n' roll."

Exhausting Time

Keep in mind that everything is new and different and you are being constantly bombarded with sorting out how things are done in this new place, where you can find the things you need, what the proper social and classroom etiquette is, all while trying to fit in. This is an absolutely exhausting time. You need to take care of yourself so you don't become sick and get behind in your classes.

 Try This: It will be all too easy to isolate yourself or use other methods to escape reality when the blues set in and you are feeling overwhelmed. Do what you need to do to take care of yourself and stay healthy. For example, get enough rest, eat well, exercise, listen to music, but then get back out there and stay connected with others.

Depression versus Grief

If someone happens to get stuck (freezes) in the crisis stage of transition shock, she or he becomes paralyzed in the sense that there is failure to move forward. If you find that you are spending your time living in the past, finding no joy in the present, or experiencing a deep sadness that will not go away even with distractions, you may be heading towards clinical depression and you need to seek professional help. Your school's student health center will be able to help you find the care you need.

Grief

We all experience various losses throughout our lifetimes and the subsequent grief that comes with each one. It is a part of life and is difficult to avoid, especially for the TCK. As mentioned in Chapter 3, loss is a common theme for TCKs. If you can identify and put a name to your losses, confront them, mourn over them, come to closure with them and move on, you can develop strength and character from the grief. You can grow from it, learn from it and end up in a better place because of it.

Grieving takes time and needs expression. It certainly helps to have someone who will listen to those expressions of grief. Call on a parent or other family member, a mentor, pastor or trusted friend. College campuses are well-equipped at providing student health counselors and other professionals who are well-versed in the grief cycle of students, international and otherwise.

Depression

Depression, on the other hand, is bigger than grief. Self-worth takes a nosedive and with it comes an amplification of negative feeling…about everything. Going to a comedy with friends won't distract you from the deep sadness you'll feel if you are depressed. There is a loss of joy in the things you used to enjoy and it is difficult to get on with life. Each day may seem insurmountable as you feel sad all the time. It is not just TCKs who are at risk of facing some degree of depression during their college years. The American College Health Association's (ACHA) National College Health Assessment (NCHA) found in a 2005 survey that 14% of over 50,000 students surveyed reported feeling so depressed they had difficulty functioning anywhere from three to eight times during the past year.

 Share It: Remember that all first-year students are also going through the same stages of transition and are likely to be experiencing the same feelings. This is not unique to TCKs. Talk with another student and share what you miss and why. Let him or her share what is being missed. Spend time grieving. Then wipe your tears and move on.

It has been my experience in speaking with mental health professionals on college and university campuses that mental health visits and complaints of depression tend to increase about six to eight weeks after the start of the term. Some of the reasons for this timing are:

- The chaos of settling in has dissipated and old unresolved issues begin to resurface.

- It is also right around the time of mid-term exams and stress levels are up.

- The days are getting shorter in many parts of the world so there is more darkness to deal with.

- The first small holiday has come and gone, perhaps leaving the international student with no place to go.

Any deep sadness that is not easily distractible and lasts two weeks or longer may be clinical depression and you need to seek professional help. Maureen Price Tillman, L.C.S.W., Founder and Director of "College with Confidence", says it is crucial that you talk to a mental health professional *immediately* if you are experiencing one or more of the following:

- You have thoughts of or made a plan for committing suicide.

- You have hurt yourself in other ways.

- You have thoughts about hurting someone else.

- You can see that your judgment is impaired.

- You have been doing things impulsively that you would never have done before.

- You have gotten involved in dangerous activities: drugs, excessive alcohol, gambling, excessive spending, reckless driving.

Sometimes someone close to you will be the one to point out that it is important for you to seek professional help. Try to be open to hearing this, even though it may be difficult. This person may be able to observe something you are not aware of and is reaching out to offer support.

 Tip to Remember: There are some wonderful antidepressant drugs now on the market. Used along with good counseling, they can make a world of difference for students dealing with depression. Such drugs should only be taken under the supervision of and along with counseling from a mental health professional.

If a person *you* know is entertaining suicidal thoughts or showing behavior indicating that they want to hurt themselves, you *must* report it. It is your moral and, in some countries, your legal responsibility to tell someone in authority that this person needs help. If someone wants to share something with you but wants you to keep it a secret and you suspect that they may say they want to hurt themselves, you must let them know that you cannot and will not make any promises if they are planning on committing self-harm.

The good news is that depression is treatable. With the help of caring mental health professionals who might also prescribe short-term antidepressant drug therapy, you can work through life's toughest problems.

Listen to Your Body

Students cannot always recognize that they are facing issues that can be helped through counseling services. Many students suffer from physical symptoms such as head, neck, back or stomach aches; vomiting or diarrhea; sometimes even ulcers that they do not recognize as psychosomatic illnesses. Their stress and suffering is manifesting itself in physical symptoms.

Dig Deeper: If you find yourself making frequent visits to the student health center, consider the possibility of your physical symptoms being related to stress or depression.

Maureen Tillman says that mental health professionals talk about vegetative signs of depression. Your body may be feeling the effects of depression and showing you in various ways:

- You may be sleeping too little or too much.

- You may feel soothed by overeating or have little appetite.

- You may have lost weight without trying.

- Your mood is impacted – the things that you used to enjoy you no longer do.

- Irritability is common when depressed.

- You may have difficulty concentrating on your academic life.

- You may experience low energy or fatigue.

Coping Strategies

Many times, particularly in persons with seasonal affective disorder (SAD), depression sets in during the winter months when the daylight hours are shortened. Be sure to get plenty of exercise and exposure to sunlight, particularly when the winter blues set in. With a doctor's supervision photo therapy with light boxes which provide illumination similar to the sun's light can be used for treatment as well as prevention.

Maureen often advises her clients to use "positive self-talk," a particularly helpful coping skill that can be used during challenging times. She says there have been many eminent mental health professionals including Albert Ellis, Aaron Beck and David Burns who have written about how feelings result from the "messages" you give yourself.

She suggests some important steps for helping yourself with positive self-talk:

1. Listen to that "voice" in your head:

   What are the kinds of thoughts that you find yourself having?

   Are they critical?

   Are they self-defeating?

   Are you seeing things in black and white terms?

2. Say those thoughts out loud, listen carefully, and consider how thinking this way can make you feel worse.

3. What would you say to a dear friend or someone you love?

   Would you feed them negativity and self-deprecation during difficult times?

   Maureen suggests we would all most likely agree that this would be extremely damaging for anyone who is struggling emotionally. She says that is why it is critical to challenge your negative thoughts.

After that, she suggests *substituting* with kind, loving, caring thoughts. Have compassion for yourself that this is a tough time but you will get through it.

4. Come up with some kind of affirmative self-statement to help yourself:

"I have had tough times before and gotten through it."

"I have had this feeling before and it passes."

You may find it is helpful to put a stop sign in your brain when you find yourself having negative thoughts and substitute them with the affirmative statement.

 Dig Deeper: Learn the difference between grief and depression. Get exposure to sunlight and plenty of exercise and sleep. Be proactive. Have a list of resources (see below for starters). Acknowledge when you need help and find out how to get help.

Use the Experts

At one time or another during our lifetimes each one of us faces difficulties that are just too complicated, too deep or too overwhelming for us to handle on our own. It helps to have someone to talk to about them – someone who knows how to listen and who can give advice, tools, or strategies for dealing with the issues. Mental health professionals are in place to do just that and more. They may prescribe medications they know can help.

> *"The ultimate show of strength is to recognize how you are feeling at any given moment. Even more courageous is to acknowledge it."*
> Dr. Aruna Jha –
> Univeristy of Illinois -
> Chicago

Unfortunately many international students are hesitant to use these services, do not know about them, or do not understand them. Some students come from families or cultures that look at seeking out help as a weakness or a failure or feel it would bring shame to their families if they were to find out.

Some cultures feel it is disrespectful to talk to their elders about their personal problems. Instead, they confide in their fellow students but they can't move forward in that kind of relationship because they are only "recycling" their problems. Friends can listen but they cannot always give the advice and strategies that a professional can.

You may find yourself being pushed to the student mental health counselors by your deans, advisors or a friend. It is in the best interest of the institution you are attending to make sure you succeed. They care about how you are doing. That is exactly why many referrals to student health counselors will come from the learning support centers on campuses. When they see a student's grades drop and the student put on academic probation, they realize he or she may need a little help.

Many counseling centers have staff that are trained specifically to work with international students. Brent from Chapter 1 found himself struggling with depression during his first semester. He finally found some help when he opened up to some of his professors, his track coach, and then to a counselor. The professors and coach took him under their wings, got him off campus for a meal now and then and gave him a lot of support. They even hooked him up with an older student who served as a mentor for him. What he appreciated the most about the mental health services was that he felt safe speaking to someone outside the classroom in a neutral and non-judgmental atmosphere.

Student Health and Counseling Services

Student counseling centers exist on nearly every college campus and many have other less overt layers of student support. In many places the first layer consists of those who are the closest to students such as Student Advisors (SAs), Resident Advisors (RAs), or House Fellows. The next layer may be the Dean of Students, Dean of First-Year Students or Dean of International Students, and lastly the counselors themselves. All of them are trained to watch for signs of stress, depression, and suicidal symptoms and behaviors in students.

Some college campuses have student-run programs aimed directly at helping fellow students deal with all kinds of issues from eating disorders to depression to the break-up of a relationship. One such example is Tufts University's "Ears for Peers," 24-hour confidential call-in hot line.

A huge amount of change goes along with becoming a new student, particularly in a new country or culture. Change is stressful. Some universities have mental health visits built directly into the cost of tuition and students are encouraged to take advantage of those services as soon as they feel the need to talk with someone. Many health insurance policies today cover mental health visits as well as counseling that might be needed above and beyond what the university health services offers.

Choose Well

That being said, it is worth mentioning that not all counselors are attuned to the issues of third culture kids/global nomads/international students. Some TCKs have reported their student mental health visits were actually counter-productive. As one American TCK who was raised in Europe said, "When my mental health counselor couldn't even tell me what was wrong with me, I felt completely hopeless – like I was so weird that no one could figure me out. So I thought I must *really* be screwed up."

You are allowed, even expected in some situations, to "try out" different counselors to see who works best with you. Try looking at your first visit as an interview process for both of you.

 Try This: When you make an appointment with a counselor ask for someone who has had experience living internationally or who knows about TCKs. You could also direct your counselor to TCKid.com which has important but often overlooked resources on counseling for TCKs.

Hot Topic

Thankfully depression and stress among college students is no longer a taboo subject. Due to an alarming increase in mental health issues in college students, depression and suicide are hot topics on today's university campuses as well as in preventive health journals, newsletters, blogs and more. Don't be surprised to see lectures, workshops and seminars on depression and suicide offered on your campus. Halfofus.com and CampusCalm.com are two helpful internet sites dedicated to the mental health of college students. They were started by students who themselves had suffered through anxiety or other psychological issues. The sites address these topics and much more.

In 2002, USA Today reported on findings presented at the American Psychiatric Association that there is not just an increase in psychological problems in college students, but they are being detected much earlier. Robert Gallagher of the University of Pittsburgh states the ages of 18-25 as the prime time for conditions such as depression to emerge. Haro Morano, editor of Psychology Today, says many students suffer from a variety of mental health conditions before ever arriving on their campuses and are either already equipped with anti-depressants or ready access to student mental health centers helps them on their way to diagnosis and treatment. The good news is:

- Depression, suicide and other mental health issues in university students are taken seriously.

- There is help available.

- You never have to face it alone.

Surviving the Chaos

Self-Centeredness

Self-centeredness (not isolation) is not a bad thing at this time in your life and your transition. Think about taking care of yourself. You're stressed and having to cope with all kinds of change 24/7. You are adjusting to new people, perhaps sharing a room with another person for the first time. You are in new surroundings, perhaps a new climate, vastly different routines and even different bedtime hours. Take some time for yourself. What do you need to do during this chaotic time to keep yourself healthy and happy? Is it working out at the gym, going for a run everyday, playing your guitar or listening to music? Maybe it's time spent in a dance studio or on Skype with friends. As witnessed by our semester abroad student, many people feel a great deal of release when journaling.

Plan Ahead

Look at the academic calendar well in advance and plan your trips early on. Don't wait for the break to be upon you before thinking about where you will go. For North American students it is a good idea to think about Thanksgiving break shortly after arrival at school. By Thanksgiving, have an idea of what you will do and where you will go for the winter break and be thinking about your next break right after that. At or after each break, be ready for the next one. It will give you something to anticipate.

 Try This: Plan your trips for the year early on. Ensure you are never left high and dry and lonely when everyone else gets off campus for holidays.

Ask Questions

As was mentioned before, all college freshmen are likely to feel clueless most of the time, but this is even truer for TCKs and other international students. They not only have to adjust to college life like everyone else, they must also adjust to a completely new culture. That is why it is so important to ask questions if you don't understand something.

 Tip to Remember: It could be that the burning question you have but are too embarrassed to ask at the risk of looking completely foolish is something other first-year students don't understand as well and it has nothing to do with the culture.

Invite Visitors

A Canadian colleague who has lived and worked in European international schools for many years, says his family prefers to invite friends to come visit them when they start heading for that dip in the culture shock curve and find themselves beginning to get negative about their host country or new environs. When entertaining visitors you, of course, want to show them around to the nicest places and make sure they have a good time. This family says it helps them see the positive things about where they are living. Students can try this by inviting friends to come visit them on their campus for a weekend. My daughters have kept up their relationships with their classmates from Switzerland who have come to college in the U.S. by visiting them on their campuses or vice versa.

 Try This: If you are feeling negative or ambivalent about your school, invite someone to come and visit so you can show them around your new environment and point out all the best things about living there.

Extend Grace

The chaos and culture shock in the transition stage may seem a bit daunting, but now that you are aware of these emotions and reactions, you won't be so surprised when they come at you. They are to be expected. They will hit some students harder than others, but be assured, everyone will feel something. Learn to be flexible at this time. Give yourself and others a little slack. Everything is so new and different and everyone deals with that differently.

 Beware: Try not to go by first impressions of other students you meet at this time because everyone is reacting to all the newness and may be feeling stressed and overwhelmed. Extend some grace. Give everyone a second chance once life settles down.

Make It an Adventure

Treat each challenge as an adventure. A young American family who had just moved to Kenya was initially freaked out by the frequency of lizards in the various rooms of their house, including in their beds. Knowing they couldn't put screens over the vented windows meant they would have to learn to live with the lizards. So they began to look at them as housemates and the children gave them names. It became a game to try to recognize returning visitors. What stories could you take away from your uncomfortable experiences?

Temporary and Unique

Learn to laugh every day, especially at yourself. In no time at all you will be entertaining friends by retelling your most embarrassing re-entry/transition stories. Be patient...with yourself and others. Remember that this is just a stage. It is unique and temporary and, in time, you will get through it.

What You Should Know:

What's Normal:	What's Not Normal:

- Cluelessness
- Chaos
- Fear
- Uncertainty
- Emotional Instability
- Disappointment
- Full of self-doubt
- Lack of self-esteem
	- Deep sadness that
	  does not go away
	- Lack of joy in what
	  used to bring happiness
	- Failure to move ahead
	- Paralysis – difficult to
	  get out of bed or
	  go to class
	- Homesickness you
	  can't shake

- It's not just you – all first-year students are likely feeling the same way.

- It's only a stage and it will pass, unless you get stuck and then you need to seek help.

- Resources are there for you – Student Advisors, Resident Advisors, Deans, friends, coaches, student counseling center – use them.

Resources:

Books

- *The Art of Crossing Cultures*, by Craig Storti, Nicholas Brealey, 2001.

- *Survival Kit for Overseas Living,* by L. Robert Kohl, Nicholas Brealey, 2001.

- *The Art of Coming Home,* by Craig Storti, Nicholas Brealey, 2001.

Websites

- The Interchange Institute – www.interchangeinstitute.org

- College with Confidence – www.collegewithconfidence.com, a comprehensive psychotherapy service that supports parents and young adults through the college experience, and provides seminars, teleconferences, and consultations for individuals and organizations involved in the teen-to-adult transition.

- TCK counseling resources – www.counseling.tckid.com, www.tckid.com/group/5-ways-therapists-can-help-third-culture-kids/, www.tckid.com/group/people/counselors-for-tckid/

- The American College Health Association – www.acha.org

Resources (cont'd):

Websites

- Interaction International – www.interactionintl.org - develops programs, services and publications to provide and contribute to an on-going flow of care that meets the needs of (TCKs) and internationally mobile families.

- www.HalfofUs.com and www.CampusCalm.com – two websites for, by and about students that address mental health issues such as depression, suicide, anxiety, stress, eating disorders, cutting, and drug and alcohol abuse on college campuses.

Chapter 5

Introduce Me

The Entering Stage

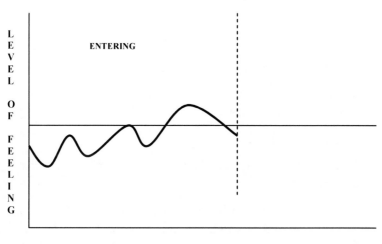

"I feel excluded (even if I am part of the group) because I do not share the same interests and values. There is a disconnect. Many people (including my parents) say I am mature – is it because I am really mature or because I just stand out from the crowd?

It is hard to feel like I don't fit in. Swimming against the current is exhausting. It's nice to feel like I am part of a group, but I am not sorry for the experiences I have had and everything I have accomplished. I am who I am; people can either accept and embrace it or not. It's too much work to be someone I am not."

Telma, ATCK from Mozambique
who lived in South Africa and the U.K. while growing up.
She is now a graduate student at a U.S. college

The fourth stage of the transition cycle is the Entering stage. This stage begins when you decide, either consciously or unconsciously, that you are going to settle in and connect with this new place. Unlike the leaving stage which ends when you land in the new place, the Transition stage does not have a clear-cut ending. Many of the emotions and reactions we talked about in the Transition stage continue on into the Entering stage. What makes the Entering stage different from the Transition stage is:

- The chaos has settled down.

- The storm is over and the dust has settled.

- One day it dawns on you that you know how to get from point A to point B without stopping and asking directions.

- You know where to find the best pizza in town and now know much more than the newcomer.

- You have routines in place.

- You are not constantly bombarded with new information that needs to be processed.

You have pretty much done what processing needs to be done, although there will still be times you are caught culturally off-guard and need to review the operative rules in this new place. Transition is a constant learning activity. In fact, some will say that you have finally finished your adjustment once you understand the jokes!

Unpack and Connect

This is the time you feel ready to unpack your mind. Up until now you have been in the survival mode and getting all your settling-in needs met such as

- finding out where to shop,

- arranging all your banking and communication needs,

- sorting out classes, finding clubs and activities to join, and

- figuring out how everything works in this new place.

You've been busy taking in all that is new and different, learning the social and cultural rules of the new community. Things are no longer overwhelming and chaotic, but you may still be feeling a bit marginal, vulnerable and uncertain.

Don't be surprised when, after the dust settles from the chaos of transition, you begin to succumb to coughs, colds, flu or other physical ailments. Your body has been producing constant amounts of epinephrine to respond to the stress associated with this stage and just when you are beginning to feel a bit more comfortable in your new environs and are more relaxed, you start feeling the effects of being in such a heightened state of alertness and readiness for so long. Your protective reflexes are down, tired out and you start to feel fatigued or become ill. This too will pass. Now is the time to take care of yourself.

 Beware: You've survived landing, learned your way around, and come to understand the in's and out's of how things work in this place so now it's time to rest, eat well and allow your body to recover.

Once the heightened alertness of the survival mode settles down, you begin to find the time, energy and interest to really connect with people. Up to this point your relationships have been fairly superficial. You have been meeting so many people at once and been receptive to all of them, but you haven't had the opportunities for developing deep relationships just yet.

...or Disconnect?

When you are ready to start developing friendships, it may come as a surprise to find yourself having difficulties making those connections. Because you can speak a variety of languages, have strange values and world views (comparatively speaking), and tell far out stories, your international upbringing has made you different from your home-country peers. You have no shared experience with them. You may not know their pop culture or common jokes. Some young adults never learned the childhood songs or games that their peers did. You may understand your peers to some degree, but they certainly don't understand you. They have no frame of reference for you and they really aren't quite sure what to do with you.

Feeling Different

Besides the unexpected reality of having to deal with culture shock, particularly when it is their home country, the inability to connect with their domestic peers is one of the major preoccupations of TCKs. In a 1998 research study of 698 ATCKs, Ruth Useem and Ann Baker-Cottrell of San Diego State University found that three-fourths of adult TCKs feel different from others who have not lived abroad as children, and especially from those who have had no international experience.

Not Belonging

In all the discussions, interviews and forums when I have asked TCKs what issues they struggled with at college or university, the issue of not fitting in/not belonging is what immediately surfaces. Global nomads feel different from their peers and therefore, aren't quite sure where they fit or belong. They know they aren't really American, British, German, or whatever their home country is, but they can't really call themselves a foreign national even though they may feel like it, unless of course, they have continued on to yet another new host country for university. In some respects, those students have a somewhat easier adjustment because they expect the culture will be different, but they still suffer the same relationship issues.

Who Am I and Where Do I Belong?

As you may remember from before, Katrina, my middle daughter, had a difficult time settling into her new school when we repatriated. We left the U.S. when she was just 15 months old. She changed cultures four times and here she was 15 years later trying to figure out how to acculturate, blend in and make friends back "home." Just when I thought she was beginning to get the hang of it, the hallways of the house once again reverberated with heartbreaking wails of defeat. I raced up to her room to find her sobbing over a homework assignment. She was supposed to write an essay explaining who she was. Heaving between sobs she said, "I don't know who I am!"

No Commonality

I wasn't as acutely aware then as I am now of what her dilemma was. Katrina really didn't know who she was because she didn't have a sense of belonging anywhere. She wasn't Asian, African, European or American, although elements of each of those places certainly helped form her sense of self. She, like all TCKs, is layered with all the cultures she has meaningfully interacted with and the experiences she has shared. She did not share a commonality with any particular group in her new school. The sense of belonging she had through her relationships was an ocean away and had no relevance here.

Identity in Belonging

As humans, we all have basic, specific needs. These needs are many but Pollock and Van Reken put emphasis on two related human needs that, if met, help us form our personal identity:

(1) the need for strong relationships

(2) the need for a sense of belonging

Therefore, our identity is not in our passport; rather it is found in belonging. The question of belonging doesn't normally rate a place on a TCK's radar screen as long as they are enjoying it, but as soon as meaningful relationships are left an ocean or a continent away, those shared emotional experiences that gave them a sense of identity are gone. Issues of identity and belonging typically surface upon transition or repatriation. The interruption of those relational and emotional needs cuts to the very core of who we are.

I love to tell the story of Sara, a bi-cultural TCK born and raised in Switzerland. She frequently visited both the United States, her father's passport country and India, her mother's home. Sara was on the international school's basketball team that I helped coach with Janneke, my oldest daughter. Each year we took a "road trip" (I use the term loosely since we usually traveled by train or plane) to an international competition. In her senior year the team captain made a video of the trip for each of the girls. Sara ended up at university in my husband's hometown of Rochester, New York. I did not understand how important that video had become for her until we went to visit her while we were on home leave. She was so excited about our visit and couldn't wait to introduce my family to her friends, who had all seen the basketball road trip video numerous times. Her friends wanted to know why she was so excited about seeing our family. To them we were just a former coach and a teammate. Her answer was telling, "Because they know me from where I am from." In other words we had a history with her (we had known her for about five years at this point in time) and we knew all about the place she called "home" and it was neither the U.S. nor India. Here were people who understood her stories or were even part of them, appreciated and affirmed her and who tied her to a place of belonging once again.

Double Whammy

Keep in mind that all first-year students venturing away from home, some for the first time away from parental influences, will be trying to figure out who they are and what other aspects of themselves lie within. TCKs have the double task of discovering their cultural as well as personal identity. Home-country peers already have a cultural identity whereas the TCK lacks clarity due to the different layering of his or her experiences. Although TCKs may not be able to conceptualize it, they are likely to feel off-balance or out-of-sync as they strive towards adaptation in their new surroundings.

Rootlessness

Too often, TCKs do not have the time they need to develop lasting relationships that affirm them or stay rooted long enough to develop a sense of belonging. This is why they feel they belong everywhere and nowhere. Pieces of each place they have lived make up who they are, but the picture isn't finished. They are constantly searching for the place they can truly call home. This sometimes leads to a pattern of what Dave Pollock and Ruth Van Reken call "rootlessness and restlessness."

Where are You From?

TCKs come to dread any version of the question which petitions where they come from or what is considered home to them. How do *you* answer the question, "Where are you from?" This question was asked on the TCKid.com forum, a website designed by and for TCKs to come together as a community to share and learn from each other. A variety of responses were posted such as the following:

- "Somewhere out there…"

- When I find out I'll let you know.

- Pick a country – any country!

- Do you want the long version or the short version?

- Please don't ask.

- Do you have enough time for this?

- You know, I wish I knew.

Many said they just rattled off a list of the places they had lived because they weren't certain of what is really meant by 'where are you from.' It could be interpreted to mean the passport a TCK travels on, what their nationality is, where their parents are living now or where they grew up. Many TCKs become so frustrated with trying to explain where they are from that they give up. This was the case with Rita from Chapter 1, the American TCK who grew up in France and India and returned to the U.S. for university. If she merely stated she came from India this very pale, Anglo-Saxon young woman would be taken for a foreign national from India. She tried several different approaches to answering the question but it always had to be followed up with a lengthy explanation. Once that was over, her home-country peers weren't quite sure of what to do with the information. She grew so weary of trying to explain her life that she decided it was just easier to avoid the question. She began isolating herself to the point that she would plan her classes around not having to eat dinner with others. She ate, studied and did most things alone. You will learn more about Rita later.

 Try This: Think ahead of time how you will answer the question, "Where are you from?" in a way that won't tire you and freak others out.

Answering the Question

Some transition experts suggest a good way of dealing with the ambiguity is to respond with, "Right now I am living in (name of place)." If the person is interested enough in knowing where you lived before, then let the questions continue. Perhaps they want to know more because they too have traveled extensively and are looking for a connection. This could be your next best friend.

 Try This: It is quite okay to say you are A + B = "I am a British German, or A + B = C: I happen to be American but have lived my life in Italy and Costa Rica, or, " I'm a global nomad. My last stop was Mozambique."

Restlessness

Pollock and Van Reken tell us this sense of belonging everywhere and nowhere is at the heart of the issue of restlessness. In the search for a place of belonging TCKs will often develop a migratory instinct that interferes with moving forward in their lives. I see it in the students I work with. Some will transfer from one college to another or change their major over and over again. In fact, several sets of adult TCK (ATCK) research data have shown that as many as one third do not stay at one college long enough to complete their degree. They are more likely to attend three or more colleges and take as long as five to nine years to complete a bachelor's level degree. Adult TCKs may move from job to job, or even from relationship to relationship. There is a sense that the next step, the next move, the next job is going to be the real thing and they can finally settle down. But on the complete opposite end of the spectrum are the TCKs who finish at university, get a job, get married, buy a house and stay in it for the rest of their lives, vowing never to move again.

Hidden Immigrant

Katrina decided to answer the essay question, "Who Are You?" with a few paragraphs on third culture kids. She had been familiar with the term and the profile and felt it was a good way to share with others how she cannot be labeled as an American just because she looked, spoke and learned to dress like one. She explained that she was really a "hidden immigrant" as Pollock and Van Reken call it when you appear like the dominant culture but think and act differently.

Look Alike/Think Differently

It is easier as a foreigner to enter a new culture when you do not resemble the dominant culture at all. Because you look different, the host culture people will expect you to think and act differently. When you look the same but don't think and act the same you can get all kinds of nasty responses from people including anger and degrading remarks. People think you are a social deviant because you don't follow the rules. But you can't follow rules you don't know exist. You may be regarded as stupid or mentally challenged when you don't understand how simple, common, everyday things work. This happened to me more times than I wish to acknowledge. I once nearly had a melt down in a department store because I thought the credit card machine had eaten my card. It returned it a few seconds later once the transaction had been recorded. But I had never seen a credit card machine like that. You should have seen the way the cashier looked at me. I know of some TCKs who will put on an accent in their home country to ask a question they know will sound stupid coming from a domestic person just so they won't feel foolish or embarrassed.

How You Look Matters

In the U.S. as well as many other countries, it matters how you physically look to the dominant culture. People don't think about culture, they think about race, about how you look. They want to be able to label you. Jennifer, our bi-racial, bi-cultural TCK at the beginning of this chapter experienced this in the U.K. She had people asking her over and over again about where she was from (something we know is difficult for TCKs to answer). She kept telling them she was from Switzerland but they could not grasp how a racially mixed person could come from such a stereotypically white country. Once she finally explained her British/ African lineage, the response she got was, "Oh, you're a mix." They had a label for her and their curiosity was satisfied. Unfortunately they did not know what to do with the information once they had it because it did not lead to any further relationship.

Not Just Re-entry

The hidden immigrant experience doesn't just happen with re-entry. If you are a FS or TCK going on to another host culture and you look like the dominant culture, you are sure to have the same reactions. An American student going to study in the U.K. will look like the host country culture. The same for a Nigerian going to the U.S. He or she will be perceived as an African American. Even an Asian student, because the U.S. is so culturally mixed, may be perceived there as an Asian/American and will take others by surprise if perfect English does not come out of his or her mouth.

Between Worlds

We talked about belonging as one of the basic human needs we all must have fulfilled in order to continue moving ahead in life. TCKs are desperate to fit in and devastated when they don't and can't figure out why.

Some of the areas in which TCKs feel different from home-country peers are that they:

> *"I think what I was most taken aback by when I first arrived [at college] is how I was identified as being different because in Switzerland such labeling didn't exist because, well, everyone was different."*
> Brent, Thai/American TCK

- Hold world views that can be 180 degrees different from their peers who have not lived outside their home country or at the very minimum, have much more expanded world views than those of their peers.

- Understand that there are many ways of doing things – not just one right way.

- Are used to having diversity in their relationships.

- Relate differently (more on that in Chapter 6).

- Are worldly, mature, well-versed in places, peoples, cultures and languages of this world.

- Have more in common with internationals than with domestic peers.

- Are hidden immigrants in that they look the same as home-country peers but think and act differently.

- Have no shared experience with home-country peers.

Neither Here

Global nomads are "caught between two worlds" in the truest sense of the phrase. Many feel they don't belong to any group – domestic or international. Such was the case with Rita who came to college a few days early to attend International Orientation (I.O.). While attending your school's I.O. is a *wonderful* idea and one that I highly encourage TCKs to do, you may not always find the connection with others you are hoping to find. Rita found that the international students split off into groups based either on ethnicity or shared language. Although she spoke French fluently and could have joined the French speakers, they were "too French" for her. She didn't own the nationality and felt it was not the right fit for her. But she also didn't fit in with the Indian students or the Americans who were invited to I.O. to interact with the group. She was neither/nor – belonging everywhere but nowhere. She was experiencing what one global nomad on TICKid.com says is "being an international without being an international."

Nor There

This is a common complaint among bi-cultural TCKs. They cannot identify with either ethnic group of their heritage. One Asian/American TCK told me she tried participating in the Asian club at her school but was rejected for not being 100% Asian. But she also did not feel 100% American either. After learning that she was a TCK and actually did belong to a group – the TCK tribe – she became comfortable with who she was as a person. More about this in Chapter 7.

Remember that everyone's experiences are different. I share these various stories to illustrate what kinds of surprises others who have gone before you have run into so you can be prepared if you experience something similar.

> **Share It:** Keep in mind that not everyone has issues of not fitting in. Your TCK lifestyle has taught you how to adapt and integrate. You know how to do it. In fact, you are better placed than your domestic peers for dealing with change and integration. Use the skills you own.

Isolation

In conversations with TCKs when I hear the phrase, "I didn't fit in," the word, "isolated" rapidly follows. What often happens as a result of the disconnect with their peers is TCKs try to avoid these uncomfortable interactions. We saw that with Rita when she realized her differences over trying to answer the "Where are you from?" question. It became uncomfortable and she relegated herself to being alone so she wouldn't have to deal with it. In fact, she told me she felt such a sense of relief when she took her first holiday break and went to visit her grandparents in North Carolina. She didn't feel different there. She was unconditionally loved and accepted and didn't have to explain anything to anyone.

Loss of Control

After returning from her break, Rita began studying excessively. If she had a good excuse for not interacting with others, it made more sense to her. She explained to me that without realizing it, her behaviors then became obsessive. They were the only things she could control when all else was out of control. She couldn't control American culture and she couldn't control who she was so she began setting rules around eating, exercising and activities. Through the help of a counselor she became more integrated in her second year and the controlling behaviors stopped. She is doing well today, has graduated from college and has plans to stay and work in the U.S.

Roger's story is one that both epitomizes the dilemma as well as celebrates the insight that led to the eventual integration of his experiences.

Roger, an American/Canadian ATCK who is currently attending college in New York City spent his early childhood in Africa but was unexpectedly repatriated at age eight and lived with his grandmother in the U.S. for two years. At age ten his family moved to France where he stayed until he graduated from a British international school. At age 18 he knew he wasn't ready to go to college just yet and he wanted to stay in Europe so he spent three years touring in a band and working at a local church.

Once he chose his school Roger was very excited about the move. As a 22-year-old first-year student he was mature and ready for the academic challenge which he threw himself into. He stayed so busy that he didn't experience the usual pangs of homesickness. But something happened during the first long holiday break when he went to stay with his grandparents in the Midwest of the U.S. Because he had been living in such a cosmopolitan city he hadn't been able to appreciate just how different the cultural norms of the U.S. were, something that hit him straight on in the Midwest. He realized he wasn't as American as he thought. Roger struggled with this reality his entire second semester.

"Just when I was trying to build deeper relationships with people being normal became a psychological issue for me. I was constantly asking myself, 'Am I different?' and the answer was always, 'Yes.' Everyone else is okay but I'm weird.

Once I started noticing the differences and not liking the differences, I started to take precautionary measures out of fear. I spent a lot of time alone in my second semester to keep from having bad experiences. I saw myself as the minority and automatically felt inferior. Instead of embracing the differences, I put a negative connotation on them."

Roger never came out of it during his entire second semester. He tried to keep busy and not have to deal with it because the more he reflected on it, the worse it got. He experienced homesickness for the first time in the second term. He did not seek the help of a mental health counselor but relied on phone calls to his parents. Roger now admits that he made the mistake of closing himself off as to 'what's next?' and wasn't mentally prepared to come back to the U.S. which is what may have triggered his emotional responses.

Roger did get through it. He spent the summer after his first year staying in the city and working at the college. The words of the mental health counselors who had helped him face intense re-entry shock when he was eight years old and his family was repatriated from Africa all came back to him once he had the relaxed summer months to mentally spend time with it. He now understands how his international experiences have made him unique but not terminally unique. He says they are an advantage to him and plans on highlighting them on his job résumés. He believes he is stronger because of his ordeal and now embraces the differences.

Coming to Understanding

I could tell you story after story of global nomads just like Roger, including tales of near-suicides out of the hopelessness that comes with feeling different, weird, inferior or worthless. My hope and prayer for you is that by reading this book, you will understand that you *will* feel different from your peers but it is a *good* kind of different. You will appreciate there are positive ways to deal with the differences and come to embrace them. In Chapter 6 you will be given tools and strategies for making friends and building relationships and in Chapter 8 you will learn how TCKs develop their identity and come to grips with who they are as international beings.

Except for Leslie (at the beginning of Chapter 1) who attended a Transition /Re-entry Seminar, all of the TCKs I have interviewed and spoken with over the years while preparing to write this book had not received any kind of preparation before returning to their passport culture. Many of them were not even familiar with the term TCK or global nomad. My purpose in writing this book is so that you will not have the negative experiences these students did. Knowledge is power. You are likely to experience the different stages of transition, and you may or may not be able to put the name on the stage, but you will know it is normal to be feeling what you are feeling and you will pass through it.

Embracing Your Experiences

Now is a good time to tell you how Brent from Chapter 1 made out in his adjustment. Unlike Roger who just felt worse with introspection, that is what eventually brought Brent to terms with how to be happy. He spent a lot of time looking at his life and asking himself questions like, "What do you need to do or stop doing to feel better and be happy?" For him it could have meant eating or drinking less, exercising more, studying more or studying less. He just kept at himself until he was happy with the changes he made to be the person he wanted to be.

One other major turning point for Brent was going on a semester abroad to Europe. While he did not go to his beloved Switzerland he did catch up with all his best friends who happen to still be hanging out with each other. According to Brent they had not changed at all and he knew he had. He tells me, "It was the nail in the coffin. I realized that even if I had stayed with them and gone to university in the U.K., I would have changed and we would have drifted apart to finally go our separate ways. Coming away from that, I realized that it was time for me to let go, albeit not completely, and embrace my new life."

Marginal, Introducing, Vulnerable

> "I am coming into a period of self-doubt again. I know it is because I am in a different place and out of my comfort zone. I also feel quite intimidated by some of my peers in the group. I feel like they are all smarter than I am, I don't know why I feel this way and it is quite annoying!
>
> Last night we were all gathered together and this gave me a better perception of certain people. Although everyone is most likely insecure themselves and are trying to build their own self-confidence, most seem to be quite arrogant about it. Many are also quick-witted and always have something clever to say. I am always in admiration of people who can do that and accredit too much to it. I deduce that they must be smarter than me and I often feel like I am left out of the circle."
>
> *Marie, journal entry*

Marginal

Just like our semester abroad student mentions in her journal entry, self-doubt can set in when you feel you are not relating well to others. You can become **self-conscious** about everything. You feel

marginalized, like you are on the outside looking in, and are not quite fully a part of this place even though the desire to belong is there.

At times your actions, words or behaviors may be misinterpreted. Your cultural signals don't work in this place You become **fearful** of making cultural *faux p*as and have to think twice before saying or doing anything that might bring another round of laughter.

Introducing

The Entering stage is a time when:

- You are constantly **introducing** yourself, looking for someone you can finally connect with.

  - This introducing will continue for quite some time.

  - You need to step out of your comfort zone and begin the introductions rather than wait for others to initiate them.

- You have some **incredible knowledge** and abilities that are completely useless here.

  - You may know how to tell the poisonous from the non-poisonous jungle snakes and the best way to kill one but no one cares about that in this place.

  - You may be the best camel racer this side of the Jordan River but if you try to talk about it, your peers look at you like you're from another planet.

  - You are an incredible person with interesting stories to tell and no one wants to hear them.

  - The status you may have enjoyed in your host country community has no merit here.

  - You feel as though you have lost your identity and along with it went your self-esteem.

Vulnerable

This is a **vulnerable** time for all college freshmen as they sort out their personal identities, but it is especially so for TCKs who are not only dealing with the new surroundings but are sorting out their cultural identity as well.

- This is the time students feel **ambivalent** about being here and begin making appointments with their deans and advisors to talk about transferring or leaving. They may call home to tell their parents or high school guidance counselors they want to come home. They doubt themselves, their abilities, and their choice of college. They feel they don't belong there. (Chapter 9 gets into some of the reasons for this and ways to avoid it.)

- The mind unpacking continues and, as it does, **grief** gets recycled and revisited. Grief processing is a continuous exercise that can be cyclic. Something reminds you of home – a smell, a sound, a song – and you are momentarily swept back in time to a place that has now become idealized or romanticized because it was so much better than this place. It was easy, comfortable, happy...or so it seemed. It is again time to name those losses, spend time with the grief associated with the loss, bring them to closure, and move forward.

Emotions Still in Flux

It is not at all uncommon in the Transition and Entering stages to have really good days interspersed with down days, blue days with happy days, wildly exciting days with it-couldn't-get-any-worse days. The grief versus depression we discussed in Chapter 4 is still an issue that hangs around in the Entering phase. Fluctuating emotions and bouts of homesickness still ply you even though things are beginning to settle and take shape in your life. Although you have the desire to settle in, it is still a stressful time. It is important to continue to pay attention to taking care of yourself and preventing stress from building up and impacting your body.

 Share It: Surround yourself with people who make you feel good about yourself. Life is too short to be hanging out with people who don't do that.

I like to play a frame game during the Transition/Re-entry seminars I give where I ask the students to write down on a 3" x 5" card the one thing, thought, activity, attitude, or anything else they consider to be the number one best way to cope with the stress and chaos of transition. Through a series of movements and comparative assessments, the ideas expressed on the cards are rated on a 1-10 scale. Some of the highest-rated stress and anxiety busters students come up with are as follows:

- Play my guitar

- Dance

- Listen to music

- Journal

- Chat with my friends on Facebook

- Laugh

- Not take myself too seriously

- Paint

- Go for a run

- Go shopping

- Take a nap

What things do you do for stress relief? Need more ideas? Visit *www.CampusCalm.com*.

Entering Well

The hustle and bustle has settled and you are committed to making this place and this experience work for you. There are a few things you can do that will ease the transition. We already talked about things like researching your country and new community. You may also want to find books or websites on cultural do's and don'ts and idiomatic expressions you may not be familiar with. See the resources section.

Expect Surprises

Things happen all the time that take us by surprise. Remember the water fountain story? I laugh at another story an ATCK tells of landing back in the US and heading off to her university in the western part of the country. After a very long bus ride into what appeared to be the middle of nowhere, the passengers stopped for a rest only to be met by riders on horseback...gobs of them. She had spent most of her childhood outside the U.S. and thought surely the days of the old west were still being enforced. Only later did she find out that the town they had stopped in was celebrating Founder's Day and they were doing a 19th century reenactment.

The point is you do end up feeling stupid a lot of the time and your own countrymen will get angry with you for things you can't help. One day you will be able to look back and laugh at some of your own experiences which will make for good storytelling.

 Tip to Remember: People tend to have more patience with the ignorance of a foreigner than the stupidity of their own countryman.

Find a Mentor

The saying goes, "You need a mentor to enter." The key to negotiating the entry stage is to find someone you can trust who will introduce you to the community and the community to you. The word 'trust' here is vital. Jenny, a nine-year-old American girl tells the story of being immersed in the local village school upon her family's arrival in France.

> "I was so relieved to find a girl in my class who could speak fairly good English. Caroline and I became good friends, or so I thought. Since I didn't understand the language, I really depended on Caroline to translate all the teacher's instructions for me. Things were going pretty well until one day when we were lined up to go into the school and I asked Caroline what the teacher just said. Caroline told me we had to cross the courtyard and go in another door. I headed off to the other door but turned around when I heard laughter. I realized I had been duped. I was the only one going in the opposite direction. Caroline had given everyone a good laugh... at my expense. It seems inconsequential now, but at the time I was mortified."

This was a traumatic incident for this young girl. Imagine the consequences of relying on someone who cannot be trusted to introduce you to the culture as a secondary school or university student. Choosing the right mentor is critical.

Look for mentors who have positive, encouraging attitudes about the community and fit well in it. You want someone who models positive behavior and has a good reputation. Your mentor should show some interest in getting to know you so that he or she can understand where you are coming from and can introduce you to the right people.

You may meet a good mentor at your school's orientation program. Student and resident advisors may also serve as mentors. They are selected for those positions under careful scrutiny and are trained to come alongside and guide first-year students. Wait and watch before deciding on your mentors. Do they display positive and encouraging attitudes? Do they hang out with the kind of people you would want to be associated with?

 Beware: Do not try to hang onto or monopolize your mentor. He (or she) is most likely not going to become your new best friend. He is there to help you adjust. If you hold on too tight or for too long he may have to try to dump you just to have a life of his own. Then you will end up feeling betrayed and unloved and even more marginalized.

You are lonely, looking for company and needing help in negotiating the new rules of your community. It is easy to be caught up in the first friendship that presents itself, but choosing the wrong mentor can be disastrous. A wrong mentor can give you a negative impression about your new community and if you are in the throes of transition shock, every negative thought will be amplified.

Look out for needy people who want to latch themselves onto you. They are most likely needy for a reason. They may be marginalized in some way. You do not want to grab onto the first person who approaches you and acts like your new best friend. This person may be looking for company out there in the fringes of society and you will be in the same category by association.

Another reason to avoid people who seem really interested in latching onto you is because threats of cults, groups of people who share misguided or extremist religious beliefs, on college campuses are real. Karen Levin Coburn and Madge Lawrence Treeger discuss this threat in *Letting Go, A Parent's Guide to Understanding the College Years*:

> "College campuses are prime targets for cult recruiters. Using coercive and deceptive techniques, cult recruiters have been known to position themselves outside the counseling service or in the student center, looking for students who appear depressed or lonely. Cult leaders know that students who are on their own for the first time, though pleased with their freedom, are anxious about taking responsibility for their own lives. Young people are searching for answers, for an identity, for some stability in their lives; they are vulnerable to the offer of instant community, a set of clear expectations, and ready answers to complex questions. International students, lonely and eager to learn about American culture, have a particularly difficult time distinguishing between genuine overtures of friendship from religious congregations and the organized recruitment by cults."

 Beware: You need to choose your own mentors. Don't let them choose you!

Embrace the Journey

Janneke, my oldest daughter, sat on the grass on a warm and sunny late August afternoon as she waited for the signal to board the bus that would take her out into the Connecticut wilderness for four days with 30 strangers. We chose to plop down on that particular piece of green because she recognized another girl she had met at a college social over the summer. They greeted each other quickly and then both proceeded to stare off into space, occasionally turning their heads in slow motion to look, with glazed over eyes, at the excitement around them. They were both frozen, timid, bundled up inside themselves as they were about to say farewell to us mothers chatting idly next to them. This was the launch of their first-year journey, an outdoor orienteering program that was to help them meet and bond with other new students.

Finally Janneke managed to utter a single sentence. "I'm going to be here for the next four years of my life!" I could just imagine the thoughts that must have been swirling around in her head before that popped out of her mouth. What if she didn't like it after all? She has just committed to spending four years in this place. She was so excited to come here, but now she was not so sure she really liked it all that much.

Make the most out of your time wherever you end up. Embrace your experience. It is a journey. You chose this place for some reason that perhaps initially escapes you, but you will remember soon enough. As with anything, give it some time.

Stay Positive

No matter how irritable or hostile you may be feeling, don't give in to the temptation to mock or belittle your culture. It is very easy to get caught up in negative emotions when someone else starts groaning about the culture, but if you join in, it can get out of hand and put you on the wrong footing to settle in and make friends in this place.

Poking fun is something everyone enjoys doing and it's not destructive, just fun. The French make fun of the Swiss, the Swiss make fun of the Germans and everyone makes fun of the Polish. While you can enjoy someone else making fun of their own culture, you need to watch yourself. It's a bit like making fun of your little brother or sister. It is okay for you to do it, but no one else better try it!

If everyone is making fun of the culture and you deem it's just in good fun, you can join in, but be sure to use words like 'we' and 'us', not 'they' or 'those.' For example: "Yeah, we Americans are so stuck on baseball we think winter should be exported," as opposed to, "Those Americans, they are so fond of baseball that..." you get the picture.

Home Again – Re-involvement

How Long Does it Take?

At one of my "Transitioning Successfully for University" seminars, a student asked the question, "How long does it take to get through the transition cycle?" So we directed it to an ATCK graduate student who often speaks at my workshops about her own personal experiences. Her response and many students concur, is that the first term at college or university is spent trying to find your way around, figuring out how everything works, and making sure you have all you need in order to function effectively (the Transition stage). By the time the second term rolls around, you are feeling pretty comfortable and start looking for friends and other people with whom you have things in common (the Entering stage). When you return from summer break for your third term, you feel like you've come home again (the Re-involvement stage).

Beware: Everyone will go through the stages at their own pace. Don't compare yourself to others and don't feel like you need to accelerate your adjustment. It will come in its own time.

I have found in talking with international students that many have a somewhat accelerated transition. The chaos of transition begins to settle down anywhere from 6-10 weeks into the first term. At one discussion group of international students on the Tufts University campus, one young woman stated that she was only then (eight weeks or half-way into the term) able to take a deep breath and not feel so scrambled. She went on to say that she was beginning to feel homesick and was experiencing vacillating emotions, things she did not have time for before. She was most likely experiencing that overlapping time between the Transition stage and the Entering stage in the second half of the first term.

Finding Friends Frenzy

The search for friends starts immediately upon hitting campus, especially during orientation – almost in a frenzied way. Everyone is looking for that new best friend. No one likes being alone. Innately, humans are social beings. Some friendships students develop at the start of school will last a lifetime and others will be short-lived. Temporary friendships meet the need at the time, but then you find other people you can really connect with. Having 20 new friends immediately isn't what makes us happy. It's finding two or three people we can share with and trust.

Changing Relationships

Some of you will find your best buddy right away and keep him or her for life. Other friends will drift away in the Entering stage. They go in search of interest groups and activities they enjoy and find people they have more in common with.

I look at my two daughters who have been through it. They both have best friends from the pre-orientation trip they opted into before the start of school. They bonded well with two or three other students in their small group. Then their group grew to include the roommates of their new friends. By Parents Weekend, we were taking my daughter's group of eight friends out to dinner. By the end of the first year, the group had changed. Over the course of the next three years, friends came and went, but the two, three or four special ones remained. Two of my middle daughter's four best friends transferred out after their freshmen year. They are still so special to each other that despite the geographical distance (Texas, Connecticut and Illinois), they continue to get together regularly.

By the time the winter break rolls around, many students have found a group or groups of people they enjoy, can hang out and have fun with. In fact, when they are back at home they have fun reconnecting with secondary school friends and swapping war stories, but then they get anxious to return to school. They can't wait to get back and to be with their new friends.

Once they get back on campus after a long hiatus such as winter or summer break, and they feel more like it has become home, they have arrived at the Re-Involvement stage. Just as in the Involvement stage when they were still at home finishing out secondary school,

> *"The journey is whatever you want it to be – or I say, whatever you decide to make it to be."*
> Dr. Aruna Jha, University of Illinois-Chicago

they once again have status. They know others and others know them. They have roles and responsibilities. They feel affirmed, safe, and secure. They once again feel they belong.

What You Should Know:

- Even though you have decided to become a part of this new place, you will still experience many emotional highs and lows. It takes time to settle in and feel normal again, but you will get there.

- It is not unusual to feel as though you do not fit in with your peers or don't belong to any particular group.

- You need to find a good mentor to help you in your adjustment.

- Enter your home country the same way you would enter a foreign culture. Treat it as though you expect it to be different.

Resources:

Books

- *Letting Go, A Parent's Guide to Understanding the College Years,* by Karen Levin Coburn and Madge Lawrence Treeger, Harper Collins Publishers, 2003.

- *Do's and Taboos Around the World,* 2nd ed., by Roger E. Axtell, John Wiley and Sons, 1990.

Resources (cont'd):

Books

- *Do's and Taboos of Body Language Around the World,* Revised and expanded edition, by Roger E. Axtell, John Wiley and Sons, 1998.

- *Kiss, Bow, or Shake Hands: How to Do Business in Sixty Countries* by T. Morrison, W.A. Conway, G.A. Borden, Intercultural Press, 1994.

Websites

- www.CampusCalm.com

- www.TCKid.com

- www.usingenglish.com/reference/idioms - idioms of the U.S. and U.K.

Chapter 6

Relationships – Past, Present, and Future

> "I feel like I have all these strings attached to my back that are pulling me backwards. The strings are things in my past like the boyfriend I left behind, my family, my friends...even my home. I'm trying to walk forward but these strings keep pulling me...holding me in the past. I wish I could just cut them all off, tie them in a bow and place them in a little box to carry around with me."
>
> *Audrey, TCK in first-year at U.K.*

In almost any discussion with TCKs the subject of relationships comes up over and over again. It is a feature on chat room discussions at TCKid.com as well as in any casual or formal TCK get-togethers. Relationships are an important part of our lives. We thrive on the sense of belonging which results from connecting and interacting with others. Understanding some of the issues that surround TCK relationships will shed some light on why it is such a hot topic.

Bows in a Box

The above analogy was given to me by a bi-national TCK who was born in and spent her lifetime in her father's passport country but was attending college in the country of her mother's passport, very near to where her maternal grandparents lived. She left behind a lot of history including a serious relationship she chose to end before leaving. She was struggling in her ability to move ahead and get settled in her new surroundings.

I have a life motto I have learned to live by through all of my family's transitions that I would regularly share with others and remind my children of: "If you are not having fun, it's your own darn fault." One hard-liner TCK makes her own rendition of it by saying, "If you're not settling in, it's your own fault." While she is trying to say that you are responsible for making the adjustment and that it is necessary to take some risks to do it, she also concedes to the fact that there may be certain barriers to settling in. One of those barriers is the strong ties mentioned above, particularly if there is a romantic relationship you have left back home. If part of your heart is still at home, it is difficult to truly want to belong in this new place.

These two students are not saying you have to sever all ties to your past; just be aware of how you can continue to cherish them while moving forward rather than living in the past, i.e. tie them in a bow, place them in a box, and keep them with you. It is possible to make new friends without being disloyal to your old friends. Hopefully, they are all doing the same thing wherever they are now. When you come together you will continue to have that unique relationship that belongs to the history you have shared in your host country.

Long Distance Relationships

While there is no easy way to handle romantic relationships that you do not want to release, there are ways to move forward while staying connected to your shared past. A Lebanese student at a U.S. university shares his personal story:

> "I have been in my current relationship for nearly three and half years and my girlfriend and I have faced and overcome enormous challenges in order to stay with one another. Family, religion, war: you name it, we have probably been through it. But for the last two years, distance has made all our previous problems seem almost insignificant. It has been the most challenging obstacle yet, not because of actual physical proximity, but that of time.
>
> My girlfriend and I met in high school and spent nearly two years together in Lebanon, spending nearly all of our time together inside or outside of school. For me, the worst part of a long distance relationship is trying to keep up that same level of involvement in each other's lives; it is nearly impossible because we no longer share experiences like we once did. All of our "shared" experiences come from conversations on Skype or instant messaging, or sending web

page links that we find interesting to one another. This works for a time, but after long semesters of stressful work/study it gets harder and harder to feel close over medias [sic] such as the internet. In short, there is a deficiency of memory-making together, and this strains the relationship.

So our solution to the long distance problem is essentially making sure we have time physically together to look forward to, like summer or winter breaks. That has really [been] what has kept us going at times. The gaps between periods of physical intimacy are a challenge, but the far more difficult part for me is actually dealing with the emotional shock when I finally am with my girlfriend. No matter how hard we try not to change, we both will to some degree, and that always takes some getting used to. To that I have no solution. But I know that as we spend more time together, things between us get much better and we once again relax around one another.

In short, the only way not to live in the past in a long distance relationship is to have something to look forward to in the future. And in my opinion, if there is no future to look forward to, then dealing with the stress and strain of long distance is nigh impossible."

Maintaining a long distance relationship is never easy, but perhaps even less so in college and university. After all, this is the time of life when you are expected to experience new things, grow, experiment and have fun. Regardless of how committed you both may feel, it still takes an extraordinary amount of energy and steadfastness to deal with the issues of jealousy, trust and intimacy that will undoubtedly surface.

Have Some Guidelines

Other students who have been in similar situations suggest that you and your boyfriend or girlfriend work out the rules for the relationship before you leave for college.

- How often will you call each other? And who will initiate which calls?

- When is it off-limits to call? For instance, calling every half hour on a Friday night isn't going to build trust. It just breeds suspicion and insecurity if your partner doesn't pick up the phone.

- Be honest with each other. If you are going to be out on the weekend when you would normally speak to each other, tell your partner ahead of time.

- Talk about how you will stay exclusive and still meet and interact with other people.

- Think about how you can create an active social life while remaining faithful to your boyfriend or girlfriend. One way to do that is to socialize in groups rather than one-on-one.

- Have an accountability partner with whom you can talk over problems and temptations. It is best to have someone of the *same sex* to serve in this role as accountability partners tend to become close friends which could be very threatening to your original boyfriend-girlfriend relationship.

If It Doesn't Work Out

If you or your partner finds that, despite all efforts to the contrary, an attraction to another person has developed, don't be too hard on yourself. If you've given it your best shot, let it die a natural death. After some time and more distance, the two of you may find that you will be able to remain good friends down the road.

Superficiality of Home-Country Peers

'Shallow' is a word TCKs use with regularity when speaking about their home-country peers. They find their peers are difficult to get to know, appear to be immature and may even be considered boring as we heard from Jennifer in Chapter 1. Just as people who have never lived abroad have difficulty understanding you because they have no frame of reference for you, the same could be said for you not having a frame of reference for them.

Beware: In any discussion of a population, we are generalizing so anything that is stereotypical of the group as a whole does not necessarily pertain to every individual person. You will meet people who don't respond like this at all and may fall at the complete opposite end of the spectrum. The majority will fall somewhere in the middle.

The Transient Community

TCKs grow up in highly mobile, transient communities where people come and go all the time. They learn to make friendships quickly. They have to. They never know when they may lose their best friend…again. So when there is a new kid at school, other children reach out to them, broadening their circle of friends in case a few get relocated on the way to graduation. As a result, TCKs tend to be very welcoming people. Students entering international schools often speak of how warmly they were greeted and how quickly they felt a part of the community.

TCKs Relate Differently

TCKs innately delve into deeper levels of relating to each other so they can quickly determine if there may be a connection with this new person. Unlike less traveled home-country peers, who historically have time to wait and see if there is a connection, TCKs don't have a lot of time. It's not surprising the student newspaper of my daughters' international school is called *Carpe Diem* (seize the day).

All cultures are different and the degree to which personal information is shared will vary greatly, but the following scenario is fairly typical among teens or young adults who have not had to change cultures or move around much.

> *Hi! You must be new. I saw you in my English literature class. My friends and I hang out for a while at Starbucks after school almost everyday. Would you like to join us?*

So you join them and that is really all they seem to do – hang out. No meaningful conversations take place. At least *you* don't think so. It may feel as though no real "getting to know you" goes on. Of course they *are* getting to know you and there *are* meaningful discussions going on; it just doesn't appear that way to you. Your cultural lens is interpreting the interactions quite differently.

This goes on day after day of joining them at Starbucks. If you are patient with your domestic peers, eventually they will share some deeper aspects of themselves with you. You share back. You become friends. So it looks like this:

Introduce → Hang out → Hang out more → Share → Become Friends

That being said, you first have to receive that initial invitation to hang out before any relationship-building can take place and that can seem to take forever. When my family first moved back to the U.S., it felt to my daughters as though they were invisible. Katrina retells the story of sitting at lunch with three girls who were on the swim team together. They talked excitedly about getting together for all their weekend plans. Not once did they think to invite Katrina even though she was sitting right there.

My youngest daughter, Kacie waited and waited for the basketball season to begin so she would at least find commonality with some of the girls in her grade. During the season the other girls were friendly enough but once the season was over, Kacie would never hear from anyone or get invited to do things. This trend continued into the next year as well. It wasn't until we had been in the U.S. for over two years that she started getting phone calls and invitations to "hang out."

This is an example of a typical TCK scenario:

Hi! You must be new. You're in my biology class with Mr. Stone. I think he is soooo boring. Don't you think so? I can barely stay awake in his class! So where did you go to school before? Do you like Starbucks?

Many TCKs can tell right away if there is going to be a connection. So they put themselves out there and share something with you about themselves so that you will share something in return. If they sense the connection, a friendship has begun and you are invited to hang out. This is how the TCK scenario looks:

Introduce → Share → Become Friends → Hang out

When a TCK tries this scenario for making friends among their domestic peers, there is usually some unfortunate fall-out. Because TCKs want information about others before they will hang out with them, they tend to give away "too much information" about themselves in the beginning. Their domestic peers don't always respond well to that. They may think you are much too intense and start backing away. There is still a need to share some aspects of your life with your peers in order for them to understand where you are coming from. But if you start talking about your life experiences, you may appear arrogant, boastful, or even worse – a pathologic liar. It's difficult for someone who may have never left his or her home state or province to fathom how anyone could have experienced the types of things you have in your relatively short life span.

As far as you are concerned, you've just been living a normal life; you do not realize that your life stories are quite exotic compared to a non-traveled person. For example, if my daughters were to talk about the loving ayahs that cared for them in Pakistan and Kenya, or to mention family vacations when they went hunting for tigers on the backs of elephants in Nepal or saw mating lions while on safari in Africa, they would appear to be wealthy, snobby, grandiose or lying. What others don't understand is that TCKs have no other stories to tell. This is their life as they have lived it.

Can't Win for Losing

It doesn't take long before you get the non-verbal cues that people are bored with your stories because they are too incredible to grasp or as one TCK shared, "They don't know what to do with the information." She explained that her university peers would always come and ask her what it was like to have lived in Singapore. So she would respond to their questions. Once their curiosity was satisfied, they had no clue where to go with the conversation so they would walk away. She once overheard someone say to another student, "Oh, don't bother talking to her. All she ever talks about is Singapore!"

So if you get bad vibes from your peers, you tend to clam up and stop talking altogether. But when you stop talking, people think you are being stuck up. You feel like you can't win for losing. If you talk about yourself, you're boasting and if you don't talk about anything, you're conceited.

Try This: When sharing stories about your life, try to leave out where they took place. In other words, instead of saying, "On the beach in Bali...," just say, "One time on the beach my friends and I..."

Interacting Successfully

Using Facetious Humor

Home-country peers tend to use facetious humor to get to know you. They really are not trying to be disrespectful or ignorant when they say things like, "So did you ride on water buffalo to get around Nepal?" or even (and this actually does happen) "So what language do they speak in Switzerland – Swedish?" One indignant TCK from Switzerland recalls an exchange with an English peer that forced her to just walk away without responding. She was asked if her beloved country was an island! Take a deep breath and remember this is how non-traveled peers try to connect with TCKs. They are not trying to be rude or make fun of your experiences. They just don't know how to talk with you otherwise. All one can do is learn to laugh with them and not at them.

Beware: Don't get angry with people who seem ignorant of your beloved host country. They are not making fun of you. They really want to connect with you but aren't quite sure how.

More Alike Than You Think

What is important to remember when dealing with home-country peers is that in many respects they are just like you or anyone else. You have more in common than you might think. Everyone has the same basic human needs: to be in relationship with others, to belong, to be understood, to be creative, to be able to express themselves, and much more. Domestics and TCKs have the same emotions, feelings, cares, concerns and problems. No one is immune to hurt, betrayal, embarrassment, frustration or confusion. Try to keep that in perspective when you find yourself becoming annoyed or things aren't moving the way you would want.

Meet Them Half-Way

Keep in mind that, through no fault of their own, students really can be geographically ignorant. Many students in the U.S. never have a world geography course, so they truly have no idea where various countries are or what languages are spoken there. That coupled with the fact that the U.S. media sadly lacks dissemination of any real world information means that many American students are not particularly interested in world events.

So how do you interact successfully with people you are beginning to think are ignorant, superficial or awkward? An Indian woman, who had attended an international boarding school in her home country and then studied abroad as an adult, says this of interacting with domestic peers:

> *"I made them meet me half-way. Without appearing arrogant I let them know I was multi-cultural by first listening to their stories. Once they shared their experiences with me I was able to share mine."*

Listen to Their Stories Too

Just as home-country peers need to understand you in order to accept you, you need to make an effort to understand them. Be genuinely interested in other people's lives. Listen to other people's stories – everyone has one to tell. People find it easy to talk about themselves. It's what they know. So when you are caught in an awkward moment, try asking your peers some questions about how they were raised. Get them talking and they might just start to ask questions back to you. You could compile a list of questions to keep on hand when socializing. You could ask things like:

- What type of music do you listen to?

- Do you play any sports?

- Do you enjoy playing video games? Which ones?

- What were your reasons for choosing this college/university?

- How far is this school from your home?

- Have you lived in any other places?

- How often do you get to see your grandparents?

- What is the farthest place you have ever traveled to?

- What do you see yourself doing five years from now?

- What does your family usually do for vacations?

- What was the strangest pet you've ever had?

All of these are good conversation starters no matter what your background and can be thrown back and forth without anyone feeling threatened. After hearing the answers to three or four of these questions, you can either delve deeper or decide that you may not have much in common.

Give It Time

It may take time to build relationships with home-country peers. Try not to judge them as they could very well turn out be your best friends later on. This is what happened with Brent and Rita. Brent, now in his fourth year of college, explained to me that the very kids who he thought were trying to make him feel bad about being different in his first year have actually turned out to be his best friends. What he misconstrued as being "picked on" was their way of trying to interact with him. They still do it, but he can appreciate now that they are joking around with him. For instance, when they talk about something very American that he doesn't understand, they laugh and wave their hands in front of their faces and say, "Language barrier." Today he is able to laugh with them.

Many young people today, particularly Americans, use sarcasm in their communications. In other words, they make remarks that are the complete opposite of what they really intend to convey. While in generations past, sarcasm was employed to tease, ridicule, make fun of or scoff at someone, young people today use it in many cases to make fun of themselves. As with Brent, these remarks are often misconstrued by the TCK as others making fun of him or her.

Rita had the same experience. The people she had tried to connect with but ended up isolating herself from in her first year ended up being her steady friends by the end of her second year at university. TCKs need to learn to use their observational skills to discern not only how things are done but also communicated before making any judgments about their new peers.

 Try This: Go easy on yourself and others, extending a bit of grace to all concerned as you reach out to build relationships.

Wrong Impressions

A word of caution must be inserted in this subject of finding friends. Because TCKs appear more worldly, mature for their years, refined, cultured and intelligent, they sometimes find that members of the opposite sex (or same sex) are attracted to them in a romantic way. You are special and it shows. People are attracted to the way you handle yourself, the way you know how to listen well and how you genuinely want to get to know someone by asking appropriate questions. This can be easily misunderstood and may give the impression that you are romantically interested in the person you are interacting with. Just be aware that this might happen and be clear with your friend what your intentions are. For instance, you might say, "I'd like to get to know you better as a friend so can we have a cup of coffee and talk some more?" There are more thoughts about romance in Chapter 9.

 Beware: Your worldliness, maturity and good listening skills may get you unexpected attention. Be clear about your intentions if you think someone has misinterpreted your interests.

Social Acceptance

Everyone worries whether they will be liked or not. Those first few weeks at college or university will be fraught with concerns like, "Am I talking too much or too loud? Am I being obnoxious? Should I speak up more or laugh more?" Despite the fact that most parents have been teaching their students since they were toddlers to be socially acceptable ("share your toys"), we all need to be reminded from time to time what it takes to "win friends and influence people" (Dale Carnegie).

Students at my seminars break into small groups and do an activity whereby the first group to come up with ten ways to be socially acceptable wins a prize. It's amazing at how simple yet effective many of their strategies are:

- Put a smile on your face to appear friendly and approachable. A smile also makes a person look more attractive.
- Be helpful. Lend a helping hand where you see the need.
- Don't talk about people. No one likes a gossip or rumormonger.
- Be truthful, even if it hurts.
- Be honest. Maintain your integrity.
- Pay attention to your personal hygiene.
- Be polite.
- Relax. No one is going to remember the mistakes you made when you first arrived. Everyone is making mistakes.
- Be yourself. Be genuine. Don't be a fake – someone you are not.
- Be a good listener.
- Be a good friend and you will get many in return.
- Be sincere
- Be responsible. Be on time for class or a job.
- If you commit to something, follow through on it.
- Be reliable.
- Think about others' needs before yours.
- Be flexible. Don't freak out when things don't go as planned.
- Don't be judgmental.
- Be humble.

This last quality is something TCKs need to focus on. It is far too easy to come off as arrogant, particularly when you have lost your patience with the perceived ignorance of home-country peers.

Finding Friends

"First impressions and first judgments are not true! Remember that knowing and formulating an opinion about someone takes time and isn't a constant. Remember to wait and see the person with different perspectives before judging or labeling them a certain way. Also, remember that you will find kindness wherever you go if you put a smile on your face and are open to new experiences."

Marie, journal entry

Looking into the semester abroad student's journal during her Entering stage reveals that she has discovered what it takes to be socially acceptable and how to look for the good in others. It is so easy to go on first impressions, but if you do, it could take months to realize that someone you thought was loud and obnoxious in the beginning of the school year is really a sweet person and doesn't usually act that way. They may have just been exhibiting their social anxieties in ways even they didn't understand.

Limitless Possibilities

The possibilities for finding friends on your college or university campus are inexhaustible. Friendships may be forged by being involved in sports, clubs, theater or singing groups, community service projects, political causes, classes (academic as well as non-academic) and various other activities. My middle daughter is still developing new friendships in her third year at college.

Orientation Opportunities

Your first opportunity to make friends quickly will be at orientation activities. At new student orientation, everyone is on equal footing. Most first-year students will know few or no other students. Everyone will be looking to make a friend. Many TCKs I have spoken with highly recommend doing a pre-orientation program whenever and wherever it is offered. This could be International Orientation, affectionately referred to as I.O. by those who went through it, or the outdoor adventure programs offered by many colleges. The people you meet at these programs may become your best friends.

International Orientation

When I speak to students at international schools, I highly encourage them to attend International Orientation. Some of you will be tempted to say that you are an American, Canadian, Brit, etc. and no one needs to teach you about your own country. But you are wrong! You are not a true American, Canadian or Brit anymore. I will risk being boringly repetitious, but you are a multi-cultural, global citizen. You need to hear what is said about culture shock because you will go through it, in one way or another. You've been out of the country and probably don't know all of the cultural expectations, what history is rooted in familiar traditions, or what is considered socially acceptable in terms of dating and other behaviors in this country. There is much to be learned if you open yourself to hearing

> *"Because I am American and go to an American university, I wasn't really considered international, but I wish I had been included in more international things in the beginning, because I was going through a lot of the same problems as international students."*
> Kim on TCKid.com Forum

things through the ears of a true foreigner, as though you are hearing it for the first time.

The University of Massachusetts at Amherst has a student panel for their International Orientation program where international students can ask upperclassmen anything that is on their minds. Many want to know how dating works in the U.S., how safe the campus is, how much students drink, and what they do for fun. These are all very cultural issues and worth finding out what the differences are.

One Tufts University TCK says of International Orientation:

> *"To do the regular orientation with everyone else is too overwhelming. There is too much going on to integrate. There's no warm up time. I.O. is much the same*

but with a smaller group of people over a longer period of time which helps you adjust easier. You feel at home faster. The I.O. leaders were all really great and I have become good friends with many of them. "

I would like to add that I.O. leaders may also turn out to be the perfect mentor for you. Keep in mind that I.O. may not provide the exact community of people you are looking for, but it is a great start to being with others in the same boat, so to speak. There is a chance you could run into TCKs like yourself there.

Outdoor Orientation Programs

More and more schools are offering outdoor orientation programs such as the one my daughters went through which took them hiking, canoeing or rock climbing for four days in the Connecticut wilderness before new student orientation began. These programs engage students mentally, emotionally and physically. You do not need to be an athlete to participate in them. They offer a variety of groups you can join depending on your interest, your activity level and how far you are willing to move out of your comfort zone.

Everyone I've spoken with highly recommends doing this. You are put into a small group for the four days and again, those people may very well become your new best friends. When my daughters got back to campus to start orientation with all the other first-year students, it was like they had already been there for a month. Four days after I dropped them at school they were introducing me to their new friends. They were excitedly arranging to meet up for dinner that night and everyone promised to bring

 Dig Deeper: Find out from your college or university what orientation and pre-orientation programs exist for first-year students. Then take advantage of one. It is a great way to feel connected early on and start making friends. A word of warning: Sign up early. Some programs have limited space and sign up may be on a first-come-first-served basis.

along their new roommates. They appeared self-assured and exuded a high degree of self-confidence. As a parent, it was such a relief to see that they had already settled in just as the other new students were arriving.

Groups and Clubs

There will be literally hundreds of activities, groups and clubs you can join to find people with similar interests. Chances are that if you have a hobby or favorite past time, it will be represented on your campus. If not, most institutions have methods (and sometimes money) in place so students can start their own club. See what is already being offered. Put yourself out there and join in a group of people who share the same passion, sports or time fillers as you enjoy. Or try something you've always wanted to do but never had the opportunity. Take up a new hobby or sport, take dance classes or get involved in a group with a good cause.

Try This: Put an ad in the school newspaper or on bulletin boards around campus that says something like, "Looking for others who enjoy _____. Please call Joe at _____ or email me at _____.

Finding Other Internationals

Another way TCKs can find people they have something in common with is to join the international clubs and activities on campus. These are great places to find people who understand you. Many TCKs will say they feel more comfortable with foreign students because they share the cross-cultural experience and many also have had a highly mobile childhood. Whenever I speak to a group of foreign students I informally do a little survey and ask how many of them had spent time living outside their parents' passport country as a child. Roughly a third of any given group also fit the definition of TCKs. It is no small wonder TCKs are attracted to internationals whether they are living outside or within their home country. They have that shared experience we talked about in Chapter 5.

Many university campuses have an international dorm where you could choose to live with foreign students. International dorms are often the center of international club activities. Many host groups who gather to speak in their favorite foreign language. The international dorm on my daughters' campus offers a dining room where you can join others for lunch or dinner as long as you speak the language of that particular table.

The International Bubble

There is a wealth of opportunity, so don't hole yourself up in an international bubble or "ghetto" as some students call it. Spread out and meet domestic students as well. Reach out to them. It may be a little difficult at first because they don't know how to relate to you and it may take longer to establish a relationship, but it is worth the effort and you may find a good mentor. Having a wide variety of friends and acquaintances will enrich your life immeasurably.

 Try This: There is no excuse for not finding ways to connect with others on your university campus. If there is a particular activity you enjoy but your university doesn't have it, approach the student activities office. Many schools will help you set up your own club.

Maintaining Identity

Sometimes TCKs feel like they have to change who they are in order to fit in and find friends. Whether it was real or perceived, Brent certainly felt pressure from his peers to conform to their way of life. Perhaps his peers actually liked the way he dressed and spoke but he interpreted it to mean that he didn't fit in. You need to decide what aspects of yourself you are willing to change and which ones must be safeguarded at all costs.

> "Because I couldn't talk about my past I felt like I was losing my identity. Through necessity I had to forget some of who I was in order to fit in. It seemed the best route to take, but I was sad to do it. I had to decide which groups were worth changing for or sacrificing my sense of self for to fit in and which groups weren't worth it."
>
> *Rita, American TCK who lived in India and France*

Ask yourself, is it really worth forgetting my past and losing myself in order to be accepted? Are those really the kind of friends you want to have if you can't be yourself around them?

 Beware: You may have to forget or ignore *some* parts of your past for a little while until your relationships are developed to the point that your new friends are ready to accept and even be curious about the other sides of you.

To Thine Own Self Be True

Keep the sense of who you are. You don't need to change to fit in. This doesn't mean you need to become what Ruth Van Reken calls, "a screamer," that is to say, someone who clearly lets everyone they come into contact with know they have no intention of ever becoming like them. Instead, feel free to keep the things in your life you have come to feel comfortable with, enjoy and find value in. This could be the style of dress you are accustomed to wearing,

> *"Be Yourself. Don't try to fit in too much. Adapt as always, but if you try too hard it won't work and you'll feel guilty about losing your old self. Make friends, but don't feel like you need to change who you are to do so.*
> "Uncle Dan" from
> TCKid.com

your methods of greeting people, or various other customs, traditions and languages from your host country. I recently met up with Brent and I noticed that he continues to enjoy dressing like a European with well-fitted slacks and a sweater over a dress shirt, but I quite prefer it to the baggy pants and baseball caps of most of his peers.

Share Your Experiences

People may actually enjoy the occasional kiss on both cheeks over the traditional hug or high five. Invite new friends to celebrate some of the holidays or traditions from your host country so they can learn a little more about you. Share the music you've come to love with others. Find opportunities to continue to speak in your host country language either through language groups, international groups or language dorms. Invite people to enjoy a special food from your host country. My daughters love inviting new friends to have a Swiss raclette meal (melted raclette cheese over boiled potatoes) with our family whenever they visit. Read newspapers and magazines from your host country.

Finding Belonging

Do you remember the lesson you took away from Chapter 1 about where TCKs find their sense of belonging? The answer is: with others of shared experience – the third culture experience. In other words, with people who have lived outside of their passport countries during childhood. TCKs need to be with other TCKs. How do you go about finding other TCKs?

We've already discussed a few possibilities like attending your school's International Orientation where you will meet other people in the same cross-cultural situation as you, but you may also meet other TCKs at I.O., particularly if it is a large school. You may even meet a TCK who doesn't even realize he or she is one. That might become evident if he or she has trouble answering the "Where are you from?" question. Or you might also ask students you meet if they have ever lived anywhere else. What a great icebreaker it is to say, "Oh, you're like me. Did you realize you are a TCK?"

> *"Knowing you are a TCK doesn't help you get connected, but at least you know why you are having difficulties getting connected."*
> Ruth Van Reken

TCK Communities

Campus TCK communities are a rapidly growing phenomenon. TCKs are beginning to understand the need to find and/or build their own communities on their campuses. Universities like Lewis and Clark have had such communities for some time now. Others are just beginning to look seriously at how they can better support this unique population. Boston College held their first-ever TCK Orientation which preceded International Orientation by a couple of days so their TCKs could do both. They will undoubtedly soon be celebrating their very own campus community.

TCKid.com has been used to help TCKs connect with other TCKs and start their own communities or join over 50 local groups from Taiwan to Colorado, meeting monthly for coffee and various activities. As with any group of people you find yourself interacting with, you may not like everyone you meet in your TCK group, but you will definitely have something in common with them.

Online Communities

Online communities like TCKid.com are growing by the day. There are many out there. You just need to know where to look. TCKs come from many backgrounds depending on the type of work which took their parents overseas. They may be from the corporate sector, the military, missionary, foreign service, humanitarian/non-profit world, education and so forth. If you can identify your sector, you will most likely be able to find an online community already established for kids that have shared your particular lifestyle. For instance the military has *www.militarybrats.com* which has blogs, chats, forums and friend finding features, and the missions sector has *www.missionary-kids.blogspot.com* and *www.mukappa.org* which lists the colleges who have started TCK communities. See the resources section at the end of this chapter for more online communities and the possibility of starting up your own campus community. Invite your domestic friends to a TCK community gathering so they can see what the draw is and perhaps gain a better understanding of you and your "tribe."

What You Should Know:

- TCKs have a totally different approach to forming relationships than their peers who have not lived in transient communities and may need to hang back from sharing too much about themselves in the beginning.

- Home-country peers may appear superficial because they aren't quite sure how to deal with someone who is coming from such a wealth of experiences that are very foreign to them.

- Relationships take time, patience, and understanding on both sides of the equation. Meet domestic peers half-way – they also have stories to tell.

- Seek out other TCKs to find your sense of belonging.

Resources:

Websites

- www.TCKid.com – for all TCKs.

- www.My.TCKid.com – for all TCKs. Blogs, forums, chats and groups to join

- www.TCKWorld.com – the first and oldest TCK website full of information and resources.

- www.Militarybrats.com – specific to military kids

- www.missionary-kids.blogspot.com – specific to missionary kids

- www.mkplanet.com – specific to missionary kids

- www.mukappa.org – specific to missionary kids

- www.tckacademy.com – training programs and teleclasses featuring TCK experts

- www.overseasbrats.com – OVERSEAS BRATS is an organization and magazine for those associated with American overseas schools

- www.fsyf.org – Foreign Service Youth Foundation

Chapter 7

Insights and Tools

> "I went to a school with a relatively high percentage of international students, but I soon discovered that I didn't fit into any particular group or sub-group of internationals. The international students bonded by nationality and since I'm American I was put into the category of someone who grew up in Iowa or Massachusetts, but I really didn't fit there. I was stuck somewhere in the middle and couldn't relate to either side."
>
> *Rita, American TCK, Tufts University Class of 2009*

Who Am I?

TCK Identity Development

Remember the story of my middle daughter, Katrina, whose first English homework assignment back in the U.S. was to write about who she was? She ended up sobbing as she stared at the blank piece of white paper in front of her. "I don't know who I am!" she blubbered out over and over again. My heart broke as she grappled with who her international upbringing had made her.

All the time we lived overseas my children would answer the "Where are you from?" question with, "I'm American." Now that we were back "home" America didn't really feel like home. Switzerland felt more like home, but she couldn't say that she was Swiss. Because TCKs build relationships with all the cultures they live in, they don't feel they have real ownership of any. They feel more like they belong everywhere and nowhere concurrently.

When I read Dr. Barbara Schaetti's addendum, "A Most Excellent Journey" to Robin Pascoe's book, *Raising Global Nomads,* I felt like the light bulb finally turned on in my brain. I got it! Up until three years ago when reading Dave Pollock's and Ruth Van Reken's *Third Culture Kids* book I had been one of those people who suffered from what Dr. Schaetti explains as "terminal uniqueness syndrome." I knew I was different but couldn't understand why.

I was so struck with Dr. Schaetti's TCK identity development model (adapted in part from William E. Cross Jr.'s seminal research on identity development), I feel compelled to share it with every TCK and ATCK I meet. It is so profound and yet the concept is so simple, I feel that every TCK needs to hear and understand it in order to grow from the third culture experience and appreciate the person they are because of it.
(Dr. Schaetti's work, including *Phoenix Rising, A Question of Cultural Identity* can be found online at *www.transition-dynamics.com/phoenix*.)

Dr. Schaetti defines the term 'identity' as "simply the sense of who each of us is." The development of identity is "the search for congruence in our sense of who we are." In layman's terms we could say it is achieving harmony in who we believe ourselves to be. She explains, and I summarize *very* briefly, that you, as any human being, are trying to sort out who you think you are as compared to who you thought you once were, and you compare that to what others believe you are and what you strive to become. In order to accomplish this, you are constantly exploring different groupings and deciding your relationship to those groups. As you go through life, things happen that bring particular groups and your place in them to your conscious awareness. For instance, early in life you may discover that you are a female but you don't consciously consider that it is a part of the gender grouping; you are light-skinned but you don't consider the race grouping; or you are Christian but you don't consider the religion grouping.

As you move through life, your attention is brought to more and more different groupings and over the course of months or even years you explore your relationship to those groupings. This begins in earnest in mid to late adolescence. Understanding your relationship within and among many different groupings that come into your conscious awareness gives meaning to who you know yourself to be.

> **Share This:** As a global nomad, your international experiences have greatly impacted your identity development. The typical TCK/ATCK/GN has been exposed to a number and variety of groupings his or her home-country peers may never encounter.

The TCK Identity Development Model

I was recently speaking with Carla, a bi-cultural ATCK who had spent the first seven years of her life living in Peru. Her mother was an American and her father was an Italian who was born and raised in Peru. He spent one year of his life as a small child living in his father's hometown in Italy learning the language. While I was telling her about Dr. Schaetti's TCK Identity Development model she said, "I remember what it was like when I went through each of those stages as you were describing them to me." I asked her if I could use her story to help bring this model to life for you.

Carla's family sold their home and left Peru when the political situation became unstable and her mother was accepted to a U.S. university for a master's program. They moved to a small New England town where they rented a home.

At age 15 Carla decided to go back to Peru to visit. "I was already in the heart of the 'awkward phase' at school in the U.S. and, in Peru I was suddenly aware of this place that I had once belonged to and how foreign I was to it," she said of the visit.

Carla's parents separated when she was in her second to last year of high school and her father moved to California for work. Shortly afterward she happened to meet another TCK who was one year behind her in high school. They really connected because they were going through similar issues. The friendship eventually developed into a romantic relationship which continued, long distance, during her first year of university.

Carla's relationship with her boyfriend unraveled at the end of that first year and they broke up. Around the same time her mother decided to relocate. With no family home and no boyfriend to come back to, Carla had no place to stay that was her own. At this point she realized her entire family network was scattered across the U.S. and she began to question the idea of where is home. She didn't feel like she belonged at her school and now she no longer felt she belonged in her old town. She had no place to really call home.

Carla felt like she had lost all points of reference. Her sense of belonging was gone...again. She then began a personal and spiritual quest to find out where home was and what it meant to her. She said, "In college I went back [to Peru] a few times on my own to try and figure it out, each time feeling more and more distant from the culture but not my family." The first visit back turned out to be a traumatic experience because she felt very different, very American, not the Italian she was raised to be while living in Peru. She had forgotten the language, wore very different clothing, didn't use make-up like the ladies there did and felt very out of place. It wasn't home.

She went on to say, "My family relations stayed strong. To some degree, I rationalized home as the spaces where you meet people you connect with rather than a singular place. That became important to me."

Carla decided to study abroad in her third year of school and used the opportunity to go to the country of her father's home. She fell in love with Italy and the way of life there and learned the language. She did all she could over the next couple of years to get back to Italy. It wasn't home but while there she realized that she really wasn't one thing or another. She wasn't fully Peruvian, American or Italian, but she instead had bits and pieces of several cultures and she became comfortable with that. She had come to terms with the fact that she had lost her home and wanted now to create her own.

As an aside, Carla mentioned that she mostly looks like her mother, who is Irish and that is the one side of her that she has not yet fully explored. She says, "I've realized that generally when I'm in Peru, I'm American; in Italy, I'm Peruvian; in America I'm Italian and this is mostly because my husband is from Florence and I have maintained that connection with language and culture."

We will follow Carla on her identity development as we look at the five stages of Dr. Schaetti's TCK Identity Development Model:

1) Pre-encounter

2) Encounter

3) Exploration

4) Integration

5) Recycling

Pre-encounter

Pre-encounter is the stage before the most profound, identity-shaking Encounter stage. Schaetti explains that in this stage TCKs are just living their incredible but usual international, cross-cultural, highly mobile lives, not understanding how that lifestyle is shaping who they are.

At some level they may already sense that they are a little different from friends and relatives who stay in one country all their lives. It becomes normal to be different. They really don't know any other way to be.

For Carla, Pre-encounter was going on in Peru. She was living in a bi-cultural home in a country that was neither that of her father or her mother. She had extended family there with her and she most likely did not appreciate that this was a somewhat unusual way to live for most Americans or Italians.

Encounter

Then one day TCKs have an experience that wakes them up on a more conscious level to the fact that their international childhoods have made them different from others. This kind of Encounter forces them into self-reflection. They start to question who they are as well as where they

141

belong. TCKs often say they belong everywhere and nowhere and this becomes crystal clear when they repatriate to a place that has been called "home" for so long they actually believe it, but they find that they really don't belong there either.

The Encounter experience could very well take place upon repatriation and the illusion that he or she knows the home country well is shattered. It could come, and I've seen this numerous times, as an accumulation of small encounters such as continuously being asked the "Where are you from?' question. This, of course, is happening several times a day when starting off at college or university. Remember Rita's story? This could have been her Encounter experience. It could have also been during International Orientation when she realized she didn't fit in with any nationality, including the one written on her passport. It could have been a combination of the two experiences.

 Tip to Remember: The Encounter experience could be triggered by any number of things, but it is a sudden and unexpected realization that you are different from others.

Remember the story of Brice Royer who had the incapacitating pain in his hands? His Encounter experience most likely came when he decided to accompany his mother to visit family in England but discovered he didn't belong there either. He was awakened to the fact that no matter where he went, he felt he was different and didn't belong.

Carla felt her Encounter experience came after her first year at university when her mother moved away from the only place Carla could call home. This opened the "where is home?" dialogue. Holiday breaks at school meant going someplace unfamiliar to visit family. She was not able to go back home as she knew it.

Exploration

Once TCKs realize they are different they naturally go into a period of Exploration to try to understand why. They get their hands on books like Pollock and Van Reken's, surf the internet, and find people to consult with to find answers. Brice immediately went into the Exploration phase to find out why he couldn't fit in anywhere. He had never heard the terms 'third culture kid' or 'global nomad'. He got on the computer and came across articles about kids that had led the same kind of life he had.

 Try This: Take a copy of Pollock and Van Reken's *Third Culture Kids: Growing up Among Worlds* along with you to university. You may want to revisit the TCK profile when you are forgetting what makes you different from domestic-country peers.

That's when he read up on the TCK profile and discovered that he had been harboring unresolved grief to the point of becoming filled with pain.

Two young graduate students from a local university desperately wanted to come to a talk I gave on third culture kids but didn't have the transportation, so I met with them on their campus. It was very clear that these Asian/American ATCKs were in the Exploration stage of their identity development. Unlike Brice, they knew the term TCK. They had always enjoyed being a little different until they came to the U.S. where they felt they didn't fit in anywhere. They didn't look or act American and yet they weren't fully Asian either and were rejected by both groups.

Carla felt her Exploration stage started when she was in university and went to Peru to visit family and try to recapture that Italian side of her heritage. She admits having gone back several times in search of the answer to the question, "Is this place home?" She also felt she was "exploring" when she decided to do her semester study abroad in Italy and traveled there again with her father to "explore her roots."

Integration

Identity Exploration can go on for months or years, as in Carla's subsequent trips to Peru and Italy. Once TCKs understand who they are and how their international life experience has shaped them, they have achieved congruence (harmony). Dr. Schaetti says that people in Integration are comfortable with being different from their home-country peers. At this point the TCK will either embrace his or her life experiences and use them to strengthen his or her success or he or she will discard them as being irrelevant.

Carla came to Integration when she went to Italy and came to terms with being "the many." She wasn't one thing or another and she was finally comfortable with that. Brice could very well have come to his Integration through his journaling, and he has continued to use his life experiences for the better good of others by founding TCKid.com.

 Share It: Once you have reached Integration and are comfortable with how your international experiences have shaped you, you can use your experiences to help others who may be working their way through the stages of identity development.

Recycling

Global nomads will often have another Encounter experience, probably not as intense as the first one but an awakening that will once again lead to self-reflection. They will engage in identity Exploration again to look at how the internationally mobile life has shaped them and then eventually move again into Integration.

Carla reports having had many more Encounter experiences but not nearly as profound as the first time around. She continuously reminds herself that her bi-cultural heritage and international lifestyle are what have made her different from most others who surround her on her university campus. She says she knows she is quirky but she deals with it by using humor. She also has found other ATCKs and internationals she enjoys hanging out with. (More on how to find belonging in Chapter 6.)

Knowing the Language Helps

As a result of her research and conversations, Dr. Schaetti found that people who had relatively easy identity Encounter experiences related to growing up globally were introduced to the terms 'global nomad' and 'third culture kid' while still living overseas, or were introduced to the terms upon repatriation via re-entry training. She mentions that even if a term such as 'military brat', 'oil brat' or 'missionary kid' was used in place of the TCK or GN term, these children at least had a notion that there was something special about their way of growing up. Knowing there is terminology for kids who have lived their lifestyle helps to validate the feelings and experiences they have had. It says to them, "You are right – you *are* different – you have experienced more than most kids your age."

People who don't know and understand the terms 'third culture kid' and 'global nomad' feel very much alone. They know they are different but cannot understand why. They think they are the only ones who feel this way and it must mean that there is something wrong with them. It doesn't occur to them that the reason they are feeling this way is because they grew up internationally. Schaetti quotes Janet Bennett, executive director of the Intercultural Communication Institute, as saying that people who don't understand that they feel different because of their international experience suffer from "terminal uniqueness syndrome." It is such a relief to ATCKs to find out there is actually a name and a profile for people like them, that they are not alone, and there is nothing wrong with them.

Keep in mind that identity development is a process, one that can take years or decades. Global nomads do eventually reach harmony in the sense of who they are. They may go through the phase of Recycling several times; that's very normal. In the three years since I have truly understood how my internationally mobile childhood has shaped me, thereby making me different, I have undergone several Encounter experiences, each of which generated a phase of Recycling. Each time I enter a period of self-reflection and remind myself that I am not just okay, I'm a part of that wonderful tribe of people who have led extraordinary and privileged lives. Once I understand that, *je me sens bien dans ma peau* (I feel good in my skin).

Third Culture Person Reacculturation Tool

Dr. Rachel Timmons, Associate Professor of Education at California Baptist University has developed a tool I give out to every student who attends my "Transitioning Successfully for University" seminar. Ever since I was first introduced to the Third Culture Person (TCP)

> *"Continue on the journey of growth and you will reach a point where you realize there are advantages to being different and you come to joy."*
>
> Dr. Aruna Jha

145

Reacculturation rubric, I have been sold on its relevance and effectiveness as a self-help tool for individuals going through transition.

A rubric is a scoring tool for subjective assessments linked to learning objectives. The TCP Reacculturation rubric serves as a guide to help international sojourners chart the progress of their adjustment while keeping an end goal clearly in mind.

The Purpose

Dr. Timmons explains that there are three reasons why an international such as you should make use of a transition rubric:

1. **To Develop Cultural Competence** – Students entering university must develop the ability to function effectively in their new home community and school culture. The rubric acts as a guide to help you make good decisions and enables you to see your progress concerning your adjustment.

2. **To Develop a Sense of Self-efficacy as a TCP** – As you work through your transition period you begin to develop a sense of self-efficacy as a third culture person. Self-efficacy in transition means you have realized that you have become someone who is able to complete cross-cultural transitions without losing your sense of personal identity along the way. A rubric helps you chart your successes and each success helps you build confidence and self-esteem.

3. **To Challenge the Fossils** – Fossils are anything which might be a stumbling block for you as you leave your host culture and readjust in your new home or school culture. Just as a fossil is hard and rigid, some people get rather hard and inflexible when they meet difficulties in their transition journey. A fossilized TCP tends to stay in the same spot too long and develop negative attitudes towards people or perhaps make destructive life choices because they feel uncomfortable in their situation.

The Tool

On the following page is a small sampling I have pieced together from Dr. Timmons' reacculturation rubric to give you an idea of its usefulness. It in no form reflects the width and breadth of the actual rubric. I have drafted six of the 16 categories from three separate sections of issues and a few descriptors in each category from what is available in the actual rubric. Dr. Timmons' rubric, which can be ordered directly from her (see resources section at end of chapter), is composed of five sections describing various reacculturation issues:

- General TCP Reacculturation Process Issues

- TCP Marginalization Issues

- TCP Support and Belonging Issues

- TCP Cultural Heritage Issues

- TCP Re-entry Preparation Issues

Each section lists two to four categories of issues and gives multiple descriptors for each area of competency. Not every reacculturation issue will apply to every person, but most people will be able to apply the majority of them to their own adjustment process. For instance, there are categories that apply to one's professional loss and career preparation that may not apply to you as university students just yet. Dr. Timmons explains that the descriptors in each of the categories is meant to provide general ideas to cause thought and reflection concerning the transition process.

	Third Culture Person Dr. Rachel	
	Limited Competencies	**Developing Competencies**
Reverse Culture Shock	▫ Experiences negative feelings toward home culture ▫ Longs for host culture experiences and relationships ▫ Disappointed in changes in home culture	▫ Begins to accept changes in home culture ▫ Finds some comfort/pleasure in home culture activities and experiences
Cultural Fatigue	▫ Experience extreme fatigue at attempting to readjust in home culture ▫ Must be hyper vigilant to interpret social cues and spoken message of home culture	▫ Asks for help or advice when confronted with confusing situation ▫ Plans ahead for new situations
Expectations of Home Culture	▫ Holds numerous unrealistic expectations of home culture ▫ Cannot deal with changes in home culture	▫ Can verbalize areas of unrealistic expectations ▫ Maintains negative or disappointed attitude in areas where expectations were not met
Stress or Health Problems	▫ Often experiences reacculturation stress related illness (stomach upset, loss of sleep) ▫ Food allergies emerge or exacerbated	▫ Experiences moderate stress related physical symptoms ▫ Able to tie events that caused stress to specific issues of readjustment
Cultural Uniqueness	▫ Believes TCP experience is only worthwhile experience ▫ Devalues home culture as having nothing unique	▫ Values the TCP experience more than the monoculture experience but does not allow view to limit progress in the reacculturation process
Social	▫ Socially unprepared for reentry	▫ Willing to persist with social efforts knowing it takes time to make new friends

Reacculturation Rubric E. Timmons		
Proficient Competencies	**Advanced Competencies**	
▫ Rarely experiences excessive homesick feeling ▫ Feels satisfied and comfortable in both home and host culture	▫ No symptoms of reverse culture shock apparent ▫ Enjoys fulfilling experiences in both cultures	**Reverse Culture Shock**
▫ Enjoys learning more about home culture ▫ Depends on new friends to help interpret social cues	▫ Encounters new situations with confidence and enjoyment without experiencing unusual fatigue/stress	**Cultural Fatigue**
▫ Notes areas of realistic/unrealistic expectations ▫ Notes realistic expectations met	▫ Able to discuss realistic and unrealistic expectations of home culture ▫ Reacts appropriately in a variety of situations	**Expectations of Home Culture**
▫ Realizes change is stressful and plans accordingly ▫ Fewer medical problems due to stress	▫ Enjoys taking on challenging/new responsibilities ▫ Physical condition is within normal range	**Stress or Health Problems**
▫ Is beginning to see value to cultural heritage in a balanced view ▫ Seems to realize +/- sides to the TCP experience	▫ Realizes that host and home culture provide worthwhile and unique experiences that enhances one's life	**Cultural Uniqueness**
▫ Has a positive attitude towards making new friends	▫ Presents a secure and healthy social perspective	**Social**

How to Use It

The rubric is best utilized over a period of time, allowing for growth and development as time goes on rather than as a one-time application. I tell students to take a colored highlighter pen and make a little circle or dash on the front page with that highlighter and write in the date. They should then go over each category that applies to their life situation, reading each of the section descriptors under each competency group. With that colored highlighter, highlight any descriptor that describes how you are feeling and what you are experiencing right now.

You may find that you have highlighted some areas in more than one competency and that is fine. That is where you are right now and it means you are showing varying degrees of comfort in certain aspects of your new situation. This is all completely normal. Even if you find that the descriptors you are highlighting mainly fall into 'Limited Competencies,' there is no need for concern. Do not worry about a score. That is not the major aim of the exercise.

Once you have completed all your highlighting, put the rubric away and don't pick it up for another three months. After three months has passed, get out another highlighter of a different color. Again put a circle or a dash and write the date next to the new color. Go over all the section descriptors again and mark the descriptors that best indicate how you are feeling and what you are experiencing now. Note whether you are highlighting more descriptors that fall in higher competencies. Perhaps you have advanced in some areas but are 'stuck' in others. Continue to repeat this three month evaluation until you feel you have 'mastered' each category. I would suggest you wait to tally your score, if you decide to do so at all, until you feel you have moved through all the competencies without being 'fossilized'.

Dr. Timmons says to keep in mind that some people may make a complete transition in a short period of time (weeks or months) like we talked about in Chapter 2 while others may take longer (one to three years). For example, Brent from Chapter 1 who is in his fourth year of college says he is still in transition.

Challenging the Fossils

A rubric helps shed light on where you might be stuck. If you see an area where you might not be moving ahead in the transition process from one culture to the next, Dr. Timmons' advice is to challenge whatever is holding you back head on. She says to purposefully continue to work hard to succeed in each area of transition difficulty and remain flexible as you learn how to fit into your new home or culture. Otherwise you risk becoming hardened to transitions between cultures much like a fossil is hard and dry.

Try This: Challenge whatever is holding you back from progressing in your transition journey. Address it head on. It will feel uncomfortable, but the satisfaction that comes from gaining a new level of comfort in your new culture will be worth it.

Dr. Timmons uses an example of someone who is feeling lonely. She suggests you must be willing to take action and work at developing healthy friendships rather than wait around and expect others to reach out to you. This is just what we talked about in Chapters 5 and 6 when we discussed how to meet people and build relationships. You must put yourself out there and take risks. This is tough because it is also the time when you are feeling vulnerable and wondering if you will be accepted. Don't give in to the temptation to compare yourself to others. This can come easier to some people than others, but it is a skill that can be developed and useful throughout your life.

In Chapter 4 we talked a lot about what to do when you are in that downward dip of reverse culture shock. Remember the family that would invite friends to come visit when they were feeling negative about their new host country? They would show their visitors around, taking them to all the lovely places they had found, pointing out the positives of life in their new country. You can do the same. Take a tour of your town or surroundings. Learn some history about it; visit the museums in the area. Look for the positive. Talk to others to find out what their favorite things are about the community. As always, be proactive.

Dr. Timmons enjoys sharing a quote from a letter sent to her by a fellow sojourner after she received her transition rubric. This woman had lived for many years in Asia and struggled with her cross-cultural transition upon re-entering her home culture. Her gratitude for the help she received was the impetus for Dr. Timmons publishing the rubric so other TCPs, including you, could take advantage of it too.

> "I've gone over so many times the rubric you sent me, and it is like finally there is something on paper that describes what I've been experiencing in words. Even though it's almost a year now that I've been home, I feel in many ways like it was yesterday. I don't think I'm much out of your rubric's stage one except for a few areas…"

What You Should Know:

- "Encounter" is often triggered by repatriation or even transition to university when you are surrounded by non-international peers. There comes a realization that you are different from others. Remember your international experiences have made you different from those who have not lived beyond their national and/or cultural borders.

- There are many resources on TCKs/GNs, many of which have already been mentioned in this book, that will help guide you through the "Exploration" stage of TCK Identity Development.

- The TCP Reacculturation rubric is a useful tool for charting the transition adjustment process and identifying areas of fossilization.

Resources:

Books

- *Raising Global Nomads* by Robin Pascoe, Expatriate Press, 2006.

- Barbara Schaetti's dissertation, "Global Nomad Identity: Hypothesizing a Developmental Model," is available through Dissertation Abstracts. It can be ordered online through Bell and Howell at www.umi.com (formerly UMI). The catalog number is 9992721.

Rubric

- To order your Reacculturation rubric or for questions on how to use it email Dr. Rachel Timmons at timmonr@sbcglobal.net.

Website

- Transition Dynamics – a consultancy serving the international expatriate and repatriate community. www.transition-dynamics.com.

Chapter 8

Practically Speaking

"He who every morning plans the transaction of the day and follows out that plan, carries a thread that will guide him through the maze of the most busy life. But where no plan is laid, where the disposal of time is surrendered merely to the chance of incidence, chaos will soon reign."

Victor Hugo (1802 - 1885)

If you have been progressing through this book by reading from front to back cover, you should at this point:

- Understand that you are a third culture kid (TCK)/global nomad (GN) and have a sense of the influence that has had on your life.

- Know that you are going through the stages of transition. You know what to expect and you understand that your wildly fluctuating emotions and sense of chaos are all a normal part of the process. And best of all, you know how to deal with it. (If not, go back and re-read!)

- Know what you need to do to enter well. You understand how important it is to find a good mentor.

- Have strategies for finding friends and building relationships.

Now let's look at some of the practicalities of attending college or university.

Get Ready, Set...Go!

You are about to undergo a rite of passage, a coming of age, a transition which takes you from adolescence to adulthood. You will be leaving behind the rules and the dependence that go with childhood and stepping forward to gain the freedom and independence of young adulthood. Other than budgetary restrictions imposed by those who hold the purse strings (your parents or caretaker or college financial aid office), you are free to decide what to do about most aspects of your life – your bedtime hour, what you eat, what you do in your spare time and where you go.

This is for Real!

Along with this new-found independence comes responsibility for your actions. You must face the consequences of poorly-made decisions and rash behavior. One mother tells each college-bound son or daughter, "Before you make a choice, take a decision or act on something, ask yourself three questions:

1) Will it hurt me?

2) How will my parents react to what I've done?

3) Can I live with the consequences of my actions?"

Preaching aside, there are many preparations to be carried out before leaving home. Some things, such as building your RAFT, have been mentioned in previous chapters, but there are other practical things you can do to prepare yourself for landing and settling in well.

Be the Tourist

Because this is such a major factor in repatriation and transition, I remind you again to consider buying a travel guide to your home (or next host) country. Treat this country the way you would a foreign one. Don't assume you know everything. I reiterate the story of my husband's colleague who gave us the guide for international newcomers to Boston, where we are now living. Even though we had been coming back every one to two years I didn't notice the changes until we were here to live full-time. I would even go so far as to suggest purchasing a book written for foreign students such as Charles Lipson's *Succeeding as an International Student in the United States and Canada* or G. Davey's *The International Student's Survival Guide: How to Get the Most from Studying at a U.K. University*. Both books have a wealth of information on the culture and practical aspects of living as a college student in the country of their expertise.

Think Ahead

Eliminate unnecessary stress. Get as many practical things in place as early as possible. The following list offers a few suggestions, but you or your parents are likely to come up with more:

- Sign up for first semester course selections.

- Decide what to pack, leave behind, put in storage or give away.

- Make a list of what needs to be purchased on arrival. Stores such as Bed, Bath and Beyond have lists you can pick up when you enter the store. Don't be fooled into thinking you need everything on the list. My daughters typically buy what they know they will need for certain and wait to finish their shopping until they see what their roommate has brought that they can share such as a TV, mini-fridge, microwave, area rug, mirrors, etc.

- Call your assigned roommate to get to know him or her and also to talk about who can bring what for the room or apartment.

- Formulate a realistic budget with your parents. Besides tuition and room and board (which they may take care of on their end), there is also the cost of text books, socializing, health care, weekends spent away, transportation and more. What are the expectations?

- Discuss banking arrangements such as money transfers, credit or debit cards, checking and savings accounts.

- Decide how you will communicate with your family. Will you use some form of Skype or other internet provider or a long-distance call plan?

- Think about cell phones. Is there a family share plan you can piggyback onto from extended family in your home country?

Activities of Daily Living

Learn appropriate life skills before leaving home.

- Learn how to write a check and balance the check book – something you may not have had the opportunity to do in your host country.

- Understand the difference between a check or debit card and credit card and how to use them.

- Talk about how to apply for a job, conduct an interview, and what you need to take with you to fill out an application. Who will you use as references? Is there anyone in your home country who you can list as a reference so the prospective employer doesn't have to phone around the globe across several time zones?

- Learn how to do your laundry.

- If you do not already have your driver's license, make a plan to complete the requirements to obtain one, preferably over the summer before the start of school. Even if you do not have a car, a driver's license is often used for identification and for other purposes.

- Become familiar with how to use the postal system, public transportation system and how your insurance works.

 Try This: You may want to consider building in time over the summer in your home or new host country before the start of school to learn some of the skills that can only take place on site.

In Case of Emergency

Know what to do in an emergency or crisis:

- Plan ahead what you will do, who you will call.

- Have emergency numbers in your cell phone.

- When in doubt of who to call, you can turn to the International Students services.

- Decide when you will inform your parents if you get in trouble, become very ill or have an accident. In the U.S. parents must have permission by the student (if they are over age 18) to speak to their health care providers, teachers or deans.

 Tip to Remember: Keep your student handbook as a ready reference for whom to call should something come up. Your college or university will have several layers of departments, services or personnel you can call for any kind of problem or situation.

Comfort Items

Bring things that make you smile, bring you comfort and tie you to your past. You will be starting a new life, but don't leave the old totally behind. It is a huge part of who you are today. Students typically bring favorite posters, items from home, scrapbooks, music, stuffed animals and yearbooks. These objects also allow you to share who you are with your new friends so they can understand where you come from. And on those blue days, pull them out and gain reassurance and comfort from them.

Ties to Your Past

Plan to maintain ties to the country you have left. It is a huge part of you and your past. Take along some of your favorite traditions, customs, music and dress. You will most likely have a chance to use them at an international gathering or a theme party. At the very least, you will be able to introduce friends to some of the things you love and what makes you the person you are.

Make New Friends but Keep the Old

While maintaining ties to your country and your past, let's not forget about friends. Plan to stay in touch, but be careful not to overdo it to the extent that you are avoiding making local friends. You have a foot in two worlds simultaneously and you will have to work hard at balancing that. It will be too easy to stay holed up in your dorm room or apartment interacting on Facebook with friends when you could be out meeting new people and having new experiences. Take risks. Put yourself out there at the risk of feeling awkward or uneasy. Try new clubs and new activities and mingle with different groups. You could start by looking for groups who like to speak the language of your host country.

Campus Life – What to Expect

While this book cannot possibly prepare you for every situation, emotion, or doubt you will encounter in your life as a college student, it can give you a glimpse of what you may or may not experience. I would suggest you also purchase and read books written for and, in some cases, written by students from your home country attending universities in your home country. I gave such a guide to two of my girls the summer before their departure called, *College Survival: A Crash Course for Students by Students* by Greg Gottesman and Friends. It is now in its seventh edition. My youngest daughter benefited from the writings of a female student: *U Chic – the College Girls' Guide to Everything* by Christie Garton. There are many others from which to choose for more detailed information about college life. Amazon.com has the U.S. guides and Amazon.co.uk has the British versions such as *Cheeky Guide to Student Life,* by Cheeky Guides, Ltd. and *A Guide to Uni Life* by Lucy Tobin.

Beliefs Tested

Your beliefs will be tested in your college setting. Professors pride themselves on helping you think about all the other possibilities besides the ones engrained in you since childhood. It is not unusual for students to question their religion, values, world view, life purpose and much more. You may feel uncomfortable – it's part of growing up, finding out who you are and what you truly believe. Some would say this is what college is all about. If we all thought the same, it wouldn't make for a very interesting or forward moving world.

Big to Little Fish

This quote reveals one of the factors that led to the depression that our TCK case study Brent (from Chapter 1) suffered during his first years at college. Quite frequently students, not just internationals, end up feeling small, incompetent or not up to the challenge once they hit college. This could be the student who came from a small school and is now at a large university, or one who excelled in a particular sport in high school but struggles to make the varsity team at college or the student who sailed through her studies in high school without much effort and is now working harder than ever to get a passing grade.

Keep working hard, use the resources available to you (teacher's assistants, writing and other labs) and don't give up. Seek out an upperclassman, perhaps on your dorm floor, to get their perspective on specific courses or instructors. You will get used to what your professors are expecting from you and learn to work with them.

> *"When I got to my college, I quickly realized how I was surrounded by brilliant, well-rounded, and extremely qualified and ambitious students. I felt insignificant and inadequate, something that took me by complete surprise."*
>
> Brent (Chapter 1)

Tip to Remember: Every college and university campus has student resources in place to help you succeed. They want you to succeed. It is in *their* best interest that their students do succeed. Be pro-active about accessing the resources, particularly on a large campus where it may be more difficult to access the resources for success and it will be easier to get lost in the crowd.

Wrong Choice?

There is a widespread phenomenon that takes place on university and college campuses within the first six to eight weeks of the start of the first term. Students, international as well as domestic, begin to second guess themselves as to whether or not they have made the correct choice of schools. I have seen it happen as early as two days after arrival on campus. There are a variety of reasons for this reaction.

- The shock of being away from family support systems, perhaps for the first time, is kicking in.

- The feelings of being out of your comfort zone are overwhelming you.

- Homesickness is having its way with you.

- You are experiencing the self-doubt we talked about in Chapter 2 that is so common in the transition stage.

 Dig Deeper: If you are feeling the emotional instability of the transition stage, remember that it (1) is to be expected, (2) is normal, and (3) will pass. If you know of someone else who is feeling the chaos and not understanding why, you can come alongside that person and help him or her through it. It's not just internationals who experience the transition cycle.

This leads into the discussion of "Did I choose the wrong school?" Many students feel as though they made a mistake in their choice of schools. One reason just mentioned is the new level of effort required to get good grades. Perhaps your decision to attend a well-respected, influential institution of higher education made you overlook the highly competitive nature of the student body. You were a high grade-earning student in secondary school, but now you feel like the dummy.

The pendulum could very well swing the other way, particularly if you are coming from a competitive International Baccalaureate (IB) program. Students who have been challenged to work hard during the IB sometimes get to university only to find they aren't challenged enough. One first-year student explained that her college insisted she complete prerequisite classes for her art major despite the fact that she did art at a higher level in the IB. She had developed an incredible portfolio during high school and was faced with learning how to draw lines in her first term. She was beginning to wonder if she had chosen the wrong school and needed to look for something more competitive. After some self-reflection she decided to stay put and use her free time to take up other activities like dance, something that had always interested her.

162

It could very well be that you *did* choose the wrong school. Students who didn't get a chance to visit the campus of their choice or who visited it early on, such as when accompanying an older sibling, may feel like they made the wrong choice. Sometimes students who made 'early decision' applications feel like they should have perhaps looked around more or applied to more schools. It could be that your preferences have changed since the time you visited the school – you thought you wanted a rural campus but now realize you like the city better or you felt like you wanted to be on a large campus but now you feel it's too impersonal. The school may have changed. You may have changed. For whatever reasons, it turns out not to be a good fit.

Try This: If you chose your college without seeing it first, try to have a visit over the summer. Spending time on campus and getting to know the town and surrounding environs will help you feel better, especially when you know what is available in terms of shopping, entertainment, restaurants and more. My daughters always tried to notice what the kids were wearing on campus so they would be prepared with their own school wardrobes.

Give It Time

The good news is that most of those students who consider leaving or transferring out to other schools do *not* actually do it. Many university advisors encourage students wanting to transfer to wait a full semester. Give it a chance. You can begin looking into where you would like to go, but it is likely that by the end of that first semester you will feel more settled and will have made some friends.

Beware: First impressions are not always accurate. Give the school, the environs and your fellow students the benefit of the doubt. Things are likely to look differently to you after the chaos has settled.

Rocky Start

Many times TCKs feel like they got off to a bad start, particularly if they are not relating well with their peers, so they want to transfer out. They feel like they've made all their mistakes in one place, learned from them, and want to start fresh somewhere else. Those unhappy feelings almost always settle down after the first or second term. My poster child, Brent, was on the verge of leaving his college three times in three years. He had been accepted and was ready to transfer, but each time, at the very last minute, he decided to stay. He says he just couldn't face the idea of starting all over, having to get acquainted with the school, the area, the culture (and all colleges do have their own culture) and most of all, making new friends.

An important note worth mentioning on Brent's case study is the fact that his family relocated from Europe back to the U.S. when he graduated from high school. So his life there was finished. He wouldn't see his friends again at school vacations. He would go home to the place his parents settled for school breaks but didn't really know anyone there. Brent couldn't wait to go to Holland for his junior year semester abroad. I spoke with him when he returned and he sounded much more content and self-satisfied. He said that going back to Europe, even though it wasn't to his beloved host country, helped him come to closure with his leaving. Each of my own three daughters found the same thing when they returned for a visit after our repatriation.

Tip to Remember: Returning to the place and people TCKs leave behind helps bring closure and allows them to move ahead.

Dormitory Life

On the subject of dormitory life, begin thinking seriously about the various living styles offered on your campus. Is a same-sex dorm or floor the only way for you to go? Maybe it is, at least for the first year, if you think you would be uncomfortable with the co-ed living that is very common and popular on most campuses today. Now is the time to begin thinking about how you will want to experience shared living. Some dormitories offer certain lifestyle living such as quiet dorms or substance-free housing. You will have three to four years to experiment with different alternatives, including fraternity and sorority houses (if your campus has Greek life) but for your first year, consider what will make you the most comfortable.

Course Load

Some students, particularly those who suffer from high school or IB burn-out, suggest limiting your course load the first semester. Along with all the rest you are dealing with in transition you must also determine how and when to study. Taking the minimum requirement of classes to maintain full-time student status could be a reassuring way to start the first term. It would give you time to settle in with the reduced stress of a full course load rather than the normally higher course load pressed upon you by advisors. You can always bump it up the second semester or take classes or online courses over the summer.

One eager TCK says she likes the flexibility of signing up for an extra class, knowing full well she can drop it if it proves to be dull or too much work. This strategy allows her to find out quickly what courses interest her and which ones don't. Since in the U.S. students are expected to declare their majors at the end of their second year, this strategy quickened the process of elimination for her.

Discrimination

Something that can come as a shock, particularly to TCKs who are used to going to school with and extending friendships to kids of all nationalities, ethnicities and races, is the discrimination that is sometimes seen on college campuses. TCKs are comfortable with diversity and thrive in mixed social settings. It can be disappointing, frustrating and infuriating to witness or be the target of discrimination. But remember that the skills you have from your TCK experiences make you good ambassadors. You may be able to build bridges to conquer the ideas that foster separateness on your campuses. Many schools are working hard to celebrate and learn from diversity and have student groups that lead the efforts.

International Considerations

Because foreign students and those who are coming home for college have the double whammy of not only learning about being a college student but also learning or re-learning the culture, those who have gone before you made a few suggestions worth considering.

- Even if you are dead-set against being labeled as an international student, consider signing in or checking in with the Office or Dean of International Students (sometimes called the International Students and Scholars Office). If you find yourself in a dilemma, they will most likely be able to help you out. This is absolutely the first telephone call for any foreign student on campus. They can help you out with anything from finding a lawyer to helping with a medical problem or finding a restaurant that serves the food you are missing.

- Think about asking for dormitory housing in the international dorm. You may find you relate well with other internationals and you may even find some other TCKs. It would also give you an opportunity to speak the languages you left behind. One drawback is that it may become so comfortable you don't reach out to make friends with domestic students. It's worth thinking about.

Coping With Change

Transitioning anywhere is exhausting, but the first year at college or university is particularly so because you are wearing your best face 100% of the time and may not have that one person yet you feel comfortable discussing your problems with. Be patient. It will come. Coping with change takes a lot of effort and involves stress. It is an immensely tiring time.

Remember to look out for yourself during this time. Find activities you enjoy and pamper yourself a little. The good news is that discomfort is normal and it will pass. Don't take yourself too seriously at this time. One day you will look back and see how comical those early days were.

 Try This: Don't forget to laugh everyday, especially at yourself.

Who's in Charge Now?

Your parents have been preparing you for this scenario since the day of your birth. They have weaned you off the bottle, taught you to feed yourself, use the potty by yourself, dress yourself and now, take responsibility for yourself. There comes a day when you are the one who is solely responsible for the consequences of your actions. Believe me, this is just as difficult (or more so) for parents as it is for you, especially those parents who have a little trouble letting go. It can be as much a lesson for us as it is for you.

It can be exciting to achieve the instant independence that comes when that umbilical chord is severed and you have your new wings, but it can also be a little scary and lonely. Parents are no longer around to bail you out. In fact, unless it is an emergency or something that would threaten your continued attendance at the school, your parents may remain oblivious to your escapades. You are 18 years old now, an adult who is legally responsible for your own behavior. Many schools assign student advisors to their first-year students who can help in the adjustment process. They are there to guide you and give out advice, but they will not parent you.

Journey into Maturity

Getting a good education aside, the college experience is also a journey into maturity. At least that's what parents would like to believe they are paying for. Not only are you responsible for your behavior but also for your health, your security, your grades, your social life, and your spending, among other things. It would be wise to understand what expectations your parents have before you embark on your new life. While you may be exempt from most family rules and guidelines that applied on the home front, you continue to be held to certain standards controlled by those holding the purse strings to your future.

Financial Considerations

Speaking of purse strings, as was mentioned earlier, setting up a budget with your parents before leaving home will help defray potential panic situations that may involve the necessity of a phone call to parents who may be dead asleep in another time zone. It will also help you determine whether a part-time campus job will be necessary to get you through the semester. Many times students will try to get a job for the summer before the start of school so they don't have the added burden of working while trying to settle into a new place and unfamiliar culture.

If you are coming from an expensive part of the world, you may find things so much more economical in your new setting. However, if you are transitioning from a developing country where essentials are relatively inexpensive, you may be overwhelmed with the cost of living expenses. In either case, do your homework with your parents ahead of time to determine your financial needs. You may want to search the internet for stores in your area to get an idea of the cost of things compared to where you are now living. Here are some things you will need to think about when making a budget:

- Dorm room essentials – bedding, lighting, storage containers, rug, refrigerator, TV, microwave, alarm clock, fan, power strip, towels.

- Food – meal plan, off-hours snacks and the occasional eating out with friends

- Books

- Computer equipment and supplies

- School supplies

- Personal hygiene items – shampoos, body lotions, make-up, shaving supplies

- Laundry supplies

- Socializing expenses

- Travel during breaks

- Health Care such as insurance co-payments

- Gifts for holidays and friends' birthdays

- Clothes – Seasonal wear, outerwear, casual wear, formal wear

- Sports gear

Setting Boundaries

Learn to set boundaries right away to avoid confusion, misunderstandings and awkward moments later. Think about how you will set limits with roommates, friends, drinking, drugs, alcohol and boy/girl friends. A good rule of thumb is to not do anything new or different from what you have been used to doing in high school for at least the first two months of school. Gaining a reputation as a party animal is a tough image to break when you want to be taken seriously later.

 Beware: Don't give in to the urge to engage in experimentation before you have created the image of who you really are as a person.

Set limits with your roommate right from the start on things like borrowing clothes, shoes or accessories without asking or when to allow visitors. Determining sensitive issues such as whether or not you will allow someone of the opposite sex to stay overnight in your dorm room will reduce the chances of confrontations. Writing out the mutually set rules with your roommate will help both of you remember and stick to them.

 Try This: Consider drawing up a contract with your roommate(s) at the very beginning of the term to establish rules everyone can agree to live by. It will help avoid conflicts later and keep issues from escalating if the limits are clearly identified early on.

Jennifer, our British/African TCK from Chapter 1 has some comments on her experience with setting boundaries:

"I know university is about finding yourself, but try and have some boundaries set up. I had a lot of boundaries and self-understandings. I knew what I wanted and what I was willing to try or participate in and what I definitely did not want to be a part of. I think that really helped me. A lot of people get lost their first year and get into trouble academically. I found that my morals and decisions helped me to resist negative temptations and keep me on track."

Drugs, Sex, Rock 'n' Roll!

Authors Coburn and Treeger in *Letting Go – A Parents' Guide to Understanding the College Years* quotes one college sophomore "who spent her first few months at college in turmoil after experimenting with drugs and alcohol" as saying, "The only thing I wish is that my parents had prepared me better for what I might face in college. There was never a discussion about sex, drugs or even money management…"

Not all parents are comfortable, nor are they prepared to discuss such delicate topics with their children. Or commonly parents' attempts to engage offspring in such conversations are met with rolling eyes, muffled remarks or literally waving their parents off as not having a clue about these things. Young adults forget their parents were once their age and while times have changed, sexual impulses, the ability to resist temptations and peer pressure have not. If anything, they have become more domineering in today's world of easy access to everything, explicit advertising and the instant gratification mentality of the Y generation. The fact of the matter is students are just as uncomfortable talking about these subjects as their parents are, but it is important for them to know how their parents feel, what the expectations are regarding such topics and what consequences bad choices will incur. I have found that choosing to place the blame on the parents takes the burden off the student to cave in to peer pressure. "Sorry man, but my folks would disown me if they ever knew I tried that. No way!"

Drugs and Alcohol

Partying involves alcohol and sometimes drugs. Alcohol lowers inhibitions, diminishes protective reflexes and interferes with the ability for rational decision making. Remember you are very vulnerable in your first year at school and everyone is looking to make friends. Do it the right way.

 Beware: Do not overestimate your ability to resist being influenced by your environment and by your desire to be accepted.

Mary Pipher, author of *Reviving Ophelia, Saving the Selves of Adolescent Girls*, brings home Shakespeare's words, "to thine own self be true." This is a must-read for any young woman heading off to university. It is a powerful reminder not to try to fit into the social scene by giving in to social pressure to drink or have sex.

Abuse of alcohol, prescription drugs and illegal drugs is on the rise. People choose to use drugs for various reasons: to fit in, out of boredom or as an escape. But drugs, particularly illegal drugs can be extremely harmful to the body. According to KidsHealth.org, illegal drugs can damage the brain, heart, and other important organs. Cocaine, for instance, can cause a heart attack — even in a kid or teen.

The web page of the National Institutes of Drug Abuse (a subsidiary of the National Institutes of Health at *www.drugabuse.gov*) outlines "What happens to your brain when you take drugs." The bottom line is this:

> Nearly all drugs, directly or indirectly, target the brain's reward system by flooding the circuit with dopamine. Dopamine is a neurotransmitter present in regions of the brain that control movement, emotion, motivation, and feelings of pleasure. The overstimulation of this system...produces euphoric effects in response to the drugs. This reaction sets in motion a pattern that 'teaches' people to repeat the behavior of abusing drugs.

This is the real threat of using illegal drugs or abusing prescription drugs. It can easily become an addictive habit. Statistics show that the younger you are when you experiment with illicit drugs or alcohol the more likely you are to become an addict in later life.

Prescription Drugs

Although marijuana is still a highly popular recreational drug on college campuses, there is a rising trend of prescription drug abuse. The infamous (and dangerous) celebrity-style partying of mixing alcohol with well known pain killers such as Vicodin™, Percocet™ and OxyContin™ has become increasingly popular with students. Watch any celebrity TV news program or read the latest dirt in popular magazines and you will understand that partying like this typically sends these celebrities to ride it out in rehab. Besides using prescription drugs for recreational reasons, more and more students are using Xanax XR® and Valium™ for self-treating sleep disturbances and anxiety.

The most surprising new trend among students is to use someone else's medicines prescribed for Attention Deficit Hyperactivity Disorder (ADHD). Adderall™ is popular with students for pulling all-nighters or preparing for and taking major tests because it increases energy, concentration and alertness while reducing fatigue. At the same time there is a significant suppression in appetite which makes it popular with young women. Students who have the drug prescribed for their ADHD benefit from selling an occasional pill here and there and their friends end up achieving their desired results. However, if used again and again these drugs can become habit forming until eventually the student feels as though he or she cannot perform efficiently without them. There is also a huge risk in taking a medicine prescribed for someone else. A doctor never dispenses medication without first taking a detailed medical history as there could be undesirable or dangerous adverse reactions to certain ingredients in the drugs.

Beware: If a drug has not been professionally prescribed for you, you are putting yourself at risk for serious health consequences.

Alcohol

The legal age for drinking across all 50 United States is 21. You can be arrested for drinking under the age of 21 or using illegal drugs whether you are on or off campus. In many other parts of the world, including Canada and the United Kingdom. the legal age for alcohol consumption is 18. What we see in the U.S. and U.K. is kids leaving home and experimenting with drinking and drugs in the relative anonymity of their campus life regardless of whether it is legal, as in the U.K., or illegal. Drinking games, binge drinking, over-drinking to the point of necessitating a visit to the emergency room (if they are lucky enough to survive) due to alcohol poisoning and getting passed-out drunk for entertainment purposes is common on some campuses. Granted, some of this behavior starts in high school and the freedom students find while attending college or university adds fuel to the fire.

> *"I was estranged from the whole 'hook up culture' that is rampant in colleges. We could say that was because going out to bars and clubs from a very young age helped get the whole 'get wasted and hook up' out of my system before reaching college."*
> British TCK raised in Switzerland and attending university in the U.S.

On the other hand, students who have been raised in societies where having a glass of beer or wine with a meal is a large part of the culture don't tend to exhibit this type of behavior. Many European countries allow wine and beer to be consumed at age 16, but they cannot legally operate a motor vehicle until age 18. They, hopefully, learn their limits with alcohol before learning how to drive.

My daughters' classmates from their international school in Switzerland would often relate tales of over-drinking at age 14 or 15. When they could legally drink at age 16, it wasn't as big a thrill and they had a better understanding of what their limits were. By the time they got to graduation they were drinking to be social. These very students now express incredulity at watching their U.S. or U.K. peers drinking with the aim of getting drunk.

The opposite is reported from the more cosmopolitan and internationally diverse Canadian universities such as McGill in

Montreal. Students say the drinking mentality comes from the historically strong French influence. Drinking is for *joie de vivre*, not for entertainment purposes. Students from several other area universities meet, mix and mingle in the city. They tend to go clubbing as opposed to on-campus partying. Part of the reason for this is that the university is so large there is only enough on-campus housing for first-year students. Raucous scenes of drunken students returning to their dorms after a night out are not common sightings

> *"I was amazed. Most of the parties I go to are all about drinking. I sit and wait to see what the entertainment for the evening is going to be and then I realize the drinking is the entertainment."*
> South African TCK who grew up in Europe and is attending university in the U.S.

on this campus. This is not to say it doesn't occasionally happen – it just is not the norm.

Risks of Overindulging

Drinking excessively puts a person at risk for anything from losing your way home to accidents, injury, or targets of crime. If drinking is part of your evening plans, be sure you stay with a group of friends. There is safety in numbers. To this day, I tell my daughters, "If one of you goes to the bathroom, you *all* go to the bathroom."

Designate a driver (D.D.) for the evening who will not be partaking of alcoholic beverages. Friends usually take turns serving this important role on different evenings out. Many U.S. bars today serve free sodas to the D.D.s as an incentive not to allow friends to drive drunk. Some colleges have organized student groups who will come and pick up fellow students who cannot and should not drive themselves home.

You may find yourself going along with the crowd when you really know better and may do things you would never have considered doing at home. Temptations of all sorts abound everywhere. You may walk into a party where shots of alcohol are being consumed. Everyone seems to be having such a good time and you want to be a part of the scene, so you take some too. Before you know it, you end up in a compromising position, sick, drunk or worse. What does that do for your reputation? I suggest reading Jennifer's advice again about deciding what your limits will be before you are in that situation.

Beware: I can't say it often enough or boldly enough that young college freshmen, men and women, are at risk because of their desire to fit in and make new friends.

Rape

Regardless of which article you read or website you browse, statistics for rape among college students is high. As many as 1 in 4 women report that they have been targets of rape or attempted rape. Statistics also point to the fact that the majority of rapes or sexual assaults are perpetrated by someone the victim knows. Before going any further with this, it is important to say that rape, the use of violence or the threat of it to force another person into having sex, is more about having power and control over another person than it is about sex. Regardless of the circumstances in which a person is raped, she (or he) is *not* at fault. No one asks to be raped. Whether they have walked alone, wore skimpy clothing or danced too seductively, they are still not asking to be raped.

Reduce Your Risk

There are commonsense precautions women can take to reduce their risk of becoming a victim of sexual assault:

- Always be alert to your surroundings and never walk alone at night or in the early morning hours. Rapists look for women who are distracted such as when talking on their cell phones.

- When going out at night, always make sure you know where you are and how to get back to your housing.

- Try to get a male friend to walk you to your car or dorm. Campus security will also get the job done if you are on campus and need to get from the library or some other building late at night back to your dorm.

- Always stay in well-lit areas and avoid big bushes or shaded areas.

- Walk quickly and with purpose as though you have someplace you need to get to in a hurry.

- Weave your car keys or other keys through your fingers to serve as an immediate weapon if needed.

- You can always carry pepper spray and/or a loud police whistle on your key chain.

- Don't worry about being rude to someone who stops to ask you a question. Just keep going. As Gavin de Becker, author of *The Gift of Fear* says, "listen to your intuition even at the risk of appearing foolish."

Self-Defense for Women

They are many programs, classes and workshops available to college students either through their communities or their universities that teach self-defense for women. Some programs, such as the RAD (Rape Aggression Defense) includes awareness, prevention, risk reduction and avoidance as well as options to use during a confrontation or attack. The Rape Aggression Defense System is a program of realistic self-defense tactics and techniques for women. RAD courses can be found by inquiring at any local U.S. police station. Their website, listed in the resources section of this chapter, also gives the location of RAD courses in Canada, the U.K. and several other countries.

Date Rape Drugs

Another important sexual assault statistic points to the fact that in the majority of rape cases one or both of the persons involved had been using alcohol or other drugs and roughly half of all rapes occur on dates. Alcohol impairs judgment – watch how many drinks you have. If you are ever beginning to feel uncomfortable on a date, you need to leave quickly and safely. Listen to what your inner voice is telling you and don't worry about offending someone.

Women as well as men need to be wary of someone putting something into their drinks, alcoholic or non-alcoholic. Watch your drink being made. Never accept a drink from another person. It is safer to drink from a bottle if you have watched it being opened and can keep a finger over the opening. Take it on the dance floor with you and, if that is not acceptable, finish it before dancing. If you have to leave it, then forget it.

Beware: Never, ever leave your drink unattended!

There are undetectable drugs sexual predators use to incapacitate their victims and induce amnesia. The drugs are tasteless, odorless, colorless, quick acting and easily dissolvable in food and beverages. Date rape drugs include Rohypnol (common street names are ruffies, roofies, rophy, roachies, forget it, or forget-me pill), Gamma Hydroxy Butyrate (GHB) and Ketamine Hydrochloride. Victims have little or no memory of what happens as long as the drug is in their system. They may make the victim act without inhibition, have difficulty thinking clearly and lose all ability for rational decision making. Victims may appear to be in a drunken stupor, barely able to walk and talk.

Be alert to your friends and others at clubs and parties particularly if they appear to have become 'intoxicated' in an unusually short period of time after consuming a beverage. Even if you are out on a date with someone you feel you can trust, continue to watch your beverage until you know this person well enough to be sure they are trustworthy and have your best interests in mind. After all, it is called the date rape drug.

Reporting Date Rape

Whether drugs are used in date rape or not, many women do not report it because they feel they are partly to blame. A woman is never to blame for unwanted sexual advances. No one has the right to touch another's body without expressed permission. Many perpetrators of date rape, especially if they get away with it, will do it again to someone else. By reporting this crime you may be able to stop this heinous activity and save other women from the same fate.

Dating

It's All Cultural

A few words on the college dating scenes are in order. As with many other things, dating appears very much to be cultural. One European-raised, American TCK likes to compare dating styles around the globe. She feels that in Europe young men and women are not afraid of relationships. There is an appreciation for romance. She says even if the dating couple realizes there are no sparks between them, the young man remains attentive and polite to his date but does not expect to have sex with her. Whereas, she says, "Hooking up is popular in the U.S." ('Hooking up' can mean anything from simply meeting for a soda pop to making out to having sex, so you must clarify with the speaker what is meant.) She knows of one young lady who has had sex with five different boys but has only been in a romantic relationship with two of them. And according to her friends at university in the U.K., "one night stands are popular." So while there is a strong basic instinct for sex, romantic relationships are not usually the order of the day.

Guard Your Hearts

With this in mind, guard your hearts. There are a lot of young people out there who just want to sow their wild oats and don't care about your emotions. They are not going to fall in love with you because they have had sex with you. You will be fortunate if they even remember your name. In fact, dating in the States has been called 'predatory.' Upperclassmen are known for vulgarly referring to first-year students as "Freshmen meat." Someone may ask you on a date, walk away excitedly after you have accepted and then return to ask your name. Now what do you suppose is on his mind?

Take Precautions

Safety experts suggest getting to know your prospective date in a group activity or on a double date before going solo. Also get to know them over the phone to get a feel for what kind of person they are. When you do go on a solo date, tell someone exactly who you are going with and where you think you will be. I know, it sounds high-school-like, but it's the safe thing to do. Also, avoid using drugs and/or alcohol as they compromise your commonsense thinking. Lastly, go to a very public place for your first few dates like a restaurant, movie theater or coffee shop. Have fun exploring together.

TCK Concerns

Now let's go back to those TCK issues and dating. Remember that because you are skilled at listening and asking appropriate questions people may misunderstand and think your genuine interest in getting to know them as a person is a sign of romantic interest. TCKs who have gone before you suggest that you make it very clear to someone you want to hang out with that it is just as friends.

TCKs also tend to give TMI (too much information) at first in their attempts to find a connection with someone. Don't bare your soul to everyone you meet. You may find yourself sharing a lot of personal things with a boyfriend or girlfriend because you feel the connection. But relationships can be fleeting, especially those formed in the first term of school. I advise students against getting into a serious relationship the entire first year of school for several reasons:

- You are very vulnerable at this time with the chaos of re-entering (or entering) and learning the culture.

- You are also limiting yourself to making new friends when you are so wrapped up in being with one special person.

- You may make friends together as a couple and then find those friends have to choose whom to remain close to if and when the relationship falls apart. If it is a bad split, one of the two in the relationship may end up with no friends and have to start from scratch.

Libby Stephens of Interaction International tells her re-entry seminar students (and I concur) that a good case scenario would be not to date at all the first year to give yourself a chance to make friends, get comfortable with college life, learn your way around and find out what kinds of people you like to hang out with. Chances are you are not going to marry the first person you date. If you end up meeting someone fabulous and you feel he or she is the perfect mate for you, start getting to know them socially. If they are meant for you, they will understand and will wait until you are ready to date in your second year.

Sex

Once you are dating, it is a good idea to review the idea of setting boundaries or limits again. Have you thought about where you stand when it comes to sex? If you are planning to wait to have sex, it is best for you to be completely up front with your boyfriend or girlfriend so there are no undue pressures or expectations put upon you that you are not prepared to handle. If he or she ends up running as a result, then perhaps it really wasn't the right person for you.

In on-going discussions about sexual health, one international health organization uses the following description to start the definition. "Sexual health is a state of physical, emotional, mental and social well-being in relation to sexuality; it is not merely the absence of disease, dysfunction or infirmity. Sexual health requires a positive and respectful approach to sexuality and sexual relationships, as well as the possibility of having pleasurable and safe sexual experiences, free of coercion, discrimination and violence. For sexual health to be attained and maintained, the sexual rights of all persons must be respected, protected, and fulfilled."

Sexually Transmitted Diseases

If you are planning on being sexually active, be certain that your partner is in agreement and not coerced into it (consensual) and take proper precautions to prevent sexually transmitted diseases (STDs) or unwanted pregnancy, i.e. use birth control and condoms. Sexually transmitted diseases are diseases which are passed from person to person through intimate contact and are among the most common infectious diseases today. According to the National Institutes of Health, more than 20 different STDs have been identified, and 13 million men and women are infected each year in the United States alone. Depending on the disease, the infection can be spread through any type of sexual activity involving the sex organs, the anus or the mouth; the infection can also be spread through contact with blood during sexual activity. Not all STDs can be cured, but all can be prevented.

Prevention of STDs

The best way to prevent STDs is to avoid sexual contact with others. According to eMedicineHealth.com if people decide to become sexually active, they can *reduce* the risk of developing an STD in these ways:

> *"The most important sex organ is the brain."*
> Regina Brett

- Be in a monogamous relationship (both sexual partners are each others' only sexual partner).

- Delay having sexual relations as long as possible. The younger people are when they become sexually active, the higher the lifetime risk for contracting an STD. The risk also increases with the number of sexual partners.

- Correctly and consistently use a male latex condom, even if you are using a spermicidal. The spermicidal nonoxynol-9, once thought to protect against STDs as well as to prevent pregnancy, has been proven to be ineffective for disease prevention. Do not rely on it.

- Have regular checkups.

- Learn the symptoms of STDs.

- Avoid having sex during menstruation. (HIV is passed more easily at this time.)

- Avoid anal intercourse or use a condom.

- Avoid douching because it removes some of the natural protection in the vagina.

Enjoying your university years means staying safe and using common sense to allow you to make the most of your time there.

What You Should Know:

- Learn the practical things you will need to know before you go off on your own. Spend some time before the start of school learning how things work in this country and get those skills under control.

- Colleges and universities have resources in place to help students succeed. Don't be shy about using them.

- The first term is exhausting. Take time to look out for your sanity and your health.

- College life is filled with a plethora of temptations. Being independent means you are now solely responsible for you choices, decisions, and actions.

Resources:

Books

- *Succeeding as an International Student in the United States and Canada*, by Charles Lipsom, The University of Chicago Press, 2008.

- *The International Student's Survival Guide: How to Get the Most from Studying at a U.K. University*, by Gareth Davey, Sage Publications, 2008.

- *The Gift of Fear*, by Gavin De Becker, Dell Publishing, 1997.

- *Letting Go: A Parent's Guide to Understanding the College Years*, by Karen Levin Coburn and Madge Lawrence Treeger, HaperCollins Publishers Inc., 2003.

- *Reviving Ophelia: Saving the Selves of Adolescent Girls*, by Mary Pipher, The Berkley Publishing Group, 1994.

Websites

- www.TCKid.com – TCKid

- www.rad-systems.com – Rape Aggression Defense

- www.KidsHealth.org – website for children's health and development.

- www.drugabuse.gov – National Institutes of Drug Abuse

Resources (cont'd):

Websites (cont'd)

- www.who.int – World Health Organization

- www.nih.gov – National Institutes of Health

Chapter 9

Health and Welfare

"A man too busy to take care of his health is like a mechanic too busy to take care of his tools."

Spanish proverb

Taking Care of Your Health

Proactive Health Maintenance

College is demanding and, particularly in the first year, requires a lot of focus and energy. It is, therefore, imperative to stay on top of your health. The last thing you need is to be down with a flu or mononucleosis at finals time. Just as you would take care of your car to keep it running smoothly, so you need to take care of your body to maintain its functionality. Rather than having a let's-wait-and-see-how-much-my-body-can-take-before-getting-sick attitude, be proactive in maintaining good health. Eating right, getting enough sleep and exercising regularly are the best ways to boost your immune system and stay healthy. It is also important to have fun, be in relationship with others and have relaxation time. College isn't all about studying, but it isn't all about socializing either. It has to be a healthy balance of both.

Think proactively about all aspects of your health. What else do you need to do to stay healthy?

- Have you considered taking a daily multi-vitamin?

- Are you keeping up-to-date with regular dental and medical check ups?

- Women (particularly if they are sexually active) need to think about having an annual pap smear.

- Steer clear of others who are experiencing cold or flu-like symptoms.

 Dig Deeper: Think about your health needs ahead of time. Find a local dentist for cleanings and exams. Don't wait for a toothache before finding a dentist you like.

Eating Right

How do you avoid the infamous "freshman 15" (gaining 15 pounds – or more – in your first year) when you have a meal card you can swipe anytime of the day or night in the campus cafeteria, various snack bars across campus or even local restaurants and take-outs?

- Avoid the buffets unless they are salad bars or offer healthy choices.

- Stay away from going crazy at fast food restaurants that serve up fried foods and high-calorie burgers and go for restaurants that offer nutritional guidelines on their food choices like Subway restaurants.

- Choose to eat at restaurants that serve seafood, vegetarian or Asian cuisine.

- Make sure you eat plenty of vegetables, fruits, and dairy products since these are the part of nutrition that help protect your immune system but are often forgotten by college students. They will fill you up and not out.

- Drink lots of water and stay away from sugary drinks that offer lots of calories with no nutritional value.

Try This: Practice healthy eating over the summer before starting school to get into a pattern of making proper food choices. You will feel good about your body and be more energetic since low fat foods vitalize the body whereas fatty foods cause lethargy. Once you get into the habit of eating well, you won't want to stop. You may overdo it or binge a little at first while getting used to the abundance of food choices, but try to remember how good you felt when you ate well.

Getting Enough Sleep

With so many activities on campus to be involved in, social events to attend, time to hang out with friends, classes to go to, and homework to get done, it may seem there is little to no time left for sleeping. But just think about it – there are 168 hours in a week. Each week if you were to:

- Spend approximately 15-20 hours in classes and labs (and this could be more depending on your field of study and number of courses you decide to take),

- Spend 45-50 hours doing course work, and

- Spend 45-50 hours socializing,

then you would be still be left with 48-63 hours to sleep. That's the equivalent of seven to nine hours per night. Notice it also means you have six and a half to nine hours to socialize and six and a half to nine hours to work on your studies each day! Now it is up to you to balance your schedule to fit your individual needs, which may vary from day to day and week to week. We will talk more about that in the following section on time management.

Exercise

Along with good eating comes regular exercise. The combination of the two will keep you energized and focused. Unlike back in my time or your parents' time, colleges and universities today compete to attract students. One way of doing that is to provide state-of-the-art exercise rooms, pristine swimming pools, and a plethora of playing fields. Lack of facilities or equipment will *not* be an excuse for not exercising.

There are many opportunities to play the sports you like without having to make the commitment to a varsity squad. Perhaps there is a sport that interests you and you would like to learn how to play. Many schools have intramural or intermural sport teams that are always looking for new players, even if you are a beginner.

Oftentimes schools will have nutritionists on staff to help you eat well and trainers available in their fitness centers to help you reach your fitness goals. Take advantage of what the school has put in place for you to enjoy.

My daughter, Katrina was introduced to rugby when we lived in Europe but she never had the chance to play seriously. She was thrilled when she discovered there was a girls' rugby team at her school. Unfortunately an unlucky tackle took her out of the game.

Once her injuries were healed, Katrina went on a quest to play another sport that had always interested her but she never had the opportunity to play – baseball. She couldn't find a girls' baseball or softball team at her college so she inquired with the boys' team. School rules stated that teams must be inclusive of all interested students regardless of gender. It turns out the boys were glad to have her on the team and are now looking for more female players. Needless to say, Katrina is having a blast.

 Tip to Remember: Getting involved in team sports at any level or other group exercise opportunities is a great way to meet people and make new friends.

Stress Prevention and Time Management

Stress, a major component in the life of a college student, if left unchecked can lead to depression, fatigue or physical illness. Stress wears away at your immune system causing viruses and bacteria that would normally be kept at bay to proliferate and cause disease.

Not managing time well is one of the leading stressors in a college student's life. While today's communications technology can be such a blessing for staying in touch with friends and family around the globe, it can also be an incredible time ravager. With internet social networking sites such as Facebook, MySpace, Twitter and others that seem to be popping up nearly everyday, students can find that they are spending more time on their cyber relationships than with the real thing. Or they may be spending more time on the computer playing games or watching movies than on their studying.

 Try This: Make a note of how much time you spend playing or communicating with friends via the internet and then set a limit. Balance your time between keeping up with old friends and socializing with your new friends.

As I mentioned earlier in the section on "Getting Enough Sleep," while it may seem that there is so much to do (both work-wise and socially) and so little time left to do it, it isn't really as bad as it seems. I remind you that, after classes and sleeping, you still have approximately 90-100 hours each week for work and socializing. It is up to you to decide how you will divide it out.

Learning time management and self-discipline now will save you grief and sorrow later. Stay ahead of the game.

- Keep a detailed calendar with all course assignment due dates and test dates marked.

- If you have a lull in your schedule where nothing is due for a while, look at your course syllabus and work ahead.

- For help with assignments, use campus resources such as writing labs, or for help with course work you don't understand, make use of math labs, tutors, and teaching assistants.

- Study regularly rather than cramming at the last minute.

- Some days will require getting up earlier or going to bed later than usual to get the work done, but try to get a steady amount of sleep whenever possible. If you need to pull an all-nighter, you can make up for the sleep later, but don't make it a regular event.

- Allow yourself more time than you actually need to get assignments or studying done.

- Take short power naps to keep your energy level and focus up.

- Build in regular study breaks with exercise or visits with friends.

- Set social, personal and academic goals.

- Prioritize your goals for the day, each week, and term.

- Establish routines to help you stay on track. Try not to get distracted, even for special occasions.

 Beware: Colds, flu and sore throats are one of the top three reasons students get behind in their course work. Stress and fatigue lower the body's ability to fight off illness.

Health Care

You would be the rare exception if you survived your entire college career without a visit to the health services, so be prepared ahead of time. Every country has definite provisions for dispensing health care but a variety of methods are used to pay for it.

In countries with fees for health care, most colleges and universities enforce mandatory health insurance for their students or (specific to the U.S.) membership in a health maintenance organization (HMO). The most cost-effective policies tend to be ones offered through the college or university itself. As with most policies, the more you pay, the more services you receive; however, many insurance plans offered by the institution cover 100% of treatment if it is obtained through the student health center. They typically do not cover serious or chronic conditions or accidents.

Dig Deeper: Don't wait for an urgent care situation to come up before knowing how you will pay for your health care needs or what is required before receiving treatment. Be sure to build co-payments or usage fees into your budget.

Countries with national health service (NHS) typically provide health care for any student as long as they are registered with the NHS and a general practitioner (GP). The clinics tend to be very busy and the quality of care may vary from country to country. Students may also take out insurance should they choose to seek the services of a private doctor instead, but it is expensive.

Canadian universities require international students to have university provided health insurance. This coverage may be supplemented by private insurance plans.

One student at McGill University in Canada explains, "There is a broad spectrum of fees and usage, depending on if you are a Quebec student, an out of province Canadian student or an international student (including Americans). If you are international you are required to have university provided health insurance (basic coverage). The clinic is always very busy as they don't have enough staff to deal with the quantities of students that go in. That being said, if you do get an appointment it is of good quality. Students can go to other clinics in the city but they can be costly/inconvenient if you don't have Quebec health insurance."

Some institutions require that the insurance carrier be based in the country of study. Many good options exist but must be compared for monthly premiums versus amount of coverage, co-payments (a small payment, usually at the time of the service, that helps offset medical costs), deductibles (an amount of money the insured party must pay before the insurance begins to cover the medical expenses), and costs associated with out-of-network providers (providers who are not contracted by your insurance carrier) and more. Be sure to read the fine print of any policy you are considering. International students will most likely be required to enroll in a comprehensive plan specific to their needs.

Dig Deeper: Check your family insurance plan for eligibility requirements. Some plans will cover children up to age 23 as long as they are pursuing an education.

Many students are surprised to discover that dental care, pharmacy costs and eyewear are not standard inclusions in their health insurance policies. Separate policies must be taken out for dental insurance. Check to see if you can continue on your family's policy.

Tip to Remember: It is imperative that you have an understanding of your health insurance policy before leaving home whether you are using your family's, one from the country where you are studying or one offered by the school.

Many, if not most, colleges and universities have campus health centers which are the student's first stop for medical concerns, wellness programs and advice. Some health centers provide only the basics and are not open on weekends or holidays, but are linked to nearby hospitals. At the other extreme you have major research hospitals practically right on campus with everything immediately available. And some universities are so large that they are practically little cities in themselves with everything from specialty clinics to dentists to psychologists to pharmacies providing any and all healthcare imaginable. Your health insurance, whether purchased through the school or privately, will cover most services at the campus health centers. There may be some fees and co-payments insurance does not cover that will be billed directly to your student account.

Medical Records

It is important, especially if you have a chronic medical or dental condition or are on regular medications, that your new physician, dentist and other providers have copies of your medical records...in the working language of where you are attending school. This means they may need to be translated ahead of time. Some large medical centers will have their own translators that can help you with that.

Bring any prescription medications you are on with a back up supply in case it takes some time to make your first appointment at your new school. Medications and medical records should be carried in your hand luggage to avoid getting lost or damaged.

Immunizations

Most schools have a list of mandatory immunizations to be completed before matriculation. Since some require a waiting period between doses, it is best to ask right away which ones your school will enforce so you can make your plan to complete them in sufficient time. Some of the required vaccines may not be available in the country in which you are currently living and will need some pre-planning for administration. Schools' policies differ even within the same country so be sure to check the institution's website ahead of time.

Following are some typical immunization requirements:

- **Diphtheria, Tetanus and/or Pertussis** (whooping cough) – 3 doses of Tetanus/Diphtheria toxoid and a booster dose of DTP within past 10 years.

- **Polio** – may not be required if over 18 years of age.

- **Measles, Mumps and Rubella** (MMR) and **Varicella** disease (Chickenpox). Both require two doses and may be waived if your child has documented proof they already had the disease such as a physician's report, or they test sero-positive for protective antibodies.

- Some schools require the completed series of **Hepatitis A** (2 doses – 6 months apart) and **Hepatitis B** (3 doses – 6 months apart).

- **Meningococcal meningitis** immunization is required at some colleges and universities but it is highly recommended for all first-year students living in dorms since they are six times more likely to be affected by this rare but often fatal or debilitating bacterial disease that affects the meninges (protective membrane surrounding the central nervous system).

Others not required for matriculation but to consider:

- **HPV** vaccine for girls and women is becoming an increasingly popular vaccine in the U.S. and guards against human papillomavirus that causes cervical cancer and genital warts.

- **Seasonal influenza** is usually given out during the school year beginning in September or as soon as the vaccine is made available and sometimes can be given right on campus.

Try This: Speak with your physician for advice on non-required vaccines and other health maintenance tips before heading off to school.

I also highly recommend you keep a copy of your full vaccination record with you, translated into the working language. This includes documentation of your baby shots which are often kept in your pediatrician's office and difficult to obtain if you've already left the country. I once worked a vaccination clinic on a large university campus where a foreign student was found to have the measles, most likely to have been exposed while on a visit back home. Every student of that college, whether they were full or part-time, graduate or undergraduate, attending day or evening classes, and living on or off campus, had to receive a measles shot if they could not provide documentation in English that they had been immunized against measles in the past.

Try This: Consolidate all your immunizations to take with you into one file, booklet or record, such as the World Health Organization's (WHO) famous "yellow book."

Campus Safety

Security Incidents

In the aftermath of the Virginia Polytechnic Institute and State University (Virginia Tech) massacre in April 2007, concerns of safe campuses have become a priority for students, parents and administrators. Historically parents and students would not have dreamed they would have to be concerned about a matriculated student committing mass murder on campus. Today, along with other issues concerning personal safety, it does cross their minds. The good news is that institutions of higher learning are taking this event very seriously. Campus security personnel are being trained on many campuses on how to deal with an event such as the one at Virginia Tech.

Many colleges and universities have set up detailed and intricate systems of immediately notifying students as well as their parents if a security incident is taking place, complete with information on where to go and what to do. Many colleges have switched over to the electronic student ID card that must be swiped to gain access to dorms and other services. Students are given emergency numbers for calling campus security to handle everything from theft to illness or accident to assault to chaperoning a female student back to her dorm late at night.

 Share It: You may be asked to give your school your cell phone number so you can be notified immediately if there is an in-progress security incident on your campus. If you change your number, be sure to inform campus security and administration. You should also make it a habit to check your campus-based email between classes.

Staying Safe

Most campuses, whether urban or rural, have security "blue lights" set up so students can call security for rides or problems. On the extremely large University of Massachusetts at Amherst campus, security's response time to a blue light call is under two minutes. This is pretty impressive given that the campus is composed of over 20,000 undergraduate students alone and sits on 1,450 acres of land.

- Students must take responsibility for their personal safety by using good common sense.

- Know who and how to call should problems or concerns arise.

- Be sure to put the campus security emergency call number into your cell phone for easy access dialing. Better yet, make it a speed dial number.

- Don't go jogging late at night or early in the morning unless you are in a group.

- Refer back to the discussion on rape in Chapter 9 for ways to stay safe when walking alone (stay in well-lit areas, avoid big bushes or otherwise shaded areas where someone can be hiding, do not talk on a cell phone, walk briskly, carry a whistle).

- Take a self defense class before heading off to college (see RAD in Chapter 9).

Theft

Theft of personal items is always a concern no matter where you are living. You may want to consider insuring some of your more valuable items such as bicycles, computers, TVs and other electronics against loss or damage. Some students will have these items engraved with an identifying mark so they can be reported if stolen.

Try This: Make a list of all your valuable items along with a description or photo and serial number and keep it in a secure place. You can even leave a copy with campus security.

Do not let strangers into your dormitory building and do not leave the doors to the building propped open and unsupervised at any time. As tempting as it may be to leave your dorm room unlocked – don't. More than one student tells the story of finding a complete stranger in his or her room upon returning from a short trip to the bathroom facilities. Keep your windows closed and locked if you are on the first floor. Female students may want to request not to have a first floor dorm room. My daughter's friend relates how she woke up to find a young man in her bed late one night. It turns out he was returning from a party where he had overindulged in alcoholic beverages and thought he had crawled into his own bed. He got the right room but in the wrong building!

All Things Monetary

To make your life less complicated check out which banks have ATMs on your college campus. Then visit each one to see who offers the best deals for setting up checking and savings accounts. Many banks in North America offer special student account packages such as checking accounts with no monthly fees up to five years, free online banking and bill paying, free check card (debit card) and overdraft protection. Compare banks for ATM fees. If you use an ATM that your bank does not own, you may incur a fee. Some banks allow you to use any ATM and never charge a fee. Ask questions and read the fine print. Also be aware that banking policies change frequently, so when they send you a new list of policies, check the list for those that are important for you.

What You Will Need

A checking account is the most fundamental way to manage your money. With a checking account you can pay your bills by using a check or online banking. A checking account is also the best way to keep track of your money. You can view your account deposits, transfers, withdrawals, and balances online any time. You can also use your check register that comes with your set of checks to note all your banking activity and check the balance against the online account summary or your monthly statement which you can opt to have arrive in the mail. If there is ever a dispute as to whether you have paid a bill or not, you can provide proof with the check you wrote (either the physical check or the printed image of the processed check found online).

A debit card (also called check card) is linked directly to your checking account. You can use your debit card to withdraw cash from an ATM or (and this is how it is different from a regular bank card) to pay for purchases at stores, restaurants and more. Even though your debit card has a Visa or MasterCard logo on it (so you can use it anywhere Visa and MasterCard are accepted), it is *not* a credit card which you can pay back monthly. *The money is taken directly from your checking account within the next 0-3 days.* It simply serves as a type of short term credit. If you are using it as a debit card you will be asked to use your PIN (personal identification number) on purchases over $50 just the way you would to withdraw cash from the ATM. If you choose to use it as short term credit you will be asked for your signature.

Beware: Always make sure you have enough funds in your account at the time you are using your debit card to cover any debits, credits or checks you use or you will be subject to overdraft charges.

A savings account – Unless you have a steady job, you may not be saving much money while you are in college, but it is still a good idea to open a savings account and have it directly linked to your checking account with an overdraft protection program. In the case of over-expenditure, money will be transferred from your savings to your checking account to make up for what is not available in your checking account. You will still have an overdraft fee but with many student packages the fees are reduced.

If you get money to cover your expenses for the whole term or school year (from your parents or guardian or from a financial aid package), put all the money for months beyond the current one in your savings account. Then, each month, transfer the amount you need for the month to your checking account. That way your money will last for the entire term or school year instead of getting spent the first part of the term "because it is there."

Beware: Savings accounts generally have a requirement that you must keep a certain minimum amount of money in them at all times, so check to make sure you will be able to meet that criterion.

Credit Cards

A credit card is basically a loan from a financial institution that you can use instead of paying cash and repay on a monthly basis either all-at-once or over time. This is how it works:

- When you pay your monthly bill, you will be paying for all your expenditures.

- If you do not pay the full amount, the balance will carry over to the following month, in addition to the new charges incurred.

- You are required to pay at least the minimum amount due each month and to make sure it reaches the credit card company by the due date.

- Late fees are a regular amount charged if your payment does not reach the company by the due date.

- You will pay the interest, according to the rate given by that financial institution, on your balance.

 Try This: Compare the interest rates and conditions for a few different cards before applying for one. Some cards use a "rewards" system in which you are paid back a percentage of what you spend in "rewards points" redeemable for cash, gift cards, hotel stays and more. There are some good deals, but you need to look for them.

We are fortunate today in that it is possible to go almost anywhere, buy anything and pay for it with a credit card, including a 99 cents cup of coffee at McDonald's. More and more places are not requiring a minimum purchase amount in order to accept credit. In New York City, for example, you can pay for taxis, ride the subway, and pay for parking with a credit card, not to mention using your credit card for shopping, restaurants and entertainment.

Your credit card will come with a set limit. A first time credit card holder may have a very low limit ($500 to $2,000) until they can establish a credit rating, at which time their financial institution will offer to increase the limit.

Tip to Remember: If you are initially offered a high limit on your credit card, you do not have to accept it. It only breeds temptation to spend more. You can ask to have the limit lowered.

Two thousand dollars is usually enough for a student starting off. Be sure you can afford the minimum monthly payment on any credit account you open. Even if you plan on never using a credit card, it is a good idea to have one you can use in the case of an emergency such as an air fare for an unexpected trip home. Our daughters got their first credit card when they went abroad for a semester since we did not want them to be stuck if something unexpected came up.

Many, many institutions offer credit cards. Everyone from airlines to member organizations like AAA (automobile club) offer cards. The days are over when "pre-approved" cards showed up in the mail practically on a daily basis. Since the economic downturn of 2009, financial institutions are being much more cautious and credit cards are no longer just handed out. My bank, for example, let my oldest daughter have a credit card from them when she was 20 years old by just filling out an application. My second daughter went in to apply when she was 20, but could only obtain a 'secured' card, meaning that we, her parents, needed to put down a $1,000 safety net before she was approved. If she demonstrates she can handle credit responsibly by paying the card off each month, the security deposit will be returned to us after 12 months

Tip to Remember: If you do receive an offer for a pre-approved card, read the fine print carefully for hidden fees. Most banks are happy to help you decide if this is a reasonable card to suit your needs even if it is not from their institution.

Types of Credit Cards

There are three types of credit cards:

▪ **General purpose credit card** – (also known as revolving credit cards) a credit card that allows you to pay for just about anything as we discussed above. Visa and MasterCard are examples of general purpose cards. You pay this off month by month.

▪ **Store card** – (also known as single or limited purpose card) are credit cards that can only be used in that particular store or chain of stores. These are very common in department stores, clothing stores, and electronics stores. Customers are enticed to apply for one and get an introductory 15% off their purchase immediately. These types of credit cards typically have higher interest rates and are not very useful unless you do most of your shopping at that particular store.

▪ **Charge cards** – American Express and Diners Club are typical charge cards. They allow you to charge your purchases on credit but then you are *expected* to pay off the *entire balance each month*. There is usually no interest for this type of credit card. The consequences of not paying of the balance each month are severe.

Identity Theft and Identity Fraud

Identity theft and fraud are crimes that take place when someone wrongfully steals your personal information in some way that involves fraud or deception and uses it for their own personal gain. Combinations of personal information such as your date of birth, social security number (SSN) or individual taxpayer identification number (ITIN) or Social Insurance Number (SIN), driver's license number (DLN), address, phone number, mother's maiden name and more can be used to apply for credit cards, take out loans, rent an apartment, open bank accounts and even take over your identity. Identity theft and fraud can completely ruin your credit rating, may take months or even years to resolve and can cost you time and money to restore your financial and personal reputation.

It is much easier than most people would suspect to have your identity stolen. Over 10 million Americans alone have their identity stolen every year. Your information can be stolen from your mailbox, your garbage, your computer, over the telephone or just by being within hearing distance. So be sure to hold your mail or have someone empty your mailbox for you if you are going to be away, shred all documents with any type of personal information on them, keep your SSN, SIN, or ITIN and credit card numbers in a safe and secure place, and do not state your information out openly if on a public telephone or in a public place. If you do receive an offer for a pre-approved credit card, destroy the application before throwing it in the trash so no one else can use it. The U.S. Justice Department suggests remembering the word **SCAM** to reduce or minimize the risk of becoming a victim of identity theft or fraud:

S – Be *stingy* about giving out your personal information unless you have a reason to trust the person or organization. If you are applying for a credit card, they will need to know specific information such as SSN, address, phone number and your mother's maiden name. But if someone calls asking you for that information, you should *never* give it out over the phone. Ask them to send you the paperwork they are requiring. Some scams involve a telephone call or email from someone claiming to be from your bank or other trusted organization or institution and asking for your personal information. Banks already have this information. There is no reason for them to be asking for it again, regardless of what they are telling you. If you are not certain, call your bank or organization directly. Never click on a link from an email claiming to be your bank. It can take you to a site that looks exactly like the official bank site but is a fraud. If there is a problem with one of your accounts, the bank will notify you and ask you to call them or to log onto the official site yourself, not to follow a link. When making purchases over the internet, make sure the website is secure. There are two ways to confirm that the site you are on is secure: there may be a yellow lock in the lower right-hand corner and/or the URL will start with 'https' instead of 'http' with the 's' meaning the site is 'secure.'

C – *Check* your financial information regularly. You should be receiving monthly statements (either online or in the mail or both) from your bank and credit cards. If you are not receiving them, call the institution. You can also check your bank and credit card account balances any time online or by calling the number on your card. Look for unauthorized purchases or withdrawals or other suspicious activity.

A – *Ask* for a copy of your credit report annually from all credit reporting bureaus. You are entitled to one free report from each bureau (Equifax®, TransUnion® and Experian®) each year. You can do this online. The reports will list all bank and financial accounts under your name. Watch for unauthorized or fraudulent accounts opened in your name or incorrect activity on any of your accounts.

M – *Maintain* careful records of your banking and financial accounts. Watch for unauthorized activity on your statements. If you do see unauthorized activity, report it to your financial institution immediately. Keep all your statements and cancelled checks for a minimum of one year in case a dispute arises.

More and more identity theft and fraud scams are coming to light on practically a daily basis. Many of these are perpetrated via the internet on social networking sites and email. Cyber-criminals have so many ways of lifting personal information from your computer that it is impossible to mention them all here. A good anti-spyware program will help detect and block someone who is trying to get into your computer with the intent to steal your personal information.

 Beware: Be sure you have a trustworthy and effective anti-virus anti-spyware program running on your computer at all times.

Despite taking all these precautions and through no fault of your own, you could still become a victim of identity theft or fraud. If you suspect this may have happened to you, contact the police and the financial institution immediately. They may advise you to close out the account that has been tampered with or opened fraudulently in your name. You should also report it to one (or all three) of the three consumer credit reporting companies mentioned earlier. Ask them to place a "fraud alert" on your file. When you report it to the police, get a copy of the police report for your records (it may cost you a small fee but you will need it as proof to deny paying bills charged to you fraudulently).

In the U.S. you can visit the U.S. Justice Department website for more information on identity theft and fraud, including what to do if you suspect you have become a victim: *www.usdoj.gov/criminal/fraud/websites/idtheft.html.*
You can also file a complaint with the Federal Trade Commission: *www.ftc.gov/bcp/edu/microsites/idtheft/.*
In Canada you should contact the Social Insurance Registration via email at: *sin-nas@hrdc-drhc.gc.ca* or go to *http://www.servicecanada.gc.ca/eng/sin/lost/lost.shtml* to replace lost or stolen identification cards.
The U.K. website for information on and the reporting of identity fraud is: *www.actionfraud.org.uk.*

Check Fraud Scams

Don't fall prey to check fraud by accepting a check written for more than the intended amount, whether it be payment for something you are selling, a service you have provided or payment for "a job" in which you receive checks from "clients" and you are instructed to take your "pay" out of it. Typically you are asked to deposit the check into your personal account and then send the "extra" money on to someone else by writing a check from your personal account. The check you deposit is typically a fake and it won't be discovered until you have already sent your check out. There are a ton of other scams out there. Remember that nothing is free and if it sounds too good to be true, it is. Just think things through and check it out with police, websites or financial institutions before agreeing to do anything with money, checks or personal information.

Banking Tips

- To make life easier and avoid unnecessary fees, try to find a bank you like with an ATM on campus.

- Sign up with your bank to have customized alerts to notify you (by email or cell phone) of low balances, daily balances, direct deposits and more.

- Keep a lump sum in your savings account for emergencies only.

- Except for emergencies, never spend more than you can pay off.

- Try to pay your credit card off every month to reduce paying interest and on time to avoid paying late fees. It also gives you a good credit rating which you will most likely need later in life when looking to take out a loan for a car or house.

 Tip to Remember: Missing even one credit card payment may drop your credit score by as much as 50 to 100 points.

- Do not spend over the credit card limit or you may incur hefty fees and demands to pay it down to the limit immediately (which may be impossible for you).

- Have the phone number of the financial institution that issued your credit card so you can call immediately if your card is lost or stolen or you feel you have been the victim of fraud.

- Don't forget to sign the back of your credit card when you receive it and use a photo ID credit card if available from your card issuer.

 Try This: Some people prefer *not* to sign the backs of their credit cards but instead write "See ID." That forces the clerk to ask for matching identification. Whichever you decide to do, just don't forget to write *something* on the back so if someone finds it, they cannot forge a signature.

- If you plan on making a lot of purchases via the internet, it is best to do so with a credit card. You have up to 30 days to dispute any purchases you feel have been made fraudulently. Or consider transferring money to a PayPal account and make purchase payments from that. If you choose not to pay with a credit card and want to use your bank debit card, consider opening a separate account solely for that purpose and maintain a set amount of money in it. If your financial information is stolen, that is the only account that will be affected since it is not tied into your other accounts. The same applies to travel expense accounts.

- Look for banks with programs to help you save money such as Bank of America's "Keep the Change." Every time you make a purchase with your debit card, the amount is rounded upward to the nearest dollar and the change goes directly into your savings account. It is a bit like putting your pocket change into a piggy bank at the end of the day.

- Ask your bank to be put on their "Do Not Call" list. This means they cannot share your phone number with any of their marketing and sales affiliates. If you do get a call from another financial institution, you will know it is fraud.

- Wait for deposited checks to be completely processed before withdrawing cash or sending a personal check on to someone else from that deposit.

In Review

Staying alert, using common sense and paying attention to what is going on with your body, your time and your finances will keep you on target for a good term, good year and good university experience. Like anything else, staying physically and financially healthy takes work and cannot be neglected.

What You Should Know:

- Time management is one of the biggest issues facing college students. The time is there. You just need to be diligent in dividing it up to work well for meeting all your needs. Set up routines early on, set goals and keep a detailed calendar to track when assignments are due.

- Eating well, getting enough sleep, exercising and balancing work and school responsibilities with recreation are vital for stress prevention.

- Banks are happy to sit down and talk with students about packages they offer. Ask a lot of questions and choose the bank that suits your needs best.

- Diligence is needed to

  $ spend wisely,

  $ safeguard your credit and

  $ prevent identity theft and fraud.

Resources:

Websites

- Experian® credit reporting – www.experian.com

- Equifax® credit reporting – www.equifax.com

- TransUnion® credit reporting – www.transunion.com

- Federal Trade Commission (U.S.) – www.ftc.gov/bcp/edu/microsites/idtheft/

- National ID Fraud (UK) – www.stop-idfraud.co.uk

- Website produced by public and private U.K. sector organizations to combat the threat of identity theft – www.identitytheft.org.uk

- For information and reporting fraud in the U.K – www.actionfraud.org.uk

- For banking information, visual examples and even videos visit www.about.com to learn how to write a check, balance your checkbook and more. Just use the 'search' function.

Chapter 10

Who Are You?

Understanding and Positively

Managing Individual Differences

Contributed by Sylvia Vriesendorp

"Leaving home in a sense involves a kind of second birth in which we give birth to ourselves."

Robert Neelly Bellah, *Habits of the Heart*, 1985

Note to the reader: I have asked Sylvia Vriesendorp, a psychologist, to write a chapter on personality differences and how understanding them can help students get along better with their roommates, fellow students, professors and others they will live and work closely with throughout their university years. After undergoing a Myers-Briggs Type Indicator with my husband, I was sold on how helpful it is in understanding personality differences. There are many different personality assessment instruments available, but I asked Sylvia to share her favorite with you.

You are All Alike!

When I first went to Africa I had a hard time remembering names and faces. I would remember a woman by the color of her dress and head scarf. But when she would show up the next day with another outfit or her hair in braids I would walk up to her and introduce myself again. It was good that most people were patient with me as I found it rather embarrassing. I never had this problem with people who belong to the same racial category as I did.

Now, in Afghanistan, I am trying to learn the names of the 30 or so drivers who work for our organization and I keep introducing myself to people who smile politely. I introduce myself over and over again to the same people and ask them who they are. It is embarrassing, but I don't see the differences yet. I am looking at their overall Afghan-ness and in that respect they all look the same.

It is no different for Africans who first come to the United States and can't seem to distinguish one blonde woman from another. It is not politically correct to admit this, but it happens to all of us.

As you get closer to people you begin to pick up more and more clues about them that differentiate one individual from another. First these clues are external characteristics such as "Ali is the one with the long curly hair or Fatima is the one with the almond shaped eyes and the coffee colored skin or Heidi has the pigtails and the blue-green eyes." As you get to know people better you start to internalize these differences and don't need to repeat them any longer to yourself. You can even recognize Heidi without pigtails and Ali after he has his hair cut off.

The less the distance between you and the other person, the more you notice about their ways of being, of doing, of speaking, and of thinking. You learn about the other's temperament, ways of reasoning and deciding, and you become more and more adept at predicting behaviors and actions. The better you get to know each other, the more you realize your differences. This is true for people who are much like you and those who are not. Of course, this does not mean you *like* everyone that you get to know better. There comes a time when you have formed a judgment that will either keep you from getting any closer to someone or invite him or her further into a relationship with you.

 Dig Deeper: The better you get to know someone, the more you realize your differences. There comes a time when you have formed a judgment that will either keep you from getting any closer to someone or invite him or her further into a relationship with you.

When I was a young girl I often clashed with my parents who believed that I should get along with everybody and that no one should be left out. I disagreed with them, giving my judgment about this or that stupid girl. I remember them arguing with me, but I would not budge. I had made up my mind that Mary was obnoxious. I wasn't sure why, but I knew I didn't like what I called obnoxious people. Of course, at the time I did not know that I was reacting to a difference, something that I could not articulate and my behavior made it impossible to discover that difference, let alone appreciate it.

I have known many more Marys since then, but I have also come to learn that these people I have wanted to remove from my life could actually contribute greatly to it – if I could only understand our differences; differences that could not necessarily be explained by radically different cultures or life experiences. These were differences that would be explained in other ways that, I discovered, were all between our ears!

Throughout the history of the world people have been fascinated, even obsessed, with understanding human differences. Typologies of temperamental differences have been recorded in ancient China, India, Persia, Greece and Egypt. Galen, who lived in what is now Western Turkey, (AD 131-200) wrote about individual differences in his *De temperamentis*, finding a physiological basis for such differences. Carl Gustav Jung, a Swiss psychiatrist (1875-1961) studied individual differences in his own practice and came to the conclusion that people have preferences for how they process information. He called these 'mental functions' and introduced the concept of "function types" or "psychological types."

Katharine Cook Briggs and her daughter Isabel Briggs Myers further developed Jung's ideas and began to write questions on index cards to help identify people's preferences. Their focus was on women who were entering the workforce to make up for the departure of men to the front during World War II. They believed that knowledge of personality preferences would help these women identify the sort of war-time jobs where they would be "most comfortable and effective." (Briggs Myers, 1980: xiii).

Their initial questionnaire eventually became the Myers-Briggs Type Indicator, which was first published in 1962. Since then decades of research by Educational Testing Services has amassed a large body of data that have validated the instrument which is now one of the most used personality assessment instruments in the world.

As I was preparing for a trip to Mali with a colleague, we had a number of clashes about how to prepare for the assignment. Things had gotten to the point that we both dreaded this common assignment: travelling together, staying in the same hotel, and working all day and many evenings together. We were grating on each others' nerves as the departure date came closer and closer.

A concerned and insightful colleague suggested that the tensions in our relationship that produced the irritations did not come from disliking each other but from profound differences in the way we mentally engaged with the demands of the task at hand. He administered the Myers-Briggs Type Indicator (MBTI) to each of us and helped us interpret our vastly different scores.

The MBTI presented us with a whole new perspective on ourselves and our differences. We learned that we made a perfect team. Our strengths and weaknesses were nearly entirely complementary: what I was good at, she was not good at; where she was very competent and confident, I was out of my element. The reason we clashed is that we each tried to make the other adapt to our own ways of doing things. Knowing that she should leave me alone as I prepared for the open-ended part of the assignment that required a great deal of intuition and associative thinking, I was able to leave her alone to take care of budget and administrative issues that required a great deal of attention to detail and coming to closure. To make a long story short, the assignment was a success and we became very good friends who greatly respected each other.

When people engage in tasks using automatic, reflexive and largely unconscious processes, they do this in very different ways. The resulting behaviors can be a source of great joy or tremendous irritation. Not understanding the root causes of their reactions can lead people to judgments about the worth, intelligence or credibility of the other. As a result, much potential for positive and productive relationships is never realized. At best, people have lost the chance to make their information gathering and decision-making processes stronger. At worst, they come to foolish conclusions or make bad decisions. In either case, what is lost is a chance to see group genius at work and enjoy the experience of complementing one another and becoming better persons as a result. The applications of this learning process are myriad as you embark on your university experience. Getting along with a roommate, surviving on your hall or in your dorm, making new friends, and understanding and interpreting the demands of your professors will only be a few of the places this understanding of yourself and others will be helpful. So let's take a look at how these mental processes differ.

Taking in Information:
Sensors and Intuitors

Your senses allow you to take in information about the world around you. You do this by hearing, seeing (including reading), tasting, touching, or smelling. Although not entirely tangible, information you receive through your senses is objective and you can share it. You can ask someone else to see, taste, smell, hear, touch the same thing you are seeing, tasting, smelling, hearing, or touching.

You can also take in information via hunches, or intuition. You cannot touch it, but somehow you know. This happens when someone says, "I think you should turn right here rather than left." But when you ask why, they cannot explain it. It's a hunch. There is much written about hunches and intuition. In many parts of North America and Europe, hunches and intuition went through a long period of being discredited as a way of collecting information because they weren't considered real or objective in a scientific sense. But we now know that hunches come from information that has been picked up without realizing it and stored for later use.

People who predominantly rely on intuition and hunches can get very irritated by people who don't trust *any* information that did not come in, consciously, through any of their senses. The same is true in the other direction. Although everyone uses both types of taking in information, everyone has a preferred mode. Those who rely primarily on their senses are called 'Sensors' while those who rely primarily on their intuition are called, not surprisingly, 'Intuitors.'

Share It: Those who prefer Sensing favor clear, tangible data and information that fits in well with their direct here-and-now experience. Those who prefer Intuition are drawn to information that is more abstract, conceptual, big-picture, and represents imaginative possibilities for the future.

Evaluating Information:
Thinkers and Feelers

The second critical mental process is what happens with the information once you have received it. As you process the data, whether sensory or intuitive, you arrive at conclusions that may lead to action or inaction, to a decision or indecision. This internal processing can follow two kinds of reasoning: one is objective and rational, using principles of linear, step-wise logic while the other process is based on subjective judgments, values, and concerns that follow another kind of logic that some would call irrational.

Once again, each person uses both processes but some people prefer the rational, logical type of reasoning while others prefer the more subjective, values-based reasoning. The former are called 'Thinkers' and the latter are called 'Feelers.'

Thinkers can get very irritated by what they consider the loose, fuzzy or touchy-feely reasoning of Feelers. They believe that individual concerns and values create chaos and arbitrary decision-making. They believe strongly in the rule of law, and, at the extreme end, in having no exceptions. On the other hand, Feelers often find the reasoning processes of Thinkers harsh and uncompassionate. They believe laws and rules are important but that one should always remember that there are human beings involved in most of our decisions.

Share It: Those who prefer Thinking have a natural preference for making decisions in an objective, logical, and analytical manner with an emphasis on tasks and results. Those who prefer Feeling make their decisions in a somewhat global, visceral, harmonious and value-oriented way, paying particular attention to the impact of decisions and actions on other people.

Interacting With the World:
Introverts and Extroverts

Jung used another dimension that most people are familiar with: introversion and extroversion. The two words, as Jung used them, were neutral, neither one was better than the other. Nowadays the word introversion has acquired a negative connotation associated with timidity, shyness and social awkwardness. But for Jung these two terms simply denoted different ways in which people stand in relation to the world and interact with it: introversion referred to their inner world of thoughts and ideas and extroversion referred to their outer world of material things and people.

Jung used the terms to differentiate between people who get energized by being with others or enjoying material things (Extroverts) and people who are energized by being with their own thoughts and ideas (Introverts). If you get energized by being around people and deflated when being alone, you are probably an Extrovert; if having people around drains you and being by yourself gets your energy back, you are probably an Introvert. This is a very quick and easy way of determining which you are.

Introverts can get very irritated by Extroverts. For example in the classroom, Extroverts tend to think aloud and spout their answers to questions quickly, even if they are not fully worked out. For Introverts this is simply 'shooting from the hip' or 'talking off the cuff' and becomes very distracting while they are thinking over carefully what they will say before opening their mouths. And when they finally do open their mouths, the instructor, especially an Extroverted one, has already moved on. Thus, sitting in a large class is hard for Introverts, but writing individual

215

reflective papers can be difficult for Extroverts. The former needs time and space to organize their thoughts while the latter needs the stimulation of other people's thoughts to formulate their own.

 Share It: Those who prefer Extroversion are drawn to the outside world – activities, people, events – as their elemental source of energy. Rarely, if ever, do Extroverted preference people feel their energy batteries are "drained" by excessive amounts of interaction with the outside world. Those who prefer Introversion draw their primary energy from the inner world of information, thoughts, ideas, and other reflections. When circumstances require an excessive amount of attention spent in the "outside" world, those preferring Introversion find the need to retreat to a more private setting as if to recharge their drained batteries.

Attitudes Towards Information:
Perceivers and Judgers

In the deeper exploration of Jung's work, and as they constructed the MBTI, Katherine Briggs and her daughter Isabel Myers discovered a fourth dimension that Jung had not mentioned even though it was, in a way, a variation on the mental processes he had observed. Briggs and Myers called this fourth dimension an attitude. They noticed that some people had a bias for the mental process that focused on taking in information while others preferred to come to conclusions.

Typically, someone with a bias for taking in information finds it hard to bring something to closure: there is always one more book to read, a study to initiate, a focus group to conduct or a few more interviews. On the other side of the spectrum are those who are impatient during the data collection phase and prefer to draw conclusions rather than looking for more information. The former are called 'Perceivers' and the latter are called 'Judgers' because the two mental processes they favor are related to perceiving (taking in information) and judging (drawing conclusions). Note that, once again, these labels are used in a neutral way rather than the more judgmental ways in which a term such as 'judger' might be used today.

You can imagine that it might be hard to work with a Judger if you are a Perceiver or vice versa. Brainstorming is generally hard for Judgers while writing the closing chapter of a thesis and drawing conclusions would be hard for a Perceiver. A Perceiver might be seen as procrastinating when he keeps doing more research rather than writing a paper or its conclusion. On the other end of the spectrum, a Judger might write a very short paper and have trouble finding or citing enough sources for the paper. Once again, in an organizational setting and at home, the two opposite types can greatly irritate each other when they don't understand they have different ways of mental processing.

 Share It: Those who prefer 'Judging' see everything in terms of either true or false, black or white, without gray areas to manage their outer life. This typically leads to a style oriented towards closure, organization, planning, or in some fashion, managing the things and/or people found in the external environment. They are driven to order the outside world. Those who prefer Perceiving rely upon their senses to run their outer life. This typically results in an open, adaptable, flexible style of relating to the things and people found in the outside world. They are driven to experience the outside world rather than organize it; in general, they easily tolerate a lack of closure.

Putting It All Together

The ingenuity of the MBTI consists in the interactions created by all the possible permutations of the four dimensions which produce 16 discernable types: Each type is indicated by a four-letter combination indicating one of the two sides of each of the four dimensions: E-I (extroversion and introversion); S-N (sensing and intuiting); T-F (thinking and feeling) and J-P (judging and perceiving).

People who have taken the MBTI will identify themselves as INFP, or ESTJ or any of the other 14 combinations. By presenting themselves as such – assuming they have been thoroughly briefed by the person who administered the MBTI – they have agreed that their overall profile fits, more or less, the general attributes of that particular type.

The more opposite letters there are for two people (i.e. ESTJ versus INFP), the more difficult it is for them to work productively together, unless they understand the sources of the differences. The beauty of the MBTI typology is that, rather than pigeonholing people, as some critics have claimed, an understanding of these differences can bring about the best possible collaborative relationships between people. After all, with all sides of the four dimensions present, two opposites have literally the best of both worlds available to them when it comes to taking in and processing information.

One final word about the questions some of you may have about nature-nurture in defining your type. Some people may argue that whether you are an Extrovert or Introvert, Feeler or Thinker, Sensor or Intuitor, Perceiver or Judger, depends on the situation. But type preferences are very much like hand preferences: some are born right-handed and others left-handed. The natural dominance of one hand, which is 'nature,' doesn't exclude competent use of the other. Everyone can adapt to use the non-dominant hand if the dominant one cannot be used for one reason or another, proving that 'nurture' can win out over 'nature.' Of course, one is clumsy at first, but eventually you can learn to write nearly as well with your left as your right hand, if you really have to. My grandfather was born a lefty, which at the time was considered some sort of a genetic flaw. Thus he was forced to write with his right hand, something he learned to do very well. Similarly, geometry courses are required in many high schools to help students learn step-wise, or Greek, logic in order to become sensors in the classroom and business world. In the same way, some people who are predominantly extroverts (or introverts) can be trained to be introverted (or extroverted) in some situations.

In Summary

EXTROVERTED (E) vs. INTROVERTED (I): How we get our energy.	
Those who prefer Extroversion are drawn to the outside world as their elemental source of energy. Rarely, if ever, do extroverted preference people feel their energy batteries are "drained" by excessive amounts of interaction with the outside world. They must engage the things, people, places and activities going on in the outside world for their life force.	Those who prefer Introversion draw their primary energy from the inner world of information, thoughts, ideas, and other reflections. When circumstances require an excessive amount of attention spent in the "outside" world, those preferring Introversion find the need to retreat to a more private setting as if to recharge their drained batteries.

SENSING (S) vs. INTUITION (I): How we take in information.	
Those who prefer Sensing favor clear, tangible data and information that fits in well with their direct here-and-now experience.	Those who prefer Intuition are drawn to information that is more abstract, conceptual, big-picture, and represents imaginative possibilities.

THINKING (T) vs. FEELING (F): How we make decisions and come to judgments.	
Those who prefer Thinking have a natural preference for making decisions in an objective, logical, and analytical manner with an emphasis on tasks and results to be accomplished.	Those who prefer Feeling make their decisions in a somewhat global, visceral, harmonious and value-oriented way, paying particular attention to the impact of decisions and actions on other people.

JUDGING (J) vs. PERCEIVING (P): How we relate to the outer or external world.	
Those who prefer Judging rely upon either their T or F preference to manage their outer life. This typically leads to a style oriented towards closure, organization, planning, or in some fashion managing the things and or people found in the external environment. The drive is to order the outside world.	Those who prefer Perceiving rely upon either their S or N preference to run their outer life. This typically results in an open, adaptable, flexible style of relating to the things and people found in the outside world. The drive is to experience the outside world rather than order it; in general lack of closure is easily tolerated.

I Hate My Roommate –
Why Can't She be Like Me?

As roommates you come to your shared dorm with different life experiences and expectations about what the other is like. You start looking at the outside and conclude that you are either fairly similar or very different. You take your first cues from the most obvious characteristics such as skin color, age, language or accent; later, after getting to know each other, you learn about differences or similarities in religion, family background, school and childhood experiences. You discover, if you didn't already know it, that someone from the south is different from someone who was brought up in the north and you begin to learn about cultural differences. If you come from a culturally homogenous background, this process can be lengthy and awkward at times.

After some time, these differences stop being important and you discover new dimensions in your relationship. It is often at this point, assuming that you have been able to move beyond the cultural differences, that you decide whether friendship is possible or not.

The conclusion you will reach is not always logical or understandable. It may be a hunch, or a series of encounters that made you decide this way or that. Once you have made up your mind, it may be difficult to change it because your behavior changes toward each other and a spiral of attraction or repulsion is set in motion.

If the relationship turns into friendship, you will find that you become more and more tolerant of each others' differences. The existence of enduring friendship and long and happy marriages is the ultimate testimony to this possibility of living happily with differences.

If the relationship is deteriorating, it may be because you don't understand the differences that are pulling you apart. A closer examination of these differences may help you become more appreciative of the other person and the gifts that are hidden inside these differences.

Try This: Take a look at the dimensions described above and see if you can identify whether different ways of mental processing are at the root of your dislike or problems with your roommate. Consider for a moment that differences in *how you function* rather than annoying attributes, or even intentional behaviors meant to irritate you, may be the cause of your deepening rift.

Might it be that your roommate's messiness is not a personal flaw that can be changed with some discipline and hard work, but rather a manifestation of how he structures the world around him? Or maybe it is just the other way around and the neatness of your roommate and her constant complaining about your messiness drives you crazy because you don't have a similar need for complete control and structure. Once again, this is not about personal shortcomings or flaws but about differences in mental processing. This explains why people tend not to change such habits, no matter how hard others try to change them.

Are there people in your class who annoy you because they don't talk enough or they talk too much? Do some of your classmates turn you off with their highly abstract and associative thinking or with their seemingly obsessive attention to detail? Do you sometimes wish that others were more like you?

Differences at Their Best

Once you start realizing that differences in the ways people behave are not just manifestations of their culture or upbringing but also differences in mental processing, you can start to look for ways to take full advantage of the opportunities offered by such differences. Here are some tips and techniques to aid you in better appreciating in someone else what you are not good at, and to begin to expose yourself to your less-favored way of being in the world and interacting with it.

If you tend to be an extrovert, make space for introverts. Leave your introverted roommate alone from time to time and respect her decision not to join in activities that involve many other people. On the other hand, if you are the introverted one, be assertive about your need to be alone, and, if this cannot be accomplished in the dorm, find another

221

place such as the library to create a quiet space for yourself. In either case, become more aware of your need to balance being alone or with others and respect others' wishes to do the same.

If you are a sensor, acknowledge that your preoccupation with facts helps you become a better scientist or researcher, but also acknowledge that there is more to science than getting the facts. On a more practical plane, when your tendency is to be very detail-oriented in your interactions with others, pay close attention to their reactions and, if they get impatient with you, know that you are simply giving too much detail. One place where this shows up is in note-taking; sensors may write down many details of a lecture, sometimes even whole sentences. On the other hand, intuitors may get drawn into associative thinking that takes them away from the here-and-now of the lecture, causing them to ignore details that are later needed to pass a test. There are probably note-taking resources available on campus or from academic counselors that can help you improve how you take notes. Mind mapping is a good method of note taking for either preference because it allows both for big picture notes and the smallest details. A mind map is a diagram used for linking words and ideas to a central key word or idea. It is used to visualize, classify, structure, and generate new ideas as well as for note taking.

If you are a feeler and your roommate is a thinker, you will probably have some heated discussions about social issues and events. Next time you engage into such a discussion see if you can identify the manner by which you each reach conclusions. Does one of you use reasoning based on rational and objective principles that are discarded by the other because they are cold and heartless? What arguments are used by each party? You can do the same in a class when listening to the reasoning of your professor or classmate and see if you can guess whether they are thinkers or feelers.

If you are a judger and your roommate is one as well, you are in luck because you won't have much friction around how you organize your living space. If you are opposite types you will need a little more patience and understanding. By taking the arguments about clutter or neatness out of the realm of personal flaws, you can come up with a compromise in which you each establish a part of your common space that is yours to control or structure as you please. Don't try to change the other to become more like you. It will never happen and you will both be miserable.

> **Share It:** Instead of trying to change another person, try to understand the way that person functions and how each of you processes information and responds to other people. Make space for differences and allow that person's strengths to make up for your weaknesses.

Dealing with Differences

Despite all your best intentions, sometimes conflict becomes unavoidable. What is avoidable is escalation of conflict to the point that one party needs to leave; leave the room, get a new roommate, drop the class, end the relationship, leave the campus, or maybe even leave the city.

Whatever the reasons that led up to the conflict, there are always three elements that are at play:

- **The story** of what happened that triggered the conflict

- **The feelings** that are generated by the conflict and

- The questioning of **the identities** of the people involved in the conflict.

The Story

Everyone looks at the world through a frame, like a window, which puts some things in the middle and other things on the periphery. When something happens that puts you at odds with someone else – a roommate or a friend, an instructor, a sibling, or a parent – your version of what happened will probably be rather different from what the other person saw or felt happened.

People tend to see themselves as the one who was right while the other was wrong. The more you retell the story to yourself, the more you pay attention to the things you did right and the other did wrong. This is why in conflict situations each party believes that the other should change, apologize, make up or repent. But like a tennis match, the way you hit the ball to your opponent influences how your opponent hits the ball back. It always takes two people or two parties for a conflict to arise.

Try to retell the story from the other's perspective by imagining what he, she or they would tell their friends. Might there be something in your behavior that was not right either? It's a daring thought, but a critical one if you are serious about resolving the conflict.

One way to find out about these different stories is to be an intermediary on the conflict two friends of yours have with each other. Listen to each story and you will soon realize that each party was right in the description about what happened. It is just that each emphasized or saw some parts of the story while de-emphasizing or ignoring (or not knowing about) other parts.

The resolution lies not in making a decision about who was right and who was wrong but in acknowledging that both parties were right and that both parties probably did something they should not have done. This is the first important step to get out of this conflict mode.

 Try This: When you have a conflict with another person, acknowledge that both parties were right and both parties were wrong. Admit areas where you may have been wrong or where the other person may have perceived you were in the wrong.

The Feelings

Everyone has feelings, even if some people claim they don't have any. When you listen to other people's stories about a conflict situation it is easy to detect the feelings behind the words. But maybe you are not very good at detecting your own feelings and have told yourself that you don't have any feelings about what happened. Don't kid yourself. Claiming not to have any feelings usually means not knowing how to name them. In some cultures the feeling vocabulary, especially for men, is very limited: angry, happy, and sad.

People with strong egos often have a hard time recognizing or acknowledging feelings because egos are about control and feelings are entirely outside the ego's control. You cannot order yourself to feel happy when you are not.

Sometimes you hear people talking about others who need 'to get in touch with their feelings.' What this really means is trying to push the ego aside and turn inward to experience how you feel without having to tell anyone. That way you can be vulnerable without risk of being discovered as a touchy-feely type, in case this label makes you nervous.

Create a quiet space around yourself and ask, "what just happened?" And then, before the ego kicks in to explain the situation in your favor, ask yourself how you really felt: did you feel betrayed, humiliated, insulted, belittled, unjustly accused, unacknowledged, put down, ignored, overwhelmed, ashamed, frustrated, jealous, disappointed, etc.? Keep silencing that quiet but persistent inner voice that keeps trying to protect you from these uncomfortable feelings. That's your ego that wants you to be right and the other wrong and that wants to present you as strong and invincible. But don't be fooled, strength comes from understanding how your feelings influenced your experience of what happened, not the other way around.

Acknowledging feelings, your own and the other's is thus the second step in turning a conflict around so that a relationship can be resumed or repaired.

 Try This: Learn "feeling" words like betrayed, humiliated, ignored, frustrated, etc. When a conflict arises, create a quiet space around yourself and ask, "What happened and how did it make me feel?" Acknowledge your feelings. Then ask the other person how they feel. Acknowledge their feelings. Acknowledgement is not agreement; acknowledgement is saying, "I hear how frustrated you are."

The Identities

Most everyone has a sense of self, a clear picture about one's identity. You may consider yourself a competent and caring person, someone who is smart and quick-thinking, relaxed, and easy-going or some other combination of positive traits. Your identity is a very central part of who you are and when someone challenges that, it is as if the earth shakes under your feet. If you consider yourself a caring person but the way you are portrayed in the other's story is selfish, this can be very upsetting. If you are a serious and honest student and find yourself accused (unjustly) of cheating, your whole sense of self is being questioned. This is the worst thing about the gossip that usually happens when conflict is not resolved.

Beware: Gossip happens when conflict is not resolved. Do not start gossip about the other person in conflict with you. And do not pass on gossip that has resulted from someone else's unresolved conflict. Gossip hurts.

The good thing about identity is that it is entirely yours. No one can define it for you and no one can take it away. This is sometimes difficult to remember when you are in the middle of such an identity 'quake' but it is a fact. Acknowledging that you are not the person that the other describes and that this is just their opinion of you, not a true reflection of who you truly are, can get you back on your feet after you have been shaken. Sometimes it helps to hear from people who are close to you that the other is entirely wrong, although in the end it is you who is in charge of naming your identity, not others, no matter how close they are.

 Tip to Remember: Acknowledging that you are not the person that the other describes and that this is just their opinion about you, not a true reflection of who you truly are, can help you get back on your feet after a conflict. Although it makes you feel better to hear from people who are close to you that the other person is entirely wrong, it is you who is in charge of naming your identity.

Together or Apart: It's Up to You

Although it can be tempting to walk away from a conflict by saying you are right and the other is wrong, it is also foolhardy. At that point, everything is lost and nothing is gained, except some misguided sense that the other is not good enough for you or not worth getting to know better. You don't, of course, have to like everyone; however, you risk exploring whether your differences are actually a source of strength in your relationship. Wouldn't everyone benefit if you could do what you are good at, and the other person could do what he or she is good at?

226

What You Need to Know:

- You don't have to like a person, but you can control your natural reflexes so you can have a productive and constructive relationship.

- Your differences probably don't have anything to do with character flaws and may have a lot to do with the ways in which you take in and process information and how you interact with the world.

- If everyone was the same, we would all be in trouble.

Resources:

Free online MBTI-like assessments

All of the mentioned links below are to assessment instruments that are based on the work of Carl Jung, Isabel Myers and Katherine Briggs but not officially endorsed as MBTI. The official and authentic MBTI is not available for free. It has to be purchased through Consulting Psychologists Press, Inc. in Palo Alta, California. One has to be licensed to purchase and administer the official version.

- www.humanmetrics.com/cgi-win/JTypes2.asp - this is a site where you can take a free adapted Myers Briggs test based on Jung Typology and get immediate results.

- www.personalitypathways.com/MBTI_intro.html - gives a good introduction to and offers another version of the MBTI.

Resources (cont'd):

- www.similarminds.com/jung.html – a 53 question adapted Myers Briggs test. The test starts by asking for your gender and then, once you submit your answers, immediately gives you a result statement and links to read more about your type.

- www.personalitypage.com/ – the Personality Pages provide descriptions of the 16 types, typical careers for each type and even information about how to apply them to relationships and your personal growth. They offer a special (free) test for children at www.personalitypage.com/kids.html

- www.keirsey.com – This website is related to the MBTI but focuses on the four temperaments. It has descriptions of the temperaments and famous people in each of the categories. There are free assessments available through this site.

Books

- *Gifts Differing – Understanding Personality Type* by I. Briggs Myers and P.B. Myers, Davies-Black Publishing, 1980.

- *Manual: A Guide to the Development and Use of the Myers Briggs Type Indicator* by I. Briggs Myers and M.H. McCaulley, Consulting Psychologists Press, Inc. 1985.

- *Please Understand Me – Character and Temperament Types* by David L. Keirsey and Marilyn Bates, Prometheus Nemesis Book Company, 1978.

- *Difficult Conversations: How to discuss what matters most* by D. Stone, B. Patton, et al. Penguin Books, 1999.

Chapter 11

Tips for Parents –

Preparing and Supporting

Your College-Bound Student

"It is hard to convince a high-school student that he will encounter a lot of problems more difficult than those of algebra and geometry."

Edgar W. Howe

Launched – Like it or Not!

I had the unusual privilege this past spring to witness the birth, upbringing and first flight of not one but two families of robins, one at the front of our house and the other at the back. I watched the mother robin leave two, then three, then four eggs in the nest. I watched in awe as they hatched and went seemingly overnight from featherless, bug-eyed babies with gaping beaks, waiting for their next meal to fully developed, beautiful creatures so big they were lying on top of one another in the tiny nest.

There came a time when I knew they were ready to fly. It got to the point that due to their size comparative to the nest, they were constantly battling for position. Then it happened. I opened the door one day and the mother, as was customary whenever I approached, flew off. This time the babies followed suit, only not very successfully. Half of them landed on the ground and either hobbled around a bit or huddled up against our fence, petrified to move any further. I could tell the mother was in distress as she watched her babies there all alone. She kept swooping down back and forth as if to say, "Come on, get up and follow me." Eventually I looked up and saw mother and four babies taking flight together. I saw them again as a family over the next couple of days, but then I don't know what happened to them or where they went, but I imagined they were well.

I couldn't help but think of the irony of witnessing this event twice just as my nest was about to empty out and I would watch as my last child takes flight. It may seem like just yesterday you were bringing that bundle of joy home from the hospital or perhaps it has felt more like an eternity just waiting for this time in your son's or daughter's life to arrive, but either way, it is here. Just like that mother robin, you have been preparing your student their entire lifetime for this day. Since the moment they were born, you have been teaching them to become independent. You've weaned them off the bottle or breast and taught them to hold their own cup, feed and dress themselves, use the potty alone, share their toys, be a good friend, be socially responsible, and on and on.

While the task of parenting never ends we are beginning to see the light at the end of the tunnel as far as having to constantly be scanning the horizon for potential deterrents to our child's well-being and future aspirations. Like the mother robin that hovered over her nest while the babies were in it, but watched from a distance as they spread their wings to fly, then swooped down to help until they could fly on their own, our

> *"A mother is not a person to lean on but a person to make leaning unnecessary."*
> Dorothy C. Fisher, *O Magazine*, May 2003

hovering days are over, but our children still need us to watch from the sidelines. Armed with the knowledge and wisdom we have been able to impart over the last 17 or 18 short years, we are preparing to send our offspring into the big world to venture forward as an independent adult to begin building his or her own arsenal of personal experience. There is no doubt about it – this is scary stuff.

Our parenting will be taken to all new levels. Our children will continue to need us but in an entirely different way. They need us to be there when things are overwhelming, chaotic, confusing, or like the baby robins, when they stumble and are uncertain. They are not always going to ask for advice as much as they just want someone to listen to them, especially when they don't have that new best friend yet to share things with. On average, I received four phone calls a day for the first three weeks of my daughter's first semester at college. While she felt guilty calling so often, I reassured her that I loved hearing from her. Once she began to settle in and find friends and activities, the phone calls became less and less frequent.

Some of us will have difficulty resisting the urge to be helicopter parents and continue to hover over our children. Others of us will gleefully send them off on their way as responsible adults and begin to carve out new lives for ourselves by making plans to travel more or begin a new career. Most of us will fall somewhere in the middle, feeling simultaneously exhilarated and anxious about the launch. I felt as though my heart was being pulled out of my chest when my first daughter left for college. When it was my middle daughter's turn, it was difficult but not quite so intense. Granted some of that was due to the fact that she was going to the same school as her older sister and overlapping by two years. Once I had adjusted to that transition, I started asking, "Now how much longer before the last one leaves?" Not to be crass about it but I knew both my daughters and I had survived this separation and I was becoming rather skilled at this long distance parenting thing, so I was no longer anxious about surviving the empty nest. However, as I write this, I am hit head-on with the impending life transition of having no more children at home. I suddenly realize it is going to be more difficult than I had anticipated at that time.

That being said, it is important to note that our children are not the only ones going through transition. Dave Pollock's transition model applies to parents at this stage in their life as well, whether they will be empty nesters or not. You too, may be able to put a name to the stages as you go through them. Not everyone will go through them the same way and even husbands and wives may find that they are not in the same stage together, but move along at different paces. It is also possible to flip-flop back and forth between stages. But just as I tell students, it is all normal and will pass with time.

Empty Nest Depression

Normal and Expected

Empty nest syndrome refers to the feelings of grief, sadness, loneliness, or loss parents or guardians, particularly women, experience when their children leave home. It is normal and expected, and as was my case, it can actually begin before the child or children have physically left the home. However, if you begin to experience symptoms of depression that prevent you from moving ahead in life, such as is discussed in Chapter 4, it is time to seek professional counseling. There come times in our lives when we need a little help getting past the bumps in the road. And for some of us moms the empty nest is occurring concomitantly while dealing with the emotional roller coaster of menopause or perimenopause (the beginning stages of menopause). How's that for a double whammy? Who couldn't use an understanding expert to talk to? If you have been waiting to repatriate or take the next international assignment until your child finishes high school, you have even more of a transition to work through, and it may help counter empty nest syndrome or, contrarily, it may make it worse.

Staying Positive

There are some things you can do to help ward off empty nest syndrome from taking hold of you. I know of one woman who looked at every event of her youngest child's entire senior year of school with a melancholy attitude. She would say, "Oh, this is the very last basketball game she'll ever play in high school...the last class picnic...the last school dance," and so on. She was basically setting herself up for how devastating it would be not to have these events to participate in anymore. If she had looked at it in a more positive light, her thoughts could have led to a more satisfying outcome. If she had chosen to think of each ending as a new beginning, she could have changed her destiny around. She could have thought of the last basketball game as, "She's had a wonderful time being a part of this team and learned some skills that will really be helpful to her in life." Focus your thoughts on how well you have prepared your child for the day they will leave home and how much you, the school, the teachers and the students have given him or her along the way. Turn it around every time you sense dread rather than delight and anticipation.

 Try This: Every time you sense dread over something that signals the end of an era, turn it around and find the positive in it.

Think About Your Future

Begin thinking about *your* future and what you want to do with your newfound freedom. After 18-plus years of focusing on your children, you can now take some of that energy and place it somewhere else, like on your spouse, traveling or a new career. Take up new hobbies, join clubs, or go on dates. Or if you really miss having someone around to mother, consider hosting a foreign exchange student.

They Come Back

Just when you begin to get used to their absence, students come back home for a school break and everything changes. They have been living on their own and have grown used to setting rules for themselves as to what and when they eat, sleep, socialize, study and more. Heads will butt if parents expect these independent young adults to follow the old high school house rules when they are back for holidays. That's not to say you can't suggest they observe reasonable limits so as not to upset the household. It is also worth thinking about what you will and will not pay for when they return home. If they are expected to buy their own personal hygiene supplies at university, then they should not empty your vanity when they are at home. These issues and more are obviously very specific to and vary much from family to family, but are worth thinking about before sparks fly.

 Dig Deeper: When your student comes back for that first long holiday, think about what household rules need to be adapted to the fact that he or she has been living independently for a while.

Assistant RAFT Builder

Leave well to enter well. Dr. Dave Pollock's RAFT model (Chapter 4) helps transitioning students do just that, but it isn't an easy task.

Reconciliation

Affirmation

Farewells

Think Destination

Students may need adults to come alongside them to strategize how to approach:

- The uncomfortable task of **Reconciliations,**
- The "I-can't-be-bothered-to-do-it-now" task of **Affirmations,**
- The difficult task of **Farewells,** and
- You can certainly start the dialogue for **Talking** and **Thinking** Destination.

Reconciling

Let's face it – it is not easy, especially for teens, to grant forgiveness when they feel they have been wronged by someone. Perhaps a good friendship has somehow gone sour, but your teen doesn't really understand why or what happened since it was never talked about. Your student probably feels he or she must have somehow offended, hurt or otherwise distanced this friend but never was able to get down to the bottom of it to understand what went wrong and what part he or she might have played in it. It's too uncomfortable so he or she just shrugged it off and went on with life. This is the time when we, as parents, may need to step in and help our children face the hurts and disappointments, ask for or grant forgiveness and reconcile relationships. Start by asking them if there is anyone they have unfinished business with. Questions to ask include:

- Is there anyone you need to apologize to and make things right with?

- Is there anyone who has hurt you in some way?

Help them map out how they will resolve the issue. Would they be willing to do it face-to-face in person or is it enough to send a note? As of the writing of this, an email is not considered to be socially appropriate etiquette for such a communication. Then follow up with your teen to be sure he or she has completed the task and not left it hanging.

Unresolved past hurts go with young people in their suitcases, baggage that will stay with them and may hinder them in making new relationships. When they come back home on holidays, they may have to face the same people again and feel the same hurt. If your family or the family of the other injured party ends up moving away, it isn't a solution since that baggage goes along. So help your child empty his or her suitcase, air such hurts and concerns and come to reconciliation so they shoulder no burdens. To free your child of the burden he must grant forgiveness from his heart whether it is accepted by the other party or not.

A couple approached me to ask for help in thinking through a possible relocation from the U.S. to Germany. They had not yet received the offer of a contract but they knew it was a serious prospect. I spent an afternoon with the couple looking at all their life considerations to see if this was really a good time for their family to make their first international move.

We looked at what they would do about their aging parents, the sale or renting of their house, whether the wife would be able to work in Germany, what they would do about their dog, and most importantly, how their children felt. This is when red warning flags started flashing before my eyes. They expressed concern that their second son had been experiencing difficulties. He had recently gotten into disagreements with his best friends and no longer associated with them. His parents confided that he had been having self-image problems and was actually struggling with depression. They also told me their son had been telling his teachers and other students that he was moving even though the parents had not yet received an offer.

This signaled to me that this young man was trying to run away from his problems. Unfortunately I did not have the opportunity to go through RAFT building with him, but I briefly discussed it with his parents. They later confessed that with all they had to do to prepare for the move they did not have the time or energy to go through it with him.

I spoke with the mother recently and while the family found the transition to be just as difficult as the training predicted, her son was suffering the most. He is receiving counseling for continued and deepened depression, but the good news is he now realizes what he did to his best friends. He "released" them too early. This is a common reaction in the leaving stage. You know it will hurt to leave someone special, so you start a fight to make it easier for them and you to leave. He is now unpacking his baggage and resolving past hurts. He has called and apologized to his friends back in the U.S. and plans to go visit and stay with them soon.

Affirming

Similarly, help your student make a list of all the people in this place he or she calls home who have been an important part of his or her life or impacted him or her in some way. Help your student come up with ways to express his or her love and appreciation to these people, affirming them for all they have done. These affirmations bring joy to both parties – the receiver as well as the giver.

Saying Farewell

Even if your student is not a big party person, work with him or her to determine how he or she will see the people he or she needs to say good-bye to. This is crucial if your family is relocating and your student will not be returning to this home for school holidays. Don't let your student walk away without proper farewells. There will be regret later and lack of a sense of closure. It is never too late for farewells. If your student later realizes he or she missed someone, encourage him or her to send a card or email at that time. If at all possible, allow your student to return to this place once more within the next year to complete the circle of transition. Let him see that life goes on and people grow and move forward even in his absence.

Thinking Ahead

Now the fun of thinking ahead to the future can begin. Among other things, talk a lot about:

- What your student will need at school,

- How you will communicate,

- How he will deal with money, and

- Where he will spend holidays.

Communicate as much as possible over the summer months before the start of school. This is the last opportunity you have to really connect with your children. Their anxiety may keep their communicativeness at bay, but this is a great time for bonding activities. Going shopping together for dorm supplies, visiting places from their childhoods and hanging out nights together will help cement that parent/child bond established years back.

Tip to Remember: It is necessary to complete each log of the RAFT so they can be tied together and used to carry your student successfully to the other side of the pond.

Limbo Land

The summer before the start of university is a truly bizarre and completely incomprehensible time. It is the leaving stage at its height, full of see-sawing emotions and ambiguity. Parents need to allow the young person (and their siblings) the time and space to leave and grieve.

Friends Frenzy

You may find your child becomes inseparable from his friends, the very ones who used to bore, annoy and otherwise irritate him. Suddenly they cannot let go of one another despite the fact that they have been together, albeit off and on for years. So finding the time to bond with him could be a real challenge. Perhaps suggesting certain days or evenings of the week be devoted to family time might help, but don't necessarily count on compliance. Schedule time for shopping, a trip to a bank, and discussion with your teen to help him know you respect his time but want and need to help him with some tasks before he leaves for university.

Pressure is Off

The months between graduation and college matriculation are like being in limbo. School is out, there may be no obligations except to hang out with friends endlessly, and the rush to get ready for college has not yet started. New graduates feel the pressure is off and they expect a well-deserved respite to lie low…really low…so low it may be difficult to get them out of bed before 2 p.m., or to get them to help with household chores, get a job or complete necessary college forms. As mothers, we may tend to feel sorry for them and let them have their way, figuring they will be working their tails off for the next few years, so why not take it easy? We feel guilty for letting them get away with it and guilty if we don't. But it is imperative that they get their forms in expeditiously. There are too many stories of horrible housing and horrendous roommates, not to mention disappointing first-year seminars because they waited until the last minute to put in their requests.

Inner Struggles

During this interminable stretch of limbo you may witness behaviors in your child which will have you wondering if he or she has developed a multiple personality disorder. You have before you a man/boy or woman/girl whose maturity level fluctuates erratically. You see them screaming independence one moment and craving nurturing the next. They vacillate between wanting to let go and not wanting to. There is an inner struggle to act like a child, because this may be the last opportunity to do so, or start acting like the adult they are expected to be. They end up behaving like both practically simultaneously, often confusing themselves as well as their parents.

Creating Distance

You may also find yourself a victim of the I'm-gonna-make-life-miserable-for-you-so-you-can't-wait-to-see-me-go syndrome. Somehow these worldly, intelligent, talented young people have this idea that if they make it difficult to be around them, we will breathe a sigh of relief when they are finally out the door. Of course, they aren't actually thinking this consciously, it is just a reflex reaction to the anticipated pain of departure – their pain and ours. It is one method of providing distance between you.

Communication – Tons of It!

This stress and responsibility-free period once high school ends and before university begins is the last chance you may have to establish or refine open patterns of communication with your son or daughter. If your adolescent has never been very communicative in the past, this may be the perfect opportunity to develop some effective ways to talk to each other. This does not mean that you both need to sit down face-to-face in the living room to get a point across about something. It could be while riding in the car. Whatever works best for you, feels comfortable and, most importantly, gets your child to open up about what is on his or her mind will pave the way for the discussions that would be helpful (i.e. "Laying Out Expectations") to have before he or she leaves for school as well as future discussions once he or she hits campus. So that the communication does not seem like endless lectures or interrogations, you might start off with some leading or open-ended questions such as the following:

- So are you beginning to get excited about starting college?

- Would you like to talk about anything that is making you anxious right now?

- What are you looking forward to the most on your campus?

- Have you thought about what kinds of clubs or activities you want to get involved in?

- Is there anything I can help you think through like packing or learning how to do your laundry?

 Tip to Remember: Just be available physically as well as emotionally in case your student feels like talking.

Listening

As parents we need to be diligent about not giving advice when that is not what our son or daughter is asking for or being critical or judgmental of anything they have shared with us which could blow the trust and confidence of our relationship. What kids really want are listeners. They want someone who will let them voice their anxieties and acknowledge their concerns without diminishing them or fixing them. They need someone who loves them unconditionally, who will remind them of their past successes and achievements and encourage them to move forward in their independence. Parents and older siblings who have been to college or university can also help clear up any misconceptions and assumptions they may have developed about university life.

Facing Loss and Grief

If both you and your child have read through the entirety of this book, it is a great tool and common ground from which to start some pertinent discussions about the upcoming transition. This time is also the opportunity to talk about the loss and grief associated with the upcoming transition (Chapter 3), particularly if your family is repatriating or relocating to yet another host country and your student will not have the opportunity to come back during school holidays. It can also be the time to confront loss and grief from multiple past relocations that might interfere with settling in and making friends. This is something that is useful for the whole family to do, especially younger siblings.

People, places, pets and possessions are obvious losses. What about the hidden losses—not being able to play a beloved sport because of a move, never again seeing a mentor who helped develop a love for music or science, or the loss of the reputation or status your child enjoyed in the community, or everything about his or her way of living in this place compared to college? Suggest names for these and allow his thought process to lead him to the point of grieving them. Adolescents are not necessarily going to open up the floodgates and pour out their emotions but the process of naming their losses and grieving them is begun.

Whenever we moved, I would ask my daughters to name four things they were looking forward to in the new place and four things they would really miss. It always started a good dialogue which validated the richness of what they were leaving behind. A friend of ours would do something similar even when her children were very small. They would go around the house or the playground and say farewell to their favorite tree, swing or bench. You might want to ask your child if there is someplace or someone they would like to visit one last time, one more routine or tradition they would like to perform or any other possibilities.

Laying Out Expectations

At some point in time before the blast-off to college, parents will want to hold a fairly one-sided discussion with their student and lay forth some expectations. Having this discussion gives both sides of the equation the confidence to know that there is a structure in place and a road map to follow. Following are some of the expectations you may want to outline.

Academic Expectations

Having a goal, such as a certain grade point average (GPA) to aim for, gives students something to work towards and if they are falling short of meeting that goal, the onus will be on them to figure out how they can pull it up. Some kids will naturally do this for themselves and others need a bit of help. Set reasonable goals, especially for their first semester since college academics can be fairly rigorous and quite different from what they are used to. Also, you wouldn't want to raise the expectation that your child will suddenly and automatically be a more serious student than she or he was in high school. Base the expectation not only on what your child has achieved in the past but also what she or he is capable of doing. This is an activity you may want to consider doing together. Let your child suggest a GPA and you can agree with it or counter it.

With so many other distractions on campus, particularly the first year, knowing what is expected in the academic arena will help students decide how and when and where they need to be spending their time and energy. It isn't only about the final grade, but also how they get there. Many colleges have classroom attendance policies in place and many courses base grades partially on attendance.

Financial Expectations

Depending on how you choose to look at it, it is either a blessing or a curse that our students' struggle for independence is retarded by purse strings that bind them to us. Ideally your student will have been working with a budget for a few years by now, learning the value of money, how far it stretches and how easy it is to waste; however, in various parts of the world, it isn't easy to set up a bank account for a minor and give them free reign with a debit card. And the issues often really don't hit home with students until they have to pay bills like food and heat out of their money.

Just as with academic expectations, students tend to feel more secure knowing what the financial arrangements will be.

- Will they need to get a job?

- What do they do if they run out of money?

- How much will they have to work with?

241

- Will it cover everything?

- How much do things cost?

In order to avoid panic phone calls in the middle of the night, these questions and more need genuine thought and input from both concerned parties.

Let your student know exactly who is expected to pay for what. Work out a budget for estimated expenses. Besides tuition, housing, meals and books, don't forget the day-to-day necessities, medical and dental care, laundry, clothes, phone, recreation and entertainment to name a few. Many students decide to take a part-time job after the first semester so they have a little extra spending money and can begin to feel a little more financially independent.

 Try This: Some parents have their students keep a running list of all their personal expenses for two or more months and work out a monthly allowance for college. They try it, penalty free, for the first two months at school and then make adjustments as needed. After that, it is up to the student to make up for any discrepancies.

Books such as *Manage Your Student Finances Now!: Easy Ways to Balance Your Budget at University and College* by Keith Houghton can help your student get started thinking about financial health at school. For parents with students in U.S. schools, the College Board puts out a wonderful parents' guide called *Meeting College Costs: What You Need to Know Before Your Child and Money Leave Home*. It is particularly useful in working your way through the maze of financial aid.

Expectations Concerning Communications

While you may not be aggravated by receiving a twice or thrice daily phone call from your darling in the first few weeks of school, he or she may not be so gracious if it were the other way around. Set up expectations before your student leaves as to how often and what method of communicating will be used. You might want to allow a grace period at the start of school whereby you both agree that any means and any times are open for getting in touch. Anxieties on both sides of the gate run high at this time. Then again, your student may be having such a wonderful time with all the orientation activities and meeting new people, he doesn't feel the need or desire to talk with you, just yet. You might just insist that an occasional email to fill you in would be in order. Personally, I always felt that no news was good news since most calls from my daughters were initiated during low moments, but that could be the exact opposite for other families. You know your student and what works best. Some students, once settled into their routines, come to look forward to a weekly phone call with family.

 Try This: Decide ahead of time when and how you will stay in touch, especially if there is a huge difference in time zones and a random call is not always convenient.

Considering distance and time zone differences for some students and their families, it would be wise to set up a calling plan along with a budget to support it. There are many more options available to consumers these days for inexpensive international calling. If you haven't already, you may want to look into Skype (computer to computer), Skype out (from computer to telephone – land line or cell phone), VoIPbuster® (voice over internet protocol). These technologies are either free or extremely inexpensive ways to connect. I would highly suggest investing in a webcam if you and/or your student do not have one already built into your computer. There is something incredibly reassuring about seeing your beloved child's face and demeanor while speaking to him or her.

There are also exceptional phone-to-phone calling rates available for making international calls such as Kallback® and the 10-10 plans in North America that charge inexpensive rates by the minute with no extra fees or charges. There are many other deals such as these that can found by looking on the internet.

International pre-paid calling cards, which can also be used for domestic calls, are one of the least expensive ways to call internationally.

Compare the major phone companies' cards for the best deal in price, ease of use and other features.

Most college students today have their own cell phones which can be more economical that using the university phone service. Students tend to use their cell phones to text message each other their location, plans for the evening and where to meet up to have a meal together rather than making calls and using up their minutes. Many parents prefer their child has a cell phone for emergency purposes. By the time you have bought your plan and paid for your line, insurance and text messaging, your final bill can be staggering.

- Shop around to see which cell phone company gives the best deal.

- Have your student see what service is more popular with their friends as some companies offer free calls to anyone using the same network. Some offer free calls nights and weekends and others will let you dial certain frequently called numbers for free.

- See what suits your student's lifestyle and then compare companies.

Signing up for a cell phone plan can be futile if you don't have a Social Security Number (SSN – U.S.) or Social Insurance Number (SIN – Canada) for credit checks. If your student cannot obtain one (foreign students in the U.S. cannot obtain a SSN) he or she can ask about pre-paid contract plans that require an activation charge and a monthly contract whereby minutes are pre-purchased at the beginning of every month and more can be bought if she or he runs out. You might want to consider calling on a relative and ask to add your student to their phone package and avoid start up costs and other fees. The student would pay their costs (line, insurance, minutes, overages and data) but avoid paying for a full package on their own and being tied to a one to two-year contract with penalties for early withdrawal from the plan.

> Our town's high school hosted an evening program for parents of seniors about to depart for college and university. A panel of college students was on hand to answer parents' and students' questions. The students all agreed that they preferred to initiate phone calls home rather than the other way around because it suited their schedule. Parents have no idea what their student is up to when they call and are often disappointed when their child says they can't talk then or they get a voice mail because their son or daughter is in class or having a meal with friends or worse yet, asleep. When asked what they thought was the best method to use to communicate with their parents, the panel unanimously answered, "Email!"

Instant messaging (IMing), SMS and Facebook are typical ways for students to interact with each other these days, but email is the favored avenue for parental communication for many reasons. Email isn't in-your-face. They can decide to look at it when they are ready (in the mood) to look at it. They can take a study break and send out long newsy mails. They can use email to zip off a quick request or to briefly touch base so parents don't worry. They can do it on their own time.

More and more parents today are learning how to text and IM in order to keep up with their sons and daughters. You too, may want to learn how to upgrade your communications, particularly when the emails stop coming as regularly as you would like. Choose a phone plan that supports unlimited texting and/or choose an IM medium such as Yahoo, AIM, AOL, MSN and others.

Regardless of the communication tool used, students just want to know their parents are still available to them, available for the occasional advice, a sympathetic ear over a break-up or friend problems or just to hear news from home. How fortunate we are in this day and age to have so many vessels at hand to support our children, some of whom are half a world away.

Behavioral Expectations

My husband's father once said to him, "If you think you are mature enough to get someone pregnant, you are mature enough to pay for your own education." Those were pretty clearly defined expectations to give a first-year college student as far as sexual behavior is concerned. Students today face many more temptations and social pressures than we experienced a generation ago. Fewer restrictions are in place to guide their behavior and repercussions for debauchery are seldom pursued to the extent they have been in the past. Despite the eye-rolling and "Yeah-what-do-you-know-about-it?" facial expressions our students display, they benefit immensely from parents holding frank discussions about the temptations they will face and the situations they are likely to encounter as well as what parental expectations will be as far their responses are concerned. I remind you of the sophomore girl's quote from Coburn and Treeger's *Letting Go: A Parent's Guide to Understanding the College Years*, "The only thing I wish is that my parents had prepared me better for what I might face in college." This young woman spent the beginning of her college career in turmoil as she gave way to every temptation including experimentation with drugs and alcohol.

We've just spent the last 17 to 18 years ensuring our children had a solid primary and secondary academic education; now we must educate them about potential pitfalls to a satisfying and successful university career. We can't beat ourselves up either if our children succumb to the temptation to experiment. We can at least feel confident that we have instilled some of our values and expectations in them. They are then responsible for how they decide to use the advice and trust we have given them. This counsel will be reinforced in many different voices since most colleges and universities today take a proactive approach to heading off disaster among their first-year students. Deans, counselors and students themselves will talk to freshmen about real-life experiences, examples, and unfortunate results of not exercising personal restraint or giving in to social pressures that have taken place on their very own campus.

Parental Practicalities

Parents of students living abroad who have gone before you have found the following information useful in helping avoid unpleasant surprises and headaches down the road to matriculation.

Summer Addresses

If you plan on spending the summer in the country where your student will be going to school, make sure the college or university has all your summer addresses so you don't miss any of the crucial information, such as roommate assignments and orientation activities that will be sent out in June, July and August. Check in with the college regularly to be sure you haven't missed anything. Sometimes the change of address doesn't go through.

If you happen to have a domestic address that is afforded you by your company, keep in mind that admissions staff that deal with your student's application may assume that he or she is a domestic student. If your student wants to be treated as an international they may be surprised that they did not receive materials which would have otherwise been very helpful to them. Such was the case with a young lady who had been living in Asia. When she got to her university she discovered that all the other international students had received instructions on how to send their belongings ahead of time and have them on campus for moving-in day. She had to go out and buy everything she was going to need all at once.

Another example of what can happen when your student doesn't clarify that they are living internationally is what happened to a young lady who had been living in Thailand for many years. Because her postal address was that of her father's company in Texas, she was given a roommate from Texas. The administration obviously thought the two young women would have something very much in common!

Part-time Jobs

With so much to adjust to during the first semester of their first year, even if your child seems keen on finding a part-time job, it might be wise to wait until they have more fully completed their cultural and school adjustment, established social networks, patterns of daily life, and study habits. Once your son or daughter settles in, there will still be opportunities to work. However, this does create a dilemma in that most work-study jobs (Federally funded jobs based on financial need) on campus are snatched up early in the beginning of the semester. Occasionally there will be some left over as well as some campus jobs that do not require a student to be on a financial aid package to apply. There may also be jobs in the surrounding town. If all else fails, students can try applying for an off-campus job over the summer for the next school year.

Parents' Weekend

If you or another relative cannot be there for Parents' and Alumni Weekend, help your student make plans to be off campus or have a relative or well-liked family friend visit your student for the weekend activities. This popular weekend is scheduled in the fall and comes right about the time your student will most likely be dealing with the lows of the dip in the curve during the transition stage. The pangs of homesickness will be intense and the "fight or flight" phenomenon may be exacerbated.

Some schools will arrange to have students, particularly internationals whose parents are not likely to be there, take a weekend excursion to a nearby big city to experience the attractions. Many schools have professors who love to entertain students in their homes during this time and surrounding churches also have members who look out for international students at this time. All of this can be said for shorter holiday breaks as well, such as Fall Break or Thanksgiving (Chapter 4).

Panic Phone Calls

Parents tend to hear from their students when they are feeling down, upset or need a reassuring voice. The good times are relegated to calling their friends. With all that your students are dealing with, sooner or later panic phone calls are bound to come in the middle of the night, either due to the time difference created by zones or by the actual lateness created by how students keep their hours. Almost every parent of a college student has a story to tell of a late night call when their child was in hysterics over one thing or another. They soothed the child and went back to bed without being able to sleep a wink until morning. Then they had to wait until they thought their student was out of bed or between classes so they could call back and see how he or she was doing only to find that their darling could hardly remember what the fuss was all about to begin with.

Sometimes your children need to turn back to the security and familiarity of home where they know they can find affirmation and unconditional love. Even if the phone calls aren't full of panic, they are likely to be full of see-sawing emotions as your child goes through the chaos of the transition stage and the ups and downs of the entering stage which may last well into the second semester or even second year.

Campus Resources

If this panic phone call does turn out to be something serious, it can be difficult to keep your wits about you, but you must try to stay calm and reassuring. Depending on the type of emergency (anything from health to academics), there will be resources in place on your child's campus to handle it.

 Try This: Familiarize yourself with the school's Parent Handbook so that you can help your student think through who or where he needs to go for the help he is seeking.

Numerous resources are in place to help your child succeed. If she is struggling with academics, she can visit the writing lab, the math lab, hire a tutor or speak directly with her professor or teacher's assistant. Highly confidential mental health services are available to help students deal with eating disorders, depression, family problems, a relationship break-up and more. Student health services and campus security will see to it that your student gets care 24/7. He or she can also contact the International Student Office.

 Share It: Tell your student about dialing national emergency call numbers such as 911 in the U.S. and Canada and 999 in the U.K. for any *off-campus* emergencies. Suggest to your student that they have emergency campus numbers in their cell phone address book and set up for speed dial.

"What Have You Done to My Room?"

The experts I have heard speak to parents of graduating secondary school students suggest we do not do makeovers of our students' rooms. That is a temptation difficult to avoid when for so many years we may have been saying to ourselves, "I can't wait to have my own office on the second floor," or "Wouldn't it be great to turn this into an exercise room?" But our students are looking for the familiarity and stability of home. They want to come home to things just as they were...a little cleaner, but otherwise the same. They may get the wrong message when we drastically alter the sacredness of their sanctuary.

Depression

When I give my "Transitioning Successfully for University" seminar in international schools I always spend an evening with parents reviewing some of the same material and presenting some things just for their ears as I am doing here. I always make a point to go over with them the difference between the sadness and depression I talk about in Chapter 4. Your children will quite naturally experience bouts of sadness due to grief, loss, and just plain emotional instability in the different transition stages and as parents, you need to stay alert to any indications they may be headed for depression. If you suspect your student is:

- Experiencing a deep sadness that is preventing him or her from moving ahead,

- Having difficulties getting motivated to attend class, do assignments or study,

- Experiencing feelings of hopelessness or loss of self-worth, or

- Isolating him or herself from others,

you need to notify someone on campus. It could be the Dean of Students, Dean of Freshmen, or the campus health center. Your Parents' Handbook will offer suggestions for the best person to call.

Share It: If your student is over 18, you may want to ask him or her to sign a permission form that allows you to speak with his or her physician or psychologist should problems arise. Otherwise, strict confidentiality rules typically apply as he or she is considered an independent adult.

Fostering Global Identities

Repatriation for the college experience is oftentimes the point of what Dr. Barbara Schaetti calls "Encounter" (Chapter 7). This is when our children are awakened to the fact that they are different from their home-country peers. If you are repatriating with younger siblings, the return home may trigger "encounter" for them as well, depending on their age and other factors such as how long they have been abroad and how integrated in other cultures they have been. Once a person realizes it is their international upbringing that makes them different, they reach "Integration" and can become satisfied with who they are as a person.

Dr. Schaetti advises parents not to help their children avoid encounter. Until they experience encounter they will not be able to understand how growing up internationally has given them unique gifts, experiences and knowledge they will be able to use in their futures. At the same time, parents should not rush their children into the encounter experience before it is time, not that they would let you. Anything you say would most likely fall on deaf ears if they are not ready. Anyway, they need to experience it for themselves.

There are things we can do to prepare our children for the encounter experience. Dr. Schaetti has noted that those people who had relatively easy identity encounter experiences were those who had been introduced to the terms "third culture kid" or "global nomad" either before repatriating or shortly after repatriating. We can teach our children from very young ages that there is a language for the experience they are living as expatriate children. In this knowledge they will begin to develop a sense of belonging, that belonging which comes from the shared experience with others who are living outside their passport countries.

While your TCK is in the "Exploration" stage of identity development, the question of nationality typically pops up. While the country of their parents is stamped on the front of their passports, it doesn't really sing to them. Their host country may feel more like "home" to them. Children don't understand when their parents excitedly talk about returning "home." To them it is as though they are relocating to yet another foreign land. So they may find it difficult to utter their nationality when asked. So why should we insist our children take on a nationality of which they have no ownership? Dr. Schaetti proposes we foster a global identity in our children. In other words, it is quite alright to let them answer that question with what is true to their hearts. For instance, a British child who grew up in Kenya might say that he is Kenyan and British or for those with multiple host country experiences, a term such as a British Global Nomad might be used to communicate this belonging everywhere and nowhere. Domestic peers may not understand the answer your child gives, but it is a starting place and perhaps one which will trigger interest in finding out more about this curious person.

As your child prepares to go to university you might want to help him think about how his international experience has changed him or made him different from his home-country peers. Have some fun and role play with her how she plans to introduce herself or answer the question, "Where are you from?" Spend some time together on TCKid.com reading over the open Forum comments. It is a real eye-opener for TCKs and parents alike.

Delayed Adolescence and Rebellion

Retarded Development

Although TCKs can appear to be more mature than their stated years, they can also be retarded in their adolescent development. While adolescents are absorbing the values, customs and traditions of the culture they live in, they are at the same time testing them in the process of determining what is culturally appropriate. An overt way of testing the rules is the typical rebellion we see during the adolescent years. But the high mobility so typical of a TCK's life means that the cultural rules are always changing. So rather than being free to move forward in their personal development to discover who they are as a person, they are once again trying to figure out what is considered to be appropriate behavior in the new culture.

Testing the Rules

Some TCKs are not as free to test these cultural rules as their home-country peers would for many reasons. Sometimes just when a teenager is ready to start exerting some independence, the family is uprooted once more and, instead of going out on his own with his buddies, he is stuck hanging out with his parents because he doesn't know anyone yet in this new place. Or perhaps he was about to start taking driving lessons but in the new country he isn't allowed to drive for another two years.

In some countries or cities it is not considered safe to be out on your own, take public transportation or hang out with friends in public places; you could be the target of robbery, kidnapping or worse. These kids are not free to decide for themselves what they want to do and where they would like to go. They are restricted as to what they can or cannot do and where they are allowed to roam for security reasons or expectations of the sponsoring organization. For some organizations such as the military or missions communities, the parent will suffer the bad choices their children make and could end up in an unexpected repatriation.

Off the Deep End

Often the normal adolescent process of testing or rebelling against parental and societal rules has to wait for later and, much to the dismay of their parents, that time could be while they are in college. Some TCKs have had to remain true to a certain expectation of behavior for so long that the freedom they feel upon leaving home for the first time releases them to dive into all the forbidden fruit. The resulting behavior appears as though they have gone off the deep end, but they are expressing the type of behavior they would have normally done years ago. The behavior may be a bit more extreme because there are no restraints, parental or otherwise.

Negative Attention

Sometimes the rebellion is a way to get attention from parents who are so far away. This happened to family friends whose daughter went back to the United States for college.

> Claire felt so alone that she was desperate for her parents to repatriate. She would plead with them to terminate their contract early and come home. Her parents recognized her need for family closeness so they did all they could to set her up with a family to live with over the summer months. But it wasn't the answer. Instead she replaced the relationship she was missing by falling into a romance with a man eleven years her senior whose reputation was a bit dubious. She actually told her father, "If you won't come home at least he will take care of me."

Anger

We have talked a lot about grief in the hope that TCKs will learn to address their losses, allow themselves to deal with them and come to closure so they do not have to deal with issues of unresolved grief like our friend Brice's story. Anger is an expression of unresolved grief and may manifest itself in this time of delayed adolescent rebellion. Oftentimes this anger is directed at the parents, the perceived cause of the pain they are experiencing. The blame for all that is wrong in their lives may be shifted to parents who they feel gave them no voice in relocation after relocation.

Constructive Rebellion

Delayed adolescent rebellion can be either constructive or destructive. Although painful for parents to witness, it is constructive if it serves to move the young adult towards independence. Knowing about delayed adolescent rebellion may help everyone be aware of it as soon as it happens and deal with it before it gets out of hand.

Parting Words

The realm of issues parents of college-age children deal with is so vast and varied that it is not possible to touch upon them all. I have tried to cover some of the particular concerns I and other parents of repatriating global nomads have found to be particularly meaningful. My sincere wish is that you and your student will feel better prepared for this exciting journey and be able to thrive through the adventure.

What You Need to Know:

- It helps to plan ahead for your empty nest or the next stage in *your* life too.

- Read the parent handbook sent by your child's college or university cover to cover. It is full of lots of great information.

- Laying out expectations ahead of time will save time, energy, and aggravation later.

- Make the time to have the discussions that need to take place *before* your student leaves home.

- Your student needs to take this book with him or her to school. It won't do just to read it through. It needs to be a ready reference and reminder when problems arise. You may also want a copy of this book at home.

Resources:

Books

- *Raising Global Nomads: Parenting Abroad in an On-Demand World,* by Robin Pascoe with *A Most Excellent Journey* by Barbara Schaetti, PhD., Expatriate Press, 2006.

- *Manage Your Student Finances Now!: Easy Ways to Balance Your Budget at University and College,* by Keith Houghton, Random House, U.K., 2003.

- *Meeting College Costs: What You Need to Know Before Your Child and Money Leave Home,* by the College Board, 2008.

- *Succeeding as an International Student in the United States and Canada,* by Charles Lipson, University of Chicago Press, 2008.

- *What to Expect When Your Child Leaves for College: A Complete Guide for Parents Only,* by Mary Spohn, Atlantic Publishing, 2008.

- *Sending Your Child to College: The Prepared Parents Operational Manual,* by Marie Carr and her daughters, Katharine Carr and Elizabeth Carr, Dicmar Publishing, 2009.

Magazine

- *Interact Magazine* by Interaction International – magazine for TCKs, their parents, caregivers and educators who deal with the challenges TCKs face.

Resources (cont'd.):

Websites

- www.Collegeboard.com – U.S. college and university information.

- www.Stattalk.org and www.Studycanada.ca – Canadian university information.

- www.internationalfamilymag.com – where family members worldwide can share their stories.

Blog

- Maureen Tillman, Licensed Clinical Social Worker who runs *College with Confidence* has a blog called College Corner that is useful to parents of students attending U.S. colleges and universities: www.maplewood.blogs.nytimes.com/author/maureen-p-.tillman/

Final Reflections

By Barbara F. Schaetti, Ph.D.

To begin: Tina, *Thank you!* And *Hip, Hip, Hurrah!* And on behalf of those who transitioned from a childhood abroad to university without this supportive resource: *It's been a long time coming!* We have needed this book for decades at least; we just didn't know it. I, for one, would certainly have found it useful back in 1977.

I graduated from the Singapore American School (SAS) in the spring of that year, and in autumn started my first year at Trinity University in San Antonio, Texas. I was eighteen years old and very accustomed to the transition experience: I had by then lived in ten countries on five continents and had been 'the new kid in school' some twelve different times. If anyone had asked me if I was prepared for this transition to university, I would have been surprised at the question. Surprised first of all because, despite all those moves, no one had ever thought to ask me that question before, and surprised certainly because, *Yes, of course*, I must be: *I had done it all before, over and over again, hadn't I?*

In those days, people like me didn't know we were *global nomads* or *third culture kids*; those terms hadn't yet been popularized and disseminated. The idea of *re-entry shock* was nowhere on our horizon, and even the idea of *culture shock* wasn't much discussed in the expatriate world. No one at SAS or Trinity understood that my peers and I, graduating from international schools all over the world, needed guidance on university-bound repatriation: on issues of identity, grief and relationships, on leaving well and arriving well, on 'home' country practicalities, etc.

Most of us muddled through; there's plenty of research now to show that most of us, my generation and the generations that came before, muddled through our university transitions to create fulfilling lives. But it could have been so much easier for all of us – less suppressing of pain through drinking and recreational drugs, through casual sex and excessive studying, and much earlier and much easier leveraging of our global childhoods into fulfilling futures. And perhaps those who got lost in the cracks, whose attempts to suppress the pain ultimately dragged them down too far, would have found their right way forward with just a little help. *The Global Nomad's Guide to University Transition* offers this and more.

It's tempting to second-guess the past: what might have been if only we had had this book back then. It's likewise important to recognize how much has changed since, for example, 1977. Non-salaried spouses of that time and earlier struggled to make meaning out of their travels; today they know that skill development is core to their life satisfaction, and in striking numbers they are using the situations of difference and change in which they find themselves to augment their intercultural competence. Expatriate parents of thirty and more years ago had no articulated knowledge of the benefits and challenges of raising their children abroad; today they are introducing their children to their global nomad/TCK heritage at earlier and earlier ages, helping to ensure that as young adults they know they have something unique to offer the professional world. International schools likewise had no systematic understanding of transitions and expatriate family concerns, nor of the implications of these on their educational mandate; today international educators are at the forefront of new research on global nomads and of new services to meet expatriate family needs.

It's clear that the zeitgeist in which global nomads are now growing up has changed. Indeed, *The Global Nomad's Guide to University Transition* demonstrates this maturation of the field. Looking back, I see people like David Pollock, Matthew Neigh, Ruth Van Reken and me paving the pathway to this book by speaking with graduating seniors at international schools around the world. International schools themselves, foremost among them the American School of The Hague, helped advance the path as they began institutionalizing transition programs for all facets of the community, including university-bound seniors. People like Norma McCaig, Bruce LaBrack, and Alice Wu placed additional stepping stones by working with colleges and universities to welcome incoming global nomads more effectively. Service organizations, especially in the Missions sector and typically inspired by David Pollock, began offering re-entry seminars. All of this created the conditions out of which comes the book you hold in your hands.

This book now paves the pathway further forward, takes it to the next milestone. In doing so, it provides a critical fail-safe. Even now, if you're a graduating global nomad it's likely you do not have a pre-departure presentation to attend, the international school from which you are graduating hasn't yet put comprehensive programming in place, the college or university receiving you hasn't got a clue, and either you don't know about or can't (or perhaps won't) access a re-entry program. Despite the maturation of the field and the new zeitgeist in which you find yourself, you're likely still to be left to manage your transition alone.

No longer! *The Global Nomad's Guide to University Transition* may be the best gift a parent or educator can give you, or which you can give yourself. There's nothing else available like it. I recommend you put it in your suitcase, right along with a copy of *Third Culture Kids: The Experience of Growing up Among Worlds*. Better yet, read both books ahead of time, give copies to your parents, teachers, and friends, and discuss the core ideas together. And if you've already made the transition to university, I still recommend this book to you; it is an important resource for you and your friends retroactively as well as proactively.

Although written to help you succeed with your university transitions, there is also a hidden promise in this book. As you apply the knowledge, guidance and resources it provides to your university transition, you will learn to think about transitions as a process, as a life experience that can be purposefully managed. Focusing on one kind of transition, you will learn more broadly how to effectively engage all the transitions you encounter, throughout your life – whether it's transition to university, transition into or out of a job, transition into or out of a relationship, or any other kind of transition. You'll put all of your transition experiences into a context, and learn to apply that context next time you're in the midst of the experience.

And as you take on leadership positions on your campus, in your community, and in your career, you will begin with a strong advantage: the skill to manage change. It has long been said that "change is the only constant." In his book *Learning as a Way of Being*, leadership consultant Peter Vaill puts it even more poetically when he says we live in a world of "permanent whitewater." Learning to proactively engage the process of transition is a core skill for success in the twenty-first century. *The Global Nomad's Guide to University Transition* marks the pathway to help you meet that challenge.

****

Barbara F. Schaetti, Ph.D., is a dual-national (Swiss and US) second-generation global nomad. Throughout her career as a consultant and coach, she has championed individuals and teams as they learn to access their capacity for mindfully and creatively engaging situations of difference and change. She is the author of numerous articles on global nomads and related topics, pioneered the concept of institutionalizing transition programming in international schools through transition teams, and is the lead author of the book *Making a World of Difference. Personal Leadership: A Methodology of Two Principles and Six Practices.*

Bibliography

Books

Andrews, Leslie A. General Editor and Ward, Ted. *The Family in Mission: Understanding and Caring for Those Who Serve*. Colorado Springs: Mission Training International, 2004.

Briggs Myers, I. and McCauley, M.H. Manual: *A Guide to the Development and Use of the Myers Briggs Type Indicator*. Mountain View: Consulting Psychologists Press, 1985.

Briggs Myers, I. and Myers, P.B. *Gifts Differing – Understanding Personality Type*. Mountain View: Davies Black Publishing, 1980.

Burns, David D. M.D. *Feeling Good, The New Mood Therapy*. New York: HarperCollins Publishers, 1999.

de Becker, Gavin. *The Gift of Fear*. New York: Dell Publishing, 1997.

Garton, Christie. *U-Chic: The College Girl's Guide to Everything*. Naperville: Sourcebooks, Inc, 2009.

Gottesman, Greg and Friends. *College Survival: A Crash Course for Students by Students*. New York: Prentice Hall, 1992.

Kadison, Richard and DiGeronimo, Theresa. *College of the Overwhelmed: The Campus Mental Health Crisis and What To Do About It*. California: Jossey-Bass, 2005.

Kiersey, David L. and Bates, Marilyn. *Please Understand Me – Character and Temperament Types*. Del Mar: Prometheus Nemesis Book Company, 1978.

Kohls, Robert L. *Survival Kit for Overseas Living*. Yarmouth: Nicholas Brealey, 2001.

Levin Coburn, Karen and Lawrence Treeger, Madge. *Letting Go: A Parents' Guide to Understanding the College Years, fourth edition.* New York: HarperCollins Publishers, 2003.

Lipson, Charles. *Succeeding as an International Student in the United States and Canada.* Chicago: The University of Chicago Press, 2008.

Pascoe, Robin. *Raising Global Nomads.* Vancouver: Expatriate Press, 2006.

Pipher, Mary. *Reviving Ophelia: Saving the Selves of Adolescent Girls.* New York: The Berkley Publishing Group, 1994.

Pollock, Dave C. and Van Reken, Ruth E. *Third Culture Kids: Growing Up Among Worlds, revised edition.* Boston: Nicholas Brealey, 2009.

Stone, D, Patton, B, et al. *Difficult Conversations: How to discuss what matters most.* New York: Penguin Books, 1999.

Storti, Craig. The Art of Crossing Cultures, second edition. Boston: Nicholas Brealey, 2001.

Storti, Craig. *The Art of Coming Home.* Boston: Intercultural Press, 2003.

Websites

"Culture shock." *Encarta Online Dictionary.* 2003. 17 Oct. 2009 <http://encarta.msn.com/encnet/features/dictionary/DictionaryRes ults.aspx?lextype=3&search=culture%20shock>

"Drugs: What You Should Know." KidsHealth.org. 29 Nov. 2009 <http://kidshealth.org/teen/drug_alcohol/drugs/know_about_drugs .html#>

"Family and parenting: What is empty nest syndrome and depression."
    eSortment, 2 Feb. 2010
    <http://www.essortment.com/family/emptynestsyndr_suoh.htm>

"Expatriates Worldwide. How many expatriates are there?" Just Landed
    Living Abroad – Guides. 27 Jan. 2010
    <http://www.justlanded.com/english/Common/Footer/Expatriates/
    How-many-expats-are-there>

"Gender and Human Rights: Sexual Health." World Health Organization.
    Jan. 2002. 7 Dec. 2009
    <http://www.who.int/reproductivehealth/topics/gender_rights/sexu
    al_health/en/>

Hill-Useem, Ruth. "Third Culture Kids: Focus of Major Study." *Newslinks,*
    Newspaper of the International School Services Jan. 1993. 15 Oct.
    2009
    <http://www.iss.edu/pages/kids.html>

"Identity Theft." Identitytheft.org. 25 Jan. 2010
    <http://www.identitytheft.org.uk/reporting-the-theft.asp>

"Identity Theft." Federal Trade Commission. 25 Jan. 2010
    <http://www.ftc.gov/bcp/edu/microsites/idtheft/>

"Identity Theft and Fraud." U.S. Justice Department. 25 Jan. 2010
    <http://www.justice.gov/criminal/fraud/websites/idtheft.html>

The Interchange Institute. "Many Expatriates Many Voices: Final Report."
    2004 Prudential Financial Relocation Study. 13 Oct. 2009
    <http://www.interchangeinstitute.org/files/Many%20Expatriates%
    20Many%20VoicesFINAL.pdf>

Pascoe, Robin. Expat Expert, Reading Room – Coming Home.
    "Repatriating Graduating Teens." *Tip sheet for repatriating grads.*
    2005. 3 Dec. 2009

<http://www.expatexpert.com/rr_coming_home.repatriating_gradu ating_teens>

Peterson, Karen S. "Depression Among College Students Rising." *USA Today*, Health and Sciences. 05/21/2002. 7 Nov. 2009 <http://www.usatoday.com/news/health/mental/2002-05-22-college-depression.htm>

Rape Aggression Defense System (R.A.D.). 14 Dec. 2009 <http://www.rad-systems.com/>

"Sexually Transmitted Diseases – Prevention." EMedicineHealth. 7 Dec. 2009 <http://www.emedicinehealth.com/sexually_transmitted_diseases/ page9_em.htm#Prevention>

"Sexually Transmitted Diseases" National Institute of Health. 7 Dec. 2009 <http://www.nichd.nih.gov/health/topics/sexually_transmitted_dis eases.cfm>

Society for the Prevention of Teen Suicide. 11 Nov. 2009. <http://www.sptsnj.org/index.html>

TCKid.com Forum, answers to the question "What kind of issues did you struggle with when you repatriated for university?" Used with permission. 12 Dec. 2009. <http://www.tckid.com/group>

Tckid.com "Uncle Dan's Blog." Used with permission. 27 Jan. 2010 <http://www.tckid.com/group/category/ask-uncle/>

Teen Health Fx. 10 Nov. 2009. <http://www.teenhealthfx.com/index.php>

Tillman, Maureen. College With Confidence. 3 Feb. 2010. <http://www.collegewithconfidence.com/>

"Transition." *Encarta Online Dictionary*. 2003. 17 Oct. 2009.
    <http://encarta.msn.com/encnet/features/dictionary/DictionaryRes
    ults.aspx?lextype=3&search=transition>

"What happens to your brain when you take drugs." National Institutes of
    Drug Abuse. 29 Nov. 2009
    <http://www.nida.nih.gov/Infofacts/understand.html>

Other

The American College Health Association's National College Health
    Assessment American College Health Association. (2005).
    Reference group data report. American College Health
    Association National College Health Assessment. Spring 2005.
    Baltimore, MD.

Cottrell, Ann Baker. *Adult TCKs: Life Choices and Personal
    Characteristics*. FIGT Conference March 2007.

Bank of America Corporation. *Student Financial Handbook*: *An easy to
    use guide to managing your money*. Sponsored by Bank of
    America. 2008.

Hudson, David. *The Great American Teen Novel*. Used with permission.

Interchange Institute's 2004 Prudential Financial relocation study, *Many
    Expatriates Many Voices*.

Kruger, Eric. Dean Foster Associates' Cross Cultural Training Program.

Aruna Jha, Ph.D. Faculty member, University of Illinois Chicago in a talk
    to international students at Tufts University.

Larsen, Jean. "Transitions and TCKs" in *Raising Resilient MKs*. Bowers,
    ed., 1998.

Maguire, Linda. LCSW. Consultant for Global CLT/Centered Life Transitions, from a personal conversation, Feb. 2008.

Stephens, Libby. Interaction International. Personal conversations, emails and Transition/Reentry Seminar. 2007, 2009/2010. Quote used with permission.

Tillman, Maureen. Creator of "College With Confidence." Personal conversations and emails. 2009/2010.

Timmons, Rachel E. "A Third Culture Reacculturation Rubric." 2006. Used with permission.

Timmons, Rachel E. *Investigating the TCP Phenomenon by Using a Rubric to Assess Cross Culture Transition Progress.* 2006. Used with permission.

Van Reken, Ruth. Personal conversations and emails. 2009/2010.

Van Reken, Ruth. *"Teaching Locally, Thinking Globally: Understanding the 'Hidden Diversity' of Cross Cultural Kids in the Classroom."* CEU seminar presented at Butler University, March 22, 2008.

About the Author

Tina Quick is a well-seasoned traveler and mother of three college-aged daughters. She is an Adult Third Culture Kid (ATCK) who, having made 18 moves (9 of them before her 10th birthday), understands well the cycle of loss and grief involved in a cross-cultural lifestyle. Tina has raised her own TCKs across four cultures on the continents of Asia, Africa, Europe, and North America.

After spending 15 adult years abroad, Tina made a career change from registered nurse to cross-cultural trainer. Her time spent substitute teaching and coaching in the International School of Geneva endeared her to many students who continue to stay in touch. Their stories and others like them have ignited her passion to work with students before, during and after their college transitions. Witnessing the struggles of students who have not yet learned how to live out the differences their international upbringing has created in them in a positive and fulfilling way has inspired her to create specialized training to suit their individual needs.

Tina is a cross-cultural trainer, writer and international speaker. She is on the Board of Directors of Families in Global Transition (FIGT) and serves as Chair Person of the Program Committee. She is a member of the Overseas Association of College Admissions Counseling. Tina works closely with colleges and universities, domestic and international schools.

If you would like to contact Tina Quick, please use the following:

Tina L. Quick

International Family Transitions
+1 781-369-1068 (office)
E-mail: tquick@internationalfamilytransitions.com
www.internationalfamilytransitions.com

Success and adventure in transition

Lightning Source UK Ltd.
Milton Keynes UK
UKOW022122061011

179864UK00002B/2/P